Modernity and What Has Been Lost

Modernity
and What Has Been Lost

Considerations on the Legacy of Leo Strauss

Edited by
Paweł Armada and Arkadiusz Górnisiewicz

St. Augustine's Press, South Bend, Indiana
The Jagiellonian University Press, Krakow

Manufactured in the United States of America

2 3 4 5 6   16 15 14 13 12 11

Library of Congress Cataloging in Publication Data
Modernity and what has been lost: considerations on the legacy of
Leo Strauss / edited by Paweł Armada and Arkadiusz Górnisiewicz.
     p. cm.
   Includes bibliographical references and index.
   ISBN 978-1-58731-511-4 (pbk.)
   1. Strauss, Leo – Criticism and interpretation. 2. Strauss, Leo –
   Political and social views. 3. Civilization, Modern – Philosophy.
   4. Political science – Philosophy. I. Armada, Paweł.
   II. Górnisiewicz, Arkadiusz.
JC251.S8M63 2011   320.092 – dc22

∞ The paper used in this publication meets the minimum requirements of the American National Standard for Information Sciences – Permanence of Paper for Printed Materials, ANSI Z39.48-1984.

ST. AUGUSTINE'S PRESS
www.staugustine.net

CONTENTS

Editors' Introduction
The Question of Modernity Meets the Question of Leo Strauss...................... 7

Heinrich Meier
Why Leo Strauss? Four Answers and One Consideration concerning
the Uses and Disadvantages of the School for the Philosophical Life............... 19

Daniel Tanguay
Leo Strauss and the Contemporary Return to Political Philosophy.................. 33

Nathan Tarcov
Philosophy as the Right Way of Life in *Natural Right and History* 43

David Janssens
The Philosopher's Ancient Clothes: Leo Strauss on Philosophy and Poetry........ 53

Paweł Armada
Leo Strauss as Erzieher: The Defense of the Philosophical Life
or the Defense of Life against Philosophy? 73

Jürgen Gebhardt
Modern Challenges – Platonic Responses: Strauss, Arendt, Voegelin.............. 83

Arkadiusz Górnisiewicz
Karl Löwith and Leo Strauss on Modernity, Secularization, and Nihilism......... 93

Emmanuel Patard
Remarks on the Strauss-Kojève Dialogue and its Presuppositions.................. 111

Piotr Nowak
Carl Schmitt and his Critic.. 125

Till Kinzel
Postmodernism and the Art of Writing: The Importance of Leo Strauss
for the 21st Century.. 135

Laurence Lampert
Leo Strauss's *Gynaikologia*.. 147

Contributors 173

Name Index... 175

Subject Index 179

THE QUESTION OF MODERNITY MEETS THE QUESTION OF LEO STRAUSS

The present volume consists of eleven chapters coming from papers prepared by a number of different scholars invited to participate in a conference on the legacy of Leo Strauss. The conference was held at the Jagiellonian University in Krakow, Poland, on June 4-5, 2009. The title of this book is the same as the title of the conference.

* * *

We are modern people. We find ourselves gathered "in the same boat" moving towards a hopefully better future. Our destination may appear to be a final state, a universal and homogeneous one, where the most important question is found to be resolved. That is the question, "How to live?" It was brought to light and explicated by the philosophers of the Socratic tradition. They bequeathed to us some truth about humanity itself, namely about the man who is participating in a constant struggle to answer the question, "How to live?" However, insofar as the question proves to be "infinite, absolute," it cannot be answered in a definite way. The final state marking its final resolution has in fact never come and is never to come, indeed. But what if we are taught, or learned, undoubtedly to believe that it really exists or just emerges from the course of history? Even granted the Socratic truth, is there still enough space within the domain of humanity for our leading truly different ways of life? Is being a poet, or a prophet, not to mention being a philosopher in a very Socratic sense, something still possible and acquirable for us moderns? Is a political science stemming from the philosophic and poetic consciousness of the most important question still to be exercised?

There have been rather few authors capable of writing on such issues. Certainly one of them is Leo Strauss. But he is also a controversial figure in the eyes of many scholars and readers who often hear of him as a founder of a mysterious sect or an intellectual "godfather of the neoconservative movement." To be sure, what cannot be forgotten is that during his lifetime Strauss was relatively neglected by his fellow academics or even somewhat derided by them especially because of his manner of reading "esoterically" and his emphatic criticism against the positivist approach in social science. He was also a teacher, and a teacher genuinely loved by his students, of a large group of political scientists who then have tried to continue the detailed research into the history of political philosophy. Their studies of political phenomena have thus turned out completely different from the studies carried out by most of the specialists in their branch of study. In such a context, Strauss's pupils or followers might have felt almost persecuted. All in all, it has become arguable whether Strauss can primarily be perceived as a profound thinker and not as a "founder" or "godfather;" or if one is able to read his texts with a kind of successful patience, but alone, to train one's mind under his books, and finally to grasp some fundamental questions that he was concerned with, without being actually involved in the "Straussian school." And yet, as the intellectual as well as political climate has begun to change, when a heterogeneity of the social sciences has generally been proclaimed and some new striking challenges in the realm of politics and society and culture have been noticed, the thinking of Leo Strauss returns to us not just as an eccentric effort in understanding a deep past but as a lively Socratic struggle to understand life itself.

So in the recent years the question of modernity as raised by Strauss, along with the whole theological-political dimension that should be gained through thinking on the "modern solution" we now seem to experience, aroused much interest in the United States and some, too, in Western Europe. There were many stages of debate with highly differentiated levels of profundity. Very little of it has been, however, recognized and seriously understood in Poland. This book was born out of our intellectual desire that has originated some time ago, during our studies that took place at the Jagiellonian University in the old beautiful city of Krakow. Then we encountered some questions about main tenets and sources of what can be called the modern way of life, and began to seek possible answers in wise books. We may, moreover, have felt ourselves witnesses to a great political and social change: It seemed that in our country the "process of transformation" had been by and large completed as Poland finally joined the European Union in 2004. So it was our personal experience that made us inclined to raise the subject of modernity and put it into the context of the legacy of Leo Strauss.

The title of this volume seems to suggest that modernity is irremediably flawed or devoid of something of utmost importance. But is the answer to the question of what has been lost ready at hand? Someone familiar with the elaborate arguments of the discontents of modernity might react with a feeling of dismay. After all, has not the situation of the modern man been analyzed endless times with the use of such prolific concepts as "disenchantment," "rationalization," "mass culture," "one-dimensionality," "commercialization," etc? But to dismiss this question simply on the basis that it has been raised too frequently would not be intellectually responsible. All the more so since in the case of Strauss's intellectual legacy the problem of modernity is being posed in such an insightful way that shuns all categories. But in what sense is our intimation of modernity's insufficiency defensible? It seems that we are led toward this problem as soon as we begin to grasp the simple fact of living in the world that has come to be almost unanimous with regard to any relevant concept of best regime. Sixteen years after Strauss's death the liberal-democratic model has been declared victorious and the idea of promoting it worldwide has been put on the top of the agenda. The vital question is, however, whether liberalism really permits many different ways of life to be exercised within it; it may also be true that the prevalent model of society works in such a way that a particular model of culture is being imposed on us, notably in the field of political discourse; the model that excludes from the outset and in the long run even destroys many ways of life which do not conform to it; and that a real tension between human beings disappears insofar as there is only one way of being "correct." It is thus clear that by pointing to the concerns in question we point toward something that goes beyond the discussion about the pros and cons of liberal democracy. It would be presumptuous to believe that the current embrace of the liberal-democratic model of culture has definitely settled the question of how to live.

One of Strauss's great achievements is certainly connected with his steadfast allegiance to that Socratic question. Strauss might have been afraid of modernity's silencing of this question, i.e., that a problem of man's good life would no longer be approached as the problem. And if the Heideggerian narrative develops the thesis that the history of Western metaphysics accounts for the forgetfulness of the question of Being, in Strauss modernity seems to bear responsibility, to some extent, not only for lowering man's goal, but also for doing away with the question, "How to live?" The complete oblivion of this question seems to be an unavoidable consequence of the coming into existence of a universal and homogenous state. Strauss saw this clearly in his famous debate with a renowned French philosopher and one of the European "founding fathers," Alexandre Kojève. For in a universal and homogenous state there would be no place for an inquiring philosophy in the Socratic sense; in such a state the most urgent questions are once and for all abolished by the final wisdom and the wisdom wins absolutely over philosophy. The shadow cast by Kojève's vision of the fulfillment of history certainly informs Strauss's concern with the consequences of modernity. Modernity conceived in terms of radical immanence, complete reconciliation with the world, and oblivion of eternity, seems to provide conditions particularly fit for a thorough oblivion of the Socratic question.

If modernity threatens to silence the most important question, it seems all the more important to show that the contemporary answers fall short of being self-evident. The importance of the so-called theologico-political problem becomes more crucial if viewed from this perspective. By confronting philosophy and the revealed religion, i.e., by juxtaposing the irreconcilable claims of Athens and Jerusalem and sharpening their contours, Strauss succeeds in putting into focus the grounds of our action, or in other words, the question, "Who is to be obeyed?" when it comes to leading one's life. However, there is much more to it than that. Strauss not only recalls the most important Western alternative concerning the way of life; the way he does it seems to involve a claim that the very possibility of raising that question depends on the existence of genuinely possible options or alternatives. Were this tension to disappear completely, the question "How to live?" would lose its urgency. In this sense one can say that Strauss's apprehension concerning modernity corresponds somehow to that formulated by Nietzsche. In the Preface to *Beyond Good and Evil* Nietzsche wrote that "the splendid tension in the spirit, something unlike anything existing on earth before" arose as a consequence of "the fight against the thousands of years of pressure from the Christian church." According to him there have been two attempts "in the grand style" to unbound the string and ease the spirit's tension: Jesuitism and the Democratic Enlightenment. He avers that the free spirits, who are neither Jesuits nor Democrats, still have "the need, the entire spiritual need, and the total tension of its bow." Without attempting to write Strauss into the Nietzschean vocabulary or even philosophy, one can justly say that Strauss understands the crucial role played by this tension of the spirit. For if the West owes its vitality to the antagonism between Athens and Jerusalem, philosophy or the philosophic way of life is in need of self-assertion and rational justification in the face of its most serious competitor, namely the life based upon recognizing the supreme authority of the Revelation. While any desire to stay confined within a faith proves fatal to any philosophy, being confronted with faith proves ultimately salutary to philosophy. As Strauss concludes, "No one can be both a philosopher and a theologian, nor, for that matter, some possibility which transcends the conflict between philosophy and theology, or pretends to be a synthesis of both. But every one of us can be and ought to be either one or the other, the philosopher open to the challenge of theology or the theologian open to the challenge of philosophy."

The defense of philosophy may be judged as Strauss's major intellectual task. The life he lived and the books he left may provide strong evidence for answering the question regarding the very possibility of the philosophic life today in the affirmative. But what are the most characteristic features of the philosophic life? Strauss, as can be learned from the present volume, studied both philosophy and poetry. The latter sometimes has the ability to voice something essential that searches deeper than some elaborate enunciations. We cannot here refrain from letting poetry speak about philosophy in this respect. It would not be presumptuous to suggest that a poem by Zbigniew Herbert, one of the most important Polish authors living in the age of the communist rule, beautifully depicts the ideal of philosophic life that had been held dear by Strauss:

Mr. Cogito
always defended himself
against the smoke of time

he valued concrete objects
standing quietly in space

he worshipped things that are permanent
almost immortal

dreams about the speech of cherubs
he left in the garden of dream

he chose
what depends
on earthly measures and judgment
so when the hour comes
he can consent without a murmur

to the trial of truth and falsehood
to the trial of fire and water

(*The Adventures of Mr. Cogito with Music*,
translated by John and Bogdana Carpenter)

After having listened to the poet let us turn to the works of the scholars whose articles form the content of this volume. The arrangement of the chapters is based on the following idea. The first part of the book may be referred to as "Leo Strauss Reconsidered" and consists of five chapters dwelling on the major themes in Strauss's thought. The second part, comprised of four chapters, may be labeled "Leo Strauss Encountered" as it attempts to explore Strauss's legacy against the backdrop of some of his major disputants. The third part may be described as "Leo Strauss Reread" as it consists of two chapters: the first one deals with Strauss's art of reading (or "learning by reading") in the context of postmodern challenge and the second one provides an example of an insightful art of reading. We believe that such an arrangement lends the book coherency that will allow the reader to grasp the thread leading from the essential question "Why Leo Strauss?" to the controversy over treatment of the text, the controversy which is nowadays considered crucial.

Heinrich Meier in the chapter entitled *Why Leo Strauss. Four Answers and One Consideration concerning the Uses and Disadvantages of the School for the Philosophical Life* claims that the question "Why Leo Strauss" can be answered separately from the recent Strauss boom in media. He unfolds his answer to the question posed at the very beginning into four answers. The first answer is that Strauss opened up a new historical and philosophical access to the history of philosophy by making us aware of the exoteric-esoteric way of writing and thereby its significance in gaining the proper understanding of the history of philosophy. The second answer is that Strauss points to the fact that philosophy is a way of life and not merely a set of doctrines. The third answer is that Strauss places political philosophy at the center of philosophy. Because political philosophy confronts seriously the question what is right, it becomes the locus of philosophy's reflection on itself. Political philosophy is responsible for defense of philosophy and its rational justification; in political philosophy the whole of philosophy is at stake. The fourth answer is that Strauss made the theologico-political problem his main theme. The rational justification of philosophy presupposes its confrontation with its strongest antagonist: the challenge of revelation; and no more powerful objection to philosophy exists than objection based on the faith in an omnipotent God. Meier's conclusion is that the possibility to turn from the history of philosophy to the intention of the philosopher may allow us to come to the insight that "leaving the historical cave" is always possible.

Daniel Tanguay in the chapter entitled *Leo Strauss and the Contemporary Return to Political Philosophy* discusses Strauss's assessment that today political philosophy is in a state of decay or putrefaction. It seems that this state of things has changed in the last thirty years due to revival of political philosophy (in France called *Renouveau de la philosophie politique*). According to him this simplistic picture of revival must be qualified in a few respects. He poses the question: "Is Strauss's judgment invalidated by this renewal?" Strauss regarded political philosophy as an attempt to answer two closely connected questions: "What is the best regime?" and "What is the best life?" The knowledge of human nature is necessary in order to judge which political regime is the best regime, which is at the same time "conducive to human excellence." Strauss distinguished between the best regime (a combination of "way of life" and "form of government") which is noble and just, and many legitimate regimes which are only just. According to Strauss modern political thought has blurred the distinction between legitimate and best regime. Modern natural law focuses on the conditions of legitimacy of a regime and not on the quest for the best regime. Strauss asked the question of the best regime and against this backdrop we can see how his renewal of political philosophy differs from other similar attempts in recent times. Almost all contemporary political philosophers believe that there is no serious alternative to the democratic regime. Contemporary political philosophy is a theory of democracy. Tanguay claims that this situation may be considered a complete departure from the traditional political philosophy.

Nathan Tarcov begins his chapter entitled *Philosophy as the Right Way of Life in* Natural Right and History with a remark that one of the most salient themes in Strauss's thought is the conception of philosophy as a way of life. This conception contrasts with the contemporary approach to philosophy as merely a branch of research. Strauss states in his response to historicism that philosophy in its original (Socratic) sense is the awareness of the fundamental problems and the

fundamental alternatives regarding their solution. Modern philosophy is politicized because it wants to establish the best order while original philosophy was
rather humanizing since it did not put itself in the service of such actualization.
The difference between philosophers and intellectuals corresponds to the difference between philosophers and gentlemen and between philosophers and sophists or rhetoricians. Granted that philosophy has awareness of its limits, it can
answer the Socratic question of how to live because it is a way of life devoted to
the quest for knowledge or wisdom. This "Socratic answer" remains in a perennial conflict with "the anti-Socratic answer." Tarcov discusses the relation between philosophic questioning and the divine law and between the philosopher
and popular opinion. The philosopher's ascent from the cave and his descent into
the cave is discussed here in detail against the backdrop of the dependence of
the philosophic life on the city. The chapter ends with asking a few compelling
questions regarding the very possibility of choosing the philosophic way of life
as one's own way of life.

David Janssens begins his chapter entitled *The Philosopher's Ancient Clothes.
Leo Strauss on Philosophy and Poetry* with a remark that we can distinguish
three quarrels in the work of Leo Strauss: 1) between Athens and Jerusalem, or
reason and revelation; 2) between Ancients and Moderns; 3) between philosophy and poetry. He argues that the third quarrel deserves more attention than it
has received up till now. His aim is to draw our attention to the importance of
ancient poetry for Strauss's understanding of the art of writing of the classical
philosophers. According to him Strauss took the third quarrel no less seriously
than the others. He argues that Leo Strauss had become increasingly doubtful
whether there is a quarrel between poetry and philosophy (as famously declared
by Plato). Janssens's main thesis is that ancient philosophy is fundamentally indebted to ancient poetry. As an example may serve the well known fact that the
word "nature" (*phusis*) appears in Homer's *Odyssey*. Strauss discovered that the
famous Greek historians such as Herodotus, Thucydides or Xenophon were not
interested in merely recording the events. Their true aim was protreptic: to help
attentive readers to free themselves from the authoritative opinions and arrive
at a genuine education (paideia). Janssens avers that Strauss's reflection reached
a point where the distinction between poets, historians, and philosophers seems
to dissolve. In order to gain the proper understanding of Plato we have to study
the writings of the pre-Platonic poets and historians. When viewed from the perspective of the art of writing (Platonic "noble lies" and Hesiodic-Homeric "tales
similar to the truth") the similarities between poets and philosophers seem to be
striking. One of the most important similarities between the two can be seen in
their ministerial and not autonomous character: they lead men to the understanding of the human soul.

Paweł Armada in the chapter entitled *Leo Strauss as Erzieher: The Defense of
Philosophical Life or the Defense of Life Against Philosophy* claims that the ques-

tion that seems to underlie Strauss's oeuvre is the question of an inevitable conflict between politics and philosophy (and these two terms have to be understood as the two ways of life). This can be also depicted in classical terms as a problem of relation between "the cave," which means the political community, on the one hand, and the struggle to ascend from the cave, led by Socratic philosophers, on the other hand. We may thus say that the *conditio sine qua non* of philosophy is the cave itself. If so, the defense of the philosophic way of life should be primarily understood as the defense of a necessary ground for any possible philosophical enterprise or, to put it in other words, of the commonsensical perception of political things which has something to do with the faith in divine source of the law of a particular community. From a certain point of view, a Straussian depiction of what philosophy originally was, of Socrates' way of life, may be construed as embarrassingly idealistic. Armada presents Strauss's judgment of the "modern solution" as being *contra naturam*. The natural conditions are to be found only within closed societies, not a world-state but, Strauss admits, this natural order cannot be simply restored in the extremely unfavorable situation that we experience today. Armada concludes that Strauss's figure of Socratic philosopher as an educator is deliberately idealized in order to redeem the claims of politics or political life or maybe human life as such. He views the Straussian concern about politics as substantially preceding the concern about the philosophic life as ascribed to Nietzsche. In other words, living in the cave comes before living "under the sky." And even with the highest estimation for the philosophy as it may be, as prudent as detached or concerning about the eternal, there is still a need for the law given by a (serious and sensible) prophet-legislator.

Jürgen Gebhardt in the chapter entitled *Modern Challenges – Platonic Responses: Strauss, Arendt, Voegelin* discusses Leo Strauss in the company of such thinkers as Hannah Arendt, Eric Voegelin, and Michael Oakeshott. All of them reacted to the crisis of the European world. Gebhardt claims we can see that the theoretical understanding behind the works of the thinkers in question is that of Plato's image of the city. They focused on the critical understanding of the disorder of their times. He speaks in terms of "platonic responses" because all these thinkers created a paradigm of order based on their reflexive understanding of the human predicament or a conception of representative humanity in the sense of the reflexive paradigm of the platonic city. The debate on the so-called decline of political theory that began in the 1950s and allegedly ended in 1971 with Rawls's *A Theory of Justice* was an intellectual blunder partly due to plain ignorance, but also to the fact that many of the thinkers in question were German émigrés formed by the German philosophy and representing an orientation that might have been threatening to some basic premises of American political science. These thinkers differed significantly, but one can discern certain agreements. Strauss analyzed the crisis of modernity using the three-wave hypothesis and focusing on the Machiavellian modification of a pre-modern political philosophy. Voegelin presented a description of a civilizational drama that ended up in the totalitarian execution of an inner-worldly eschatology emerging from sectarian Christianity (the thesis of the Gnostic character of modernity). Arendt, in turn, regarded the crisis as primarily political and having its roots in the demise of the Roman trinity of religion, tradition, and authority. The four did not work out blueprints for direct political action, but evoked the unseen measure that is indispensible as an ordering force in the life of citizens.

Arkadiusz Górnisiewicz in his chapter entitled *Karl Löwith and Leo Strauss on Modernity, Secularization, and Nihilism* explores Strauss's and Löwith's views of modernity with a particular emphasis put on the notions of "secularization" and "nihilism." He claims that at a first glance their stances on modernity seem to be quite similar: same dissatisfaction with the outcome of modern civilization, its soullessness, its conquest of nature, same rejection of the prevailing historicist understanding of man. Modernity for Strauss constitutes above all a break with the classical thinking. Strauss speaks in terms of the project of modernity: modernity is not a by-product of some objective processes or the development of Hegelian Spirit, but rather it was actualized by the means of some positive project. In turn, Löwith elaborates the problem of modernity not on the plane of political philosophy, but on the plane of philosophy of history. Löwith conceives modernity not as a radical break, but in terms of the persistence of the basic eschatological pattern after which the secularized modern philosophies of history are fashioned (the secularization thesis). He focuses on the demise of the cosmological reflection which brings forth existentialism and historicism. Both Strauss and Löwith claim that modernity ended up in a crisis which may be called nihilism. The recognition of the crisis of modernity led them both to reflect on the possibility of return. But the problem of return is ambiguous since the Western civilization consists of two main elements: the Bible and Greek philosophy, or in a more metaphorical language: Jerusalem and Athens. In turn, for Löwith the problem of return emerged not in the form of the conflict between Jerusalem and Athens, but above all in the form of two interpretations of nihilism given by Kierkegaard and Nietzsche. The chapter analyzes the grounds of their rejection of the homogenous and universal state.

Emmanuel Patard begins his chapter entitled *Remarks on the Strauss-Kojève Dialogue and Its Presuppositions* with brief remarks on the current grave state of the modern project of universal Enlightenment. Alexandre Kojève, the famous commentator of Hegel, still stood for the modern project, the aim of which he called "universal and homogeneous State," the End-State which is supposed to fulfill the fundamental aspirations of Man, to solve all contradictions and conflicts in human thought and action. Kojève challenged *On Tyranny*, Leo Strauss's defense and illustration of the classical view of the fundamental problems through a commentary on Xenophon's *Hiero*. Kojève's critical review was for Strauss a fitting opportunity to confront the philosophical quarrel between Ancients and Moderns, in a "Restatement" which appears to be the most extensive and the deepest reply to the critiques which have been addressed to his achievement. In the famous concluding paragraph of his "Restatement," Strauss stated the conflicting presuppositions of his discussion with Kojève. Patard discusses the debate in a detailed way. Kojève equated Hegel's key statement *"Geist* ist Zeit" with the following one: *"Man is* Time," Time exists insofar there is History, i.e., human existence, driven by Desire (oriented toward future: what is absent, present insofar it is absent), Desire of Desire (desire as constituting man in his humanity, i.e., anthropogenic desire), "Man is Desire for Recognition," and eventually the "historical evolution which finally comes to the universal and homogeneous State." Patard discusses the problem of the last men with regard to the universal and homogenous state and the grounds of Strauss's objection to it. He also draws our attention to the final, well-known sentence from Strauss's concluding paragraph that clearly alludes to Heidegger's revival of the question of Being (*Seinsfrage*), and it implies that a common agreement between Strauss and Kojève against Heidegger is crucial in their debate.

Piotr Nowak in his chapter entitled *Carl Schmitt and his Critic* claims that Carl Schmitt, like Hobbes before, was considered to be an intellectual pariah for many years. According to him Hobbes and Schmitt certainly share a few concepts, first formulated by Hobbes and then filled with new meaning by Schmitt such as *bellum omnium contra omnes*, "protection in exchange for obedience," "man is a wolf to another man." The two authors shared the anthropological axiom – similar understanding of *human nature*, of its evil character. Nowak discusses a masterly critique of Schmitt by Leo Strauss. For Hobbes, the state of nature is a constant struggle against adversity, against physical and social power, the influence and wills of other people. In this sense, the state of nature is impossible. One cannot live in such conditions. According to Schmitt, however, the state of nature does not concern individuals but separate totalities, states which have deadly enemies (deadly – because a political conflict is always a struggle for life and death) as well as potential allies and neutral states. The state of nature defined in this way is not a fiction. However it may become a fiction when the world is completely depoliticized. Hobbes pictured the mechanics and the workings of the power apparatus of the modern state. According to Nowak it was Schmitt who penetrated the beast from the inside and who found the direct opposite of the Leviathan.

Till Kinzel in his chapter entitled *Postmodernism and the Art of Writing: The Importance of Leo Strauss for the 21st Century* speaks about Strauss within the context of postmodernism in order to highlight today's very strong prejudices to Strauss's understanding of philosophy. These obstacles are based on the extreme historicism or culturalism that is dominant in the current academic discourse and which denies any transcultural standards as well as the ability to overcome the limitations of time. The thought of Michel Foucault or Jacques Lacan claims something contrary to Strauss, namely that writers are not masters of their words but rather the servants of some mysterious unconscious that speaks through them. Kinzel stresses the importance of Leo Strauss whose work presents a serious challenge to the reigning orthodoxies about how to read texts. Strauss rejected the current presupposition that the "humanities" always historicize and the dogma that denies the very possibility of philosophy in the original sense. Strauss's conception of philosophy aims to preserve an awareness of the necessity not to stop thinking, which is identical with asking questions. These questions in turn always imply the crucial questions "Why philosophy?" and "What is philosophy?" And these questions cannot be questions about anything, but about most important and weighty matters. Strauss takes up Plato's famous allegory and talks about the so-called second cave into which we have fallen. The second cave of which Strauss speaks in the 1930s constitutes our modern predicament which is an unnatural situation. It is necessary to use (and it is paradoxical) unnatural means to retrieve something of the natural horizon that constitutes the starting point for philosophy as originally understood. We can try to ascend from the cave by means of "lesendes Lernen" (learning by reading). So the task of philosophical education for the 21st century may thus well be to teach students the art of reading. Kinzel concludes emphatically: Reading is a form of action in behalf of philosophy: *Legere est agere.*

The last chapter entitled *Leo Strauss's* Gynaikologia, written by Laurence Lampert (who himself could not be present at the conference), gives a significant example of an art of reading deeply inspired by Strauss's concept of esoterism. Lampert refers to the two late books by Strauss that convey Xenophon's picture of Socrates. The method he uses is a kind of very careful exegesis whose aim consists in recovering the twofold meaning of the text; an exegesis that should be considered an invitation to study the text in order to confirm or refute the claims made by the commentator. Thus, from Lampert's point of view, a philosophic text is esoteric, which means that it "has hidden marvels" for the most selected audience. According to him, such an art of esoteric writing was practiced by the classic pupil of Socrates as well as by Strauss philosophically commenting on his works. Now, the title "gynaikologia" is given by Strauss and it covers four chapters containing Socrates' narration of his conversation with Ischomachos. These are: Marriage according to the gods and according to the law (Chapter VII); Order, I (Chapter VIII); Order, II (Chapter IX); Cosmetics (Chapter X). Lampert shows that Strauss's commentary deliberately reflects the structure of Xenophon's book. Not leaving the plane of exegesis he expresses the suggestion that "Xenophon's mature Socrates offered his teleotheology" (with this term, also coined by Strauss, meaning that "Socrates teaches a theology and a cosmology that maintain that gods manage a cosmos end-directed for human benefit") "as Plato's mature Socrates offered his doctrine of ideas;" they occur to be the teachings susceptible to "difficulties or logical refutation, but salutary or useful for young gentlemen and prospective philosophers." In Lampert's words, "while the peculiarly Socratic philosophizing was taken up in various ways by Xenophon, Plato, and Aristotle it remained a never ceasing consideration of nature and human nature sheltered behind a salutary teaching on nature and human nature that it knew to have difficulties." Then it seems that we are left with a fundamental question of the philosopher's ability and willingness to create a new political order to replace a dying world he still lives in, or some new values regarding gods and virtue to be pursued, by means of his salutary teaching on human nature.

* * *

First and foremost, the editors of this volume want to thank all the authors for their excellent contributions to the book.

We would also like to express our deep gratitude to the following: Bogdan Szlachta, Dean of the Department of International and Political Studies and Chair of Political Philosophy, Jagiellonian University, for his generous support of this publication (we keep also in mind his support of the conference and, generally, of our academic initiatives); Bruce Fingerhut, the director of St. Augustine's Press, for his being most sympathetic to our project and ready to cooperate on it; Marta Czerwonka from the Jagiellonian University Press, for her assistance; Lisa Fretschel, for her advice on language.

Our fruitful encounters with Professor Heinrich Meier in Munich – one of us traveled there in May, 2008, and next we both paid a visit to him in November that year – deserve special acknowledgment as they provided us with many insights and suggestions indispensable for the final outcome of the conference on Leo Strauss and this publication as well.

Paweł Armada, Arkadiusz Górnisiewicz
Krakow, April 2010

Heinrich Meier

WHY LEO STRAUSS?
FOUR ANSWERS AND ONE CONSIDERATION
CONCERNING THE USES AND DISADVANTAGES
OF THE SCHOOL FOR THE PHILOSOPHICAL LIFE[*]

There are good reasons to study Leo Strauss. Philosophical, existential, and po-litical reasons. Those reasons existed before Strauss's star rose on both sides of the Atlantic on the media horizon in the year 2003, and those reasons will con-tinue to exist long after the quarrel over Strauss's alleged influence on the foreign policy of the only remaining world power has become completely a thing of the past. I do not want to discuss that short-lived quarrel more closely here. Instead, I want to give an answer to the question "Why Leo Strauss?," a question that can most definitely be separated from the latest Strauss boom. In fact, it was not only after Strauss came to be on so many people's lips that the question was put to me; no, I have come up against it as long as I have seriously studied his work and his thought. It may be appropriate for someone coming from Old Europe to address this question as the opening question at the first conference on Strauss taking place in what once was called New Europe.

The question "Why Leo Strauss?" can be the expression of either dismissive surprise or open-minded wonder. First of all and most often it is the result of in-sufficient knowledge. Strauss, who was born in Kirchhain, Germany in 1899 and died in Annapolis, USA in 1973, was long the great unknown among the thinkers of the twentieth century. During his lifetime he doubtless drew far less attention to himself than Martin Heidegger or Ludwig Wittgenstein, Carl Schmitt or Karl Barth. Yet the lack of familiarity is not everything. How often I was asked by students of Strauss's and by students of his students in the U.S. during the 1980s and '90s why I confronted Strauss so intensively, and how often that question was followed by another, namely who had pointed me to Strauss, who had told me to read his books carefully. The second question tacitly assumes that a care-ful reading of Strauss's oeuvre is very unlikely without someone else's guidance,

---

if not to say authoritative instruction. An intensive confrontation with Strauss's thought, the question implies, could hardly grow solely out of an encounter with his books. Members of a school are all too inclined to regard as indispensable what for them was of special significance, and thus to overvalue personal contact, the teacher's example, the oral tradition, in a word: everything to which the school gives rise, everything it preserves and passes on. This may explain in large part the fact, which seems at first glance to be paradoxical, that in the orbit of the school precisely the books of the teacher are not believed to be capable of achieving what is ascribed to the books of other philosophers – provided they are great philosophers and provided they are great books: the ability to win over, on their own merits, unknown readers in an unknown place in an unknown future, to challenge them seriously, to teach them to read, to move them to think, and, in the best case, to lead them to the philosophical life.

The institution of the school plays an important role in the history of philosophy, and the quarrel over Strauss we have been witnessing since 2003 would not even exist without the school. Thus I shall return to the school later. But first I leave it behind in order to answer without further ado the question of why I study Strauss. Well, for the same reasons I study other philosophers: To enter into a dialogue about the most important questions that move us. To gain clarity on the fundamental alternatives of human existence. To explore the possibilities that philosophy holds in store for thinking the whole. To further my knowledge of myself. I did not know Strauss personally. I was never the student of one of his students. I was never told by anyone to study his writings. I read his books as I read the books of Rousseau or Plato, Nietzsche or Lucretius. Though I soon came to read these authors differently than I had read them before. The confrontation with Strauss gave me a new access to them. Through nothing and no one have I learned to read better, more attentively, more fruitfully than through reading Strauss.

In saying that, I have already arrived at my answer to the question "Why Leo Strauss?" in the precise sense. Namely, the answer to the question of what distinguishes Strauss, what is his special place in the history of philosophy, what original insight he holds in store, what is to be found in him, or what discloses itself to us more easily in him that otherwise would be difficult to find. I shall unfold my answer into four answers, which in the end you may put together into one answer.

First answer: Leo Strauss opens up a new historical and a different philosophical access to the history of philosophy. The cause that more than anything else was long associated with the name Leo Strauss was the exoteric-esoteric art of writing. The discovery of the way in which philosophers communicated different things to different addressees of their writings and gave them different things to think about over more than two millennia is of fundamental significance for the proper understanding of the history of philosophy. It makes one fully aware of a fact that had fallen increasingly into oblivion after the French Revolution, namely that the philosophers of the past wrote under conditions of censorship and persecution – even if this was by no means the only reason why they availed themselves of the exoteric-esoteric distinction – a situation that every interpretation has to take into account that wants to do historical justice to its object. An adequate understanding of the philosophical tradition therefore presupposes an in-depth study of and intimate familiarity with that "forgotten kind of writing" which Strauss brought to light and revived in his writings.

The fruitfulness of Strauss's rediscovery for historical research can hardly be overestimated. This holds no less regarding the philosophical consequences that follow from it. If the philosophers of the past directed their books at quite different addressees, between whom they themselves carefully distinguished, if they spoke to the vast majority of their contemporaries – or never lost sight of them as their audience – and if they directed their discourse at the same time to the small number of those capable of philosophy or wrote for future philosophers, then it becomes clear that they took the opinions of their contemporaries and the authoritative positions of faith proper to the commonwealths in which they lived into consideration when presenting their teachings in order to give the few who know how to understand, to give those few to understand in the same books what separated the philosophers from precisely those opinions and positions of faith or the extent to which they subjected those opinions and positions of faith to a fundamental critique.

For the interpreter of their books it follows that he must respond to the art of careful writing with the art of careful reading and that for him there is no other way to find out what the authors thought about the matter of concern to them than to get completely involved in the movement of thought that underlies the exoteric-esoteric presentation, and, with such guidance, to think the matter himself that is in question. In other words, the interpreter must inquire starting from a given work, which calls for his complete attention both in its rhetorical details and as an articulated whole, back to the author's intention; the interpreter must summon up all his powers in order to live up to the philosophical activity that found its expression in that work without having been absorbed by it or being identical with it. That is ultimately what Strauss's famous hermeneutic maxim – that it is necessary to understand a philosopher exactly as he understood himself – aims at, that is where it leads.

I would like to name by way of summary three philosophical consequences of the access Strauss opened up. The first concerns the assertion of historicism that all thought is essentially conditioned by history. If there is a decisive difference between the double-faced, exoteric-esoterically presented teaching and the thought of the philosophers, it cannot be concluded from the "historically conditioned" writing and speaking of philosophers – which takes the expectations, opinions, and prejudices of their contemporaries into consideration in order to fulfill its political purpose – that in their thinking the authors were subject to the same expectations, opinions, and prejudices. The historical dependence of their philosophy is therefore no longer a self-evident presupposition but first and foremost an object of inquiry for a philosophically adequate confrontation with the history of philosophy.

Secondly, such a confrontation will not stop with the historical reconstruction of the doctrines that have made or can make their way into the textbooks on the history of philosophy. Rather, it will transform the awareness of the distinction between doctrinal content and philosophical activity into a fundamental reflection on the relationship between teaching and thought, work and philosophical existence. In doing so, it is able to counteract the petrification of philosophy in the history of its doctrines and systems more radically and emphatically than was the so-called "destruction of the tradition," which sought to wrest the concealed, forgotten, or unraised questions from the predominance of answers in the tradition and to regain them for thinking. The undertaking of the early Heidegger, whose philosophical impulse Strauss took up and carried farther, is exceeded by the confrontation just sketched especially insofar as it makes the turn from the diversity of historical contributions that separates the philosophers to the common ground of natural capacities that connects the philosophers and then to the one matter of concern that unites them.

To this fundamental turn from history to nature corresponds, on the level of interpretation, the movement from the articulated whole of the work to the unifying intention of the author and with it – to name the third consequence – an understanding, if one succeeds, that in the final analysis is based on the encounter of kindred natures. This encounter is what allows the communication and sharing of experiences that are intrinsically bound up with the philosophical activity, and it is the ultimate prerequisite of the hermeneutic openness Strauss demands, of the effort to understand a philosopher as he understood or understands himself, in the hope that on this path something is to be learned that is of the greatest importance for us.

Second answer: Leo Strauss draws our attention to the fact that philosophy is a way of life. What I have said about the access to the history of philosophy opened up by Strauss – beginning with the distinction between the doctrinal level and the philosophical activity that precedes it, via the attempt to break open the congealment of the tradition in the movement of penetrating inquiry back into the intention of the philosopher, to the common insights and experiences that connect philosophical natures in dialogue above and beyond all historical breaks and material differences between teachings – all that has its vanishing point in the fact that philosophy is to be grasped neither as a body of doctrines nor as a discipline but as a way of life. Philosophy is the way of life that is grounded in unreserved questioning and that finds its inner unity through a questioning and inquiry that does not stop at any answer that owes its authentication to an authority. Strauss showed, as no other philosopher during his lifetime and as few philosophers before him, that philosophy is a special way of life on which special demands of justification and consistency are to be made. In giving prominence to the philosophical life, one takes account of a historical constellation in which philosophy is in danger of failing to answer the question of its right and its necessity, to answer the question "Why philosophy?"

Third answer: Leo Strauss places political philosophy at the center of philosophy. To grasp philosophy as a way of life means to grasp it as an answer to the question of what is right: The philosophical life is the life that philosophers have chosen for themselves as the right life and have recognized to be the best life. As a distinct way of life that rests on a conscious choice and is held fast in the face of all resistance, philosophy sees itself confronted not only with competing but also with authoritative answers to the question of what is right and just for man. It meets political obligations and moral demands that oppose it with the will to enforcement. It is subject to the law of the commonwealth, divine or human commandments and prohibitions. The question of what is right is posed in the sphere of the political. In this way both the rank of the political things is indicated and the urgency for philosophy of confronting them is designated.

Political philosophy makes the political things the object of inquiry: the foundations of the political community, the duties and rights of its members, the ends and means of their action, war and peace internally and in relation to other commonwealths. Yet although political philosophy, as far as its subject matter is concerned, denotes merely a part of philosophy, it by no means has a narrowly circumscribed segment of human life as its object. Nor do we meet in this object, say, an autonomous domain of life that exists alongside a number of autonomous domains of life or "provinces of culture" of equal rank. The central questions of political philosophy – the questions of the best political order, of the right life, of just rule, of the necessary weight of authority, knowledge, and force – can be adequately raised only in conjunction with those other questions of the nature of man, of his place between beast and God, of the abilities of the human mind, the capacities of the human soul, and the needs of the human body. The object of political philosophy is thus the human things in the comprehensive sense.

Because political philosophy carries out the confrontation with the question of what is right with the seriousness and circumspection required by the sphere of the political, political philosophy becomes the locus of philosophy's reflection on itself. The contemplation of the political conditions of its existence and the ascertainment of the natural foundations of philosophy belong just as much to political philosophy as does the insight into the insuperable tension between the right and the nature of philosophy on the one hand and the requirements of the political community on the other, and therefore the reflection on the rhetoric needed to do justice to that tension. Political philosophy is charged with the political defense of philosophy, and the rational justification of philosophy can take place nowhere but here. Political philosophy thus proves to be the part of philosophy in which the whole of philosophy is at stake.

Fourth answer: Like no philosopher before him, Leo Strauss makes the theo-logico-political problem his theme. The rational justification of the philosophical life is neither to be achieved by means of theoretical positings and deductions nor can it be made dependent upon the accomplishment of systematic efforts, the conclusion and success of which lie in an uncertain future. Philosophy must demonstrate its rationality elenctically, in confrontation with its most powerful antagonists and with the most demanding alternative. And it must undertake this confrontation in the present. A confrontation that is literally *fundamental* for the philosophical life cannot be postponed any more than it can be delegated.

When in 1964 Strauss characterized in retrospect the theologico-political problem as *the* theme of his studies, he said in almost as many words that his entire work revolved around philosophy as a way of life and that he had its jus-tification in view. For the talk of the theologico-political problem serves Strauss as an abbreviation for the urgency of the confrontation with the theological and the political alternative to the philosophical life or for the necessity of including in the philosophical investigation the opinions and objections that are, or can be, raised against philosophy by appealing to a human or superhuman authority. If philosophy is able to justify its right and its truth only elenctically, then it has to concentrate on that way of life by which its own answer to the question of what is right might be defeated. If philosophy is able to demonstrate its rationality only by knowing how to repel and refute the most powerful objection to philosophy, it has to seek out that objection and make it as strong as it possibly can, as strong as only philosophy can make it. It is in this sense that Strauss turned to the political life and the life of the obedience of faith in his theologico-political treatises. It is in this sense that he sought out the challenge of revelation and made it strong for philosophy. Because there is no more powerful objection to the philosophical life imaginable than the objection that appeals to faith in the omnipotent God and his commandment or law.

Two digressions may help to clarify what is at stake in my fourth answer. The first digression addresses the challenge of faith in revelation directly and makes Strauss speak to us in his own words. The second is meant to explain how the theologico-political treatises by Strauss himself or those inspired by him relate to the well-known theologico-political treatises of the early moderns.

First digression: In a lecture about "philosophy and revelation" which he gave in January 1948 at the Hartford Theological Seminary in Hartford, Connecticut, under the prescribed title "Reason and Revelation," Strauss presents the conflict between philosophy and revelation more sharply and more outspokenly than in any of his writings before or after. Strauss works out the opposition in which the freedom of questioning and knowing that philosophy requires and the obedience to the sovereign authority that revelation commands stand to one another: "To the philosophic view that man's happiness consists in free investigation or insight, the Bible opposes the view that man's happiness consists in obedience to God."

The opposition in principle between philosophy and revelation regarding man's happiness already proves in the next sentence to be the truly radical opposition regarding the right and the necessity of philosophy:

> The Bible thus offers the only challenge to the claim of philosophy which can reasonably be made. One cannot seriously question the claim of philosophy in the name, e.g., of politics or poetry. To say nothing of other considerations, man's ultimate aim is what is really good and not what merely *seems* to be good, and only through *knowledge* of the good is he enabled to find the good.

Strauss steers from the truly radical opposition directly towards the absolutely fundamental alternative, on which the conflict between philosophy and revelation is based and which concerns man as man:

> But this is indeed the question: whether men can acquire the knowledge of the good, without which they cannot guide their lives individually and collectively, by the unaided efforts of their reason, or whether they are dependent for that knowledge on divine revelation. Only through the Bible is philosophy, or the quest for knowledge, challenged by *knowledge*, viz. by knowledge revealed by the omniscient God, or by knowledge identical with the self-communication of God. No alternative is more fundamental than the alternative: human guidance or divine guidance. *Tertium non datur.**

That philosophy can seriously be called into question only in the name of revelation means two things: Revelation appears as *the* challenge to philosophy since it holds the prospect of the fulfillment of the deepest desire that moves philosophy, the knowledge of truth, and at the same time radically negates that desire itself as a free desire. The God of revelation claims to have at his disposal in perfection, without restriction, and without distortion, precisely that at which the eros of philosophy aims; but he makes access to it subject to his sovereign decision to reveal the truth he harbors within himself to whom he wishes, when he wishes, where he wishes, and how he wishes, in the bounds that his will establishes and to the ends that his judgment determines. For philosophy, revelation represents both a theoretical and an existential challenge. Revelation challenges philosophy theoretically by confronting philosophy with the question of whether the truth, the all-important truth, is not missed when it is sought after freely by man, whether the sole possible access to truth does not instead consist in its devout acceptance of him who *is* the truth. Revelation challenges philosophy existentially by confronting philosophy with the commandment of obedience, which rejects the philosophical life in the name of the highest authority conceivable and imposes on that life the severest sanction imaginable. Politics or poetry are incapable of *seriously* calling philosophy into question since they or so long as they – do not negate the philosophical life by appealing to the knowledge, truth, and power of the omniscient, the omnipotent, the unfathomable God and cannot

---

* Leo Strauss, *Reason and Revelation*, in Heinrich Meier, *Leo Strauss and the Theologico-Political Problem* (New York: Cambridge University Press, 2006), p. 149 [*editors' note*].

add weight to their objection to philosophy with the prospect of eternal salvation or eternal damnation. The theologico-political problem draws our attention to the requirement to defend the right and the necessity of philosophy against the double challenge that revelation and the life based on it, the life of the obedience of faith, represents for philosophy. The precise formulation with which Strauss chooses to characterize the unifying theme of his studies, namely, as a theologico-*political* problem contains a hint about the path on which the right and the necessity of philosophy are capable of being justified and on which the confrontation with revelation is capable of being carried out successfully.

Second digression: Strauss's mention of the "theologico-political problem" calls to mind the theologico-political enterprise that drove modern philosophy forward. From Strauss's perspective this enterprise was unsuccessful in at least one respect: it was unable to settle the theologico-political *problem*. The political success of the enterprise, the establishment of liberal society, gave the problem merely, but consequentially, a new twist: the old theological difficulty was left unresolved, whereas the new political challenge consisted henceforth in restoring the rank of the political and in making the dignity of the political life visible once again. The historical process initiated by the theologico-political enterprise of modern philosophy led to the parceling of human life into a multiplicity of "autonomous provinces of culture." In the supposedly amicable cooperation and coexistence of the economy, politics, religion, art, science, etc., philosophy loses the serious alternatives, and with them fades the awareness that philosophy is a special way of life. In the world of modern culture that it decisively helped to bring about, philosophy is less equipped than ever to carry out the confrontation with revelation successfully and to justify its right and its necessity rationally.

In 1935, in an enigmatic footnote to his book *Philosophy and Law*, Strauss raises in passing, as it were, the question of the appropriate philosophical treatment of the theologico-political problem. A radical critique of the modern concept of "culture" – as one crux of which he names the "fact of religion" and as its other crux the "fact of the political" – is possible, Strauss says, only in the form of a "theologico-political treatise." However, such a treatise would have to have, "if it is not to lead once again to the founding of culture, exactly the opposite tendency of the theologico-political treatises of the seventeenth century, especially those by Hobbes and Spinoza." The thrust of the theologico-political treatises of the seventeenth century aimed at the recovery and the persistent safeguarding of the *libertas philosophandi* by means of an effective separation of politics from theology. Peace and security – thus read philosophy's conceptual offering in its secular alliance with the political sovereign – could be achieved on the path of the progressive domination of nature and the transformation enabled thereby of human living conditions in general. Philosophy would supply the reliable and manageable knowledge required for the methodical conquest of nature and the rational reorganization of society, while the sovereign would have to take care of political protection. With this comprehensive project, the battle of the theologi-co-political treatises against the "kingdom of darkness" and "superstition" took the lead. What begins with the emancipation of politics from theology results ultimately, after the successful unleashing of a world of increasing purposive rationality and growing prosperity, in a state of incomprehension of and indif-ference towards the original sense of the theologico-political critique, a state in which the demands of politics are rejected with the same matter-of-factness as those of religion. This state finds its conspicuous expression in the existence of the bourgeois, who closes himself to all claims that aim at the whole, and in a phi-losophy that no longer knows how to answer the question "Why philosophy?." A theologico-political treatise with "exactly the opposite tendency" of the trea-tises that founded the historical development of liberal "culture" – though their intention and achievement went beyond that founding – would thus have to bring once again to awareness, in perfect clarity, the claims that the "original facts" of politics and of religion contain and reawaken the understanding of the connection that exists between the two. When Strauss speaks of a theologico-political trea-tise, he is speaking of a philosophical writing that faces the theological and the political alternative and that leads, by way of the confrontation with the demands of politics and religion, to philosophy. The theologico-political treatise has, in other words, both an elenctic and a protreptic character.

The four answers I have given – Strauss opens up a new historical and a dif-ferent philosophical access to the history of philosophy. He draws our attention to the fact that philosophy is a way of life. He places political philosophy at the center of philosophy. Like no philosopher before him, he makes the theologico-political problem his theme – these four answers outline corner points of a contri-bution to philosophy that, like few others, causes us to see the new in the old, the foreign in the familiar, one's own in one's counterpart, and depth in the surface, and whose radicality fills us with all the more wonder the farther and the more freely we move in the space that this contribution discloses to self-knowledge. For those among and after us for whom the cause of philosophy is of vital im-portance there are good reasons to study Strauss's work and thought intensively.

Let me return now to the school. In June 2002, a few months before the quar-rel over Strauss's influence on U.S. foreign policy began to preoccupy the media, I said in a lecture at the Munich symposium "Living Issues in the Thought of Leo Strauss" that Strauss, having learned from historical experience, was not willing to pay the price that philosophers from Plato to Nietzsche had been willing to pay for their teachings of political founding and their projects of counter-founding. The sole political endeavor, I noted, the sole political act of consequence that Strauss brought himself to launch was to found a school, which the offer of a pro-fessorship in political philosophy at the University of Chicago in 1949 provided him the opportunity to do. Then I added that Strauss surely was aware of the price he had to pay for making this political decision. I was asked at the time what price

I was speaking about. A question that presumably would not have been asked a year later. But let us begin with two other questions: What can move a philosopher to found a school? And in what sense does the founding involve a political decision?

The school has uncontestable advantages for the development of a comprehensive teaching, for the pursuit of a research project, and for the formation of an interpretive approach. It makes it easier to test philosophical arguments and to experiment with rhetorical figures. It makes possible both the thorough differentiation of an edifice of thought in directions, and the application of an interpretation to objects, the pursuit or execution of which would surpass an individual's powers. In the best case, the semi-public sphere of the school permits the combination of the playful treatment of possible answers that presupposes the release from the demands of public self-assertion, and the serious involvement with the true questions that requires agreement about the fundamental points of a common agenda. The institution of the school helps to gain an audience for a new orientation of philosophy and to lend it stability. It is the means of choice when the aim is to found a tradition and thereby to make it more likely that an oeuvre will remain accessible to future generations. The school offers, not least, the possibility of making some citizens familiar with philosophy and educating them in such a way that, when they later assume responsibilities in the commonwealth, those citizens will treat philosophy favorably or at least respectfully and, if necessary, grant it protection and support.

Strauss used all of these advantages of the school. He also took the opportunity – following Plato's and Aristotle's example – to foster the politically gifted and the gentlemen among his students. As a citizen of the United States of America, he was loyal to the country that had given him refuge from persecution. He showed himself to be a friend of the liberal democracy that allowed him to lead a philosophical life. He prompted a number of his students to investigate the historical, constitutional, and political foundations of the United States and encouraged them to defend those foundations. He respected their patriotism and taught them to understand the dignity that is proper to the political life. Yet he made it clear: "patriotism is not enough," and he – no less than Socrates, the citizen of Athens – left no doubt about the fact that he did not consider the political life to be the best life.

The founding of a philosophical school, however, becomes a political decision not only insofar as the founding makes it possible to exert a salutary influence on the commonwealth – no matter how mediate, no matter how variously refracted that influence may be. It is a political decision already insofar as the school like the commonwealth comprises quite different natures, it too consists of philosophers and non-philosophers who (bound together to varying degrees) cooperate in different ways, and therefore the central determinations that apply to the tension between the political community and philosophy remain valid in the relationship of the school to philosophy. For the school, no less than for the commonwealth, it holds true that different addressees have to be addressed differently, that they grasp the teaching differently and pass it on differently. The school demands political action and is fraught with political risks.

If the school gains a larger audience for the philosophical teaching, it also contributes to strengthening and oversimplifying the doctrinal content of philosophy, to emphasizing everything that allows of being taught and reduced to formulas, and, without any in-depth confrontation with the cause or the matter at issue, can be repeated, applied, and communicated. And if the school is able to exert some political influence, then it is in danger of accommodating philosophy to a particular regime or underscoring its closeness to this regime in such a way that the philosophically gifted in the future or in other regions of the world who have a genuine philosophical interest in that teaching must once again loosen the link to the political regime in order to free the teaching from the odium of being bound to an order prevailing at a certain time and in a certain place or being subservient to an ideology.

The founding of a school will be successful only if the teacher adapts his oral teaching to his students' ability to understand it. It is very likely that he will entrust his farthest-reaching reflections, his most profound thoughts, and his most challenging considerations to his carefully written books. Members of a school, however, are inclined, as I mentioned, to value the oral tradition more highly. They tend to overestimate or to regard as indispensable what for them was of special significance. This may explain in part why the school is so susceptible to apologetic tendencies regarding the teacher's philosophical radicality, why precisely in its orbit his thought is often rendered innocuous, and why pieties of all kinds are able to take root there.

Strauss was as familiar as anyone with the problem of the school and the tradition in philosophy. He knew the history of Platonism, of the Aristotelian, Epicurean, and Stoic schools, their successors and their latest heirs. In his dialogue with Alexandre Kojève on tyranny and the politics of the philosophers, he commented in no uncertain terms in 1950 on the formation of sects and drew a sharp line between the philosopher and the sectarian. Precisely because he had confronted the philosophical tradition so intensively, he was aware that the petrification of philosophy in the tradition can be cleared away again and again, he was aware that philosophical energy can be set free ever anew from its encapsulation in doctrines. And precisely because he was familiar with the history of the schools of the ancients, he was also aware that those schools helped essentially to make philosophy conspicuous as a way of life. In modernity, Rousseau and Nietzsche attempted to give the philosophical life a visible shape by emphatically drawing attention to their own lives. The alternative was the founding of a school, which does not have to produce only members of a school. Aristotle was a member of Plato's school for twenty years, nearly twice as long as he was able to teach in his own school, the Lyceum. Aristotle left the Academy as a philosopher, and from his school emerged other philosophers in turn. Just as from the school that Strauss founded philosophers have emerged – and by no means only "Straussians."

At the end of my lecture I should like to come back to the beginning and, leaving the school behind, return to the philosophical reader. Strauss's deepest response to the challenge of historicism, his answer to the question of whether philosophy is at all possible in the original meaning of the term, I stated in my first argument, Strauss's deepest response is contained in the movement from the history of philosophy to the intention of the philosopher. It is not the subject of Strauss's teaching in the sense in which, for instance, his reconstruction of the "three waves of modernity," historically inaugurated by Machiavelli, Rousseau, and Nietzsche, respectively, can be the subject of teaching and learning. It is disclosed solely in consciously and independently carrying out the hermeneutic venture itself that Strauss exemplified in his penetrating interpretations. Whoever is wholly devoted to understanding a philosopher exactly as he understood himself, and whoever allows himself to be led in the study of that philosopher by the maxim that the greatest effort and care is to be employed in order to discover whether his oeuvre contains truth, may reach the point at which it no longer makes any difference to him whether he thinks the thoughts of the philosopher or his own, because he moves on a plane on which the arguments take the lead and the alternatives visibly emerge that, beyond the "historical embeddedness" of both the author and the interpreter, determine the issue towards which the thought of both is directed. Strauss's interpretations show that this point can be reached in the study of Nietzsche or Rousseau as well as in the study of Plato or Maimonides. And it is no less reachable in the confrontation with Strauss, who clothes his philosophy almost exclusively in the garb of commentary. "It may be added" – as Strauss asserted of Alfarabi in an essay full of self-explicative statements – "that by transmitting the most precious knowledge, not in 'systematic' works, but in the guise of a historical account," Strauss "indicates his view concerning 'originality' and 'individuality' in philosophy: what comes into sight as the 'original' or the 'personal' 'contribution' of a philosopher is infinitely less significant than his private, and truly original and individual understanding of the necessarily anonymous truth."*

If it is possible to return from the history of philosophy to the intention of the philosopher, and if the individual "contribution" of a philosopher can direct our attention to the truly individual understanding of the necessarily anonymous truth, then the contributions to the history of philosophy themselves appear in a different light. Do they not allow us to come to the insight that "leaving the historical cave" was always possible at those times for which the traditional contributions give testimony? And do they not at the same time provide us with the opportunity

---

* Leo Strauss, *"Farabi's 'Plato'*," in *Louis Ginzberg Jubilee Volume* (New York 1945), p. 377 [*editors' note*].

to undergo, in turn, the liberating experience that accompanies the ascent from opinion to knowledge? The contributions to philosophy would thereby gain a justification that reaches deeper than their history and carries more weight than the danger of their petrification in the tradition. For despite their material or doctrinal content in the more restricted sense, those contributions have in common that they introduce and lead some of us to the philosophical life. Consequently, they refer to a reflection that precedes the individual contributions and convinces the most diverse philosophers that the philosophical life is good – that it will be good for kindred natures even if they are to reach answers that considerably deviate from their own. Precisely the same reflection is the ultimate ground of the art of careful writing. Thus Strauss can say of the works to which the philosophically inspired art of writing gives rise that they are "written speeches caused by love."

Daniel Tanguay

LEO STRAUSS AND THE CONTEMPORARY RETURN TO POLITICAL PHILOSOPHY

In a famous essay asking the question "What is Political Philosophy?" Leo Strauss boldly assessed the state of the discipline in his times: "Today, political philosophy is in a state of decay and perhaps of putrefaction, if it has not vanished altogether," he wrote. In the same passage, he repeated again his gloomy observation: "We hardly exaggerate when we say that today political philosophy does not exist anymore, except as matter for burial, i.e. for historical research, or else as a theme of weak and unconvincing protests."[1]

It seems at first glance that this state of affairs has been completely reversed in the last thirty years. Political philosophy appears to have been resurrected. Even in France, so reluctant to deal with the questions raised by political philosophy for most of the twentieth century, there is a strong *"Renouveau de la philosophie politique."* In the French context, the standard story-line of this revival goes as follows: in the fifties, sixties and in the first half of the seventies, Marxism, structuralism and the social sciences prevailed in French thought and political philosophy was seen as the harbor of "suspicious liberals" like Raymond Aron, Raymond Polin or Eric Weil. In the middle of the seventies, critics of totalitarianism demolished the stronghold of Marxism.

The void created by the decay of Marxism and more generally by the end of ideologies was filled in the eighties by the import of American political thought and of the new ethics of discourse from Germany. This double movement was accelerated by the final failure of communism in the nineties. During that decade, French political philosophy became acquainted with the American debate between liberals and communitarians, between moderns and post-moderns, etc. Today, there is a certain institutionalization of political philosophy in France, even though a contemporary form of political radicalism has rejected the new liberal

---

[1] Leo Strauss, *What is Political Philosophy? and Other Studies* (Chicago: The University of Chicago Press, 1959), p. 17.

consensus and categorizes much of current philosophy as a kind of ideological justification for the neo-liberal order.

This story-line is certainly partial and simplistic: it does not take into account the rich movement of "deconstruction," the French Heideggerian resistance, the sociology of Pierre Bourdieu, the apparent transformation of the Althusserian school, and many other philosophical explorations that have nothing to do with the new political philosophy. But in spite of those necessary correctives to the general picture, political philosophy has undoubtedly gained a new status in France and it would not be hard to prove that this revival has also changed the landscape of German and American philosophies.

So Strauss's judgment seems to be invalidated by the strong renewed interest in political philosophy. We say "seems," since a closer look at the works of contemporary philosophers shows that they do not mean quite the same thing as Strauss when they refer to "political philosophy." Strauss considers that political philosophy attempts to answer two closely related questions: "What is the best regime?" and "What is the best life?" To find a satisfactory answer to these questions, one must first know the nature of human beings. The best regime would be in fact the regime that corresponds most adequately to the proper hierarchical ends of human nature. Furthermore, the best regime or *politeia* will be the kind of society "that is most conducive to human excellence."[2]

The definition of "human excellence" or "virtue" constitutes one of the cruxes of classical political philosophy and consequently of Strauss's thought. Political philosophy cannot though limit itself with the quest for human excellence in "words." It should also reflect on the concrete conditions of its actualization. If there is only one best regime, i.e., a combination of "way of life" and "form of government," that permits the actualization of true human excellence, there are nevertheless a variety of legitimate regimes. While the best regime is both noble and just, the legitimate regime is only just. So one practical task of political philosophy would be to determine what regime could be just in a set of given circumstances while keeping the concept of the best regime in mind.

The quest for the best regime defines the theoretical task of political philosophy. But the political philosopher should not forget the natural tensions between the just and the noble, between the legitimate regime and the best regime and, in the final analysis, between politics and philosophy. In accordance with this task, Strauss often uses the concept of the best regime as a means to stimulate an unending dialectic between the just and the noble, the possible and the desirable. It was essential for Strauss to keep a delicate balance between the legitimate and the best regimes insofar as he deems that the most fatal error of modern political thought is precisely to blur the distinction between the two.

---

[2]　Leo Strauss, *Natural Right and History* (Chicago: The University of Chicago Press, 1953), p. 135.

According to Strauss, modern natural law as exemplified in the doctrines of Hobbes, Locke and Rousseau, has been more interested in defining the conditions of legitimacy of a regime than in the quest of the best regime.[3] Strauss describes vividly in *Natural Right and History* what he called the "doctrinairism" of modern political thought:

> Natural public law intends to give such a universally valid solution to the political problem as is meant to be universally applicable in practice. In other words, whereas, according to the classics, political theory proper is essentially in need of being supplemented by the practical wisdom of the statesman on the spot, the new type of political theory solves, as such, the crucial practical problem: the problem of what order is just here and now.[4]

This modern doctrinairism constitutes for Strauss a major obstacle to the revival of an authentic philosophical questioning of political philosophy.

Strauss dares to repeat in all its depth the question of the best regime. His proposal for the renewal of political philosophy distinguishes itself from all other similar attempts in contemporary political philosophy. One of the main reasons for the hostility against Strauss's thought is related to his refusal to give a ready-made answer to the question of the best regime, an answer that would correspond only to the needs of the present situation. In this respect, political philosophy is for Strauss an untimely discipline.

By contrast, the contemporary political philosopher wishes to define the best regime for the Here and Now, instead of searching for the best regime as such. Furthermore, one can say that the question of the best regime is already settled for him by the progress of history: the best regime is democracy as understood by modern philosophy. There is surely a large realm of discussion concerning what is the hierarchy of goods in this regime, what is the best model of democracy, how to implement a true democracy and other difficult and important political and philosophical questions. But these questions are asked with the common conviction that there are no serious alternatives to the democratic regime. Contemporary political philosophy almost always presents itself as a theory of democracy.

This is a complete departure from the traditional understanding of political philosophy. Alain Renaut, editor of a monumental *Histoire de la philosophie politique* in five volumes, underlines in his general preface to the work that Rousseau's proclamation of the sovereignty of the people in the *Contrat social* marks the end of traditional forms of political philosophy and represents the "*a priori* of political culture of democratic societies."[5] This *a priori* is today the absolute point of departure for any political philosophy. In the best cases, political philosophers still try to build some sort of philosophical foundations for this *a priori*.

---

[3] Leo Strauss, "On Natural Law," in *Studies in Platonic Political Philosophy* (Chicago: The University of Chicago Press, 1983), pp. 143-144.

[4] Strauss, *Natural Right and History*, p. 192.

[5] Alain Renaut, ed., *Histoire de la philosophie politique*, vol. 1, *La liberté des anciens* (Paris: Calmann-Lévy, 1999), p. 20.

In the last forty years, many honest efforts have been spent on the quest for the correct foundations for democracy. The scholarly output on John Rawls, Jürgen Habermas or Charles Taylor has reached astronomic proportions. In considering this literature, one sometimes has the impression of confronting a kind of *Second Spanish Scholasticism*, where the art of commenting on the commentators of some canonical texts was elevated to a degree of almost absurd perfection. The sessions of the major political science associations can be easily compared to the long, exquisite and often boring *Disputationes* in Salamanca, Alcalà or Coimbra. You have only to substitute the vocabulary of the "*distinctio formalis*" for that of "reflective equilibrium" to get the picture. Like all scholastics, the new scholastics in political philosophy are all the more ferocious in their disputes over details given that they agree on the basic principles. For them, there is no doubt that the best regime is democracy, and even the specific form of democracy known as "liberal democracy." In this sense, they have already answered the traditional question of political philosophy: what is the best regime? Their question is rather: how to transform the real society more fully into the best regime?

It is very hard then today to distinguish between political philosophy and political theory. Both seem more concerned with providing an understanding and a philosophical legitimization of the political regime in its current form than with reflecting in a non-dogmatic and non-moralistic spirit on generally accepted principles and opinions. This kind of reflection is the prerequisite for an authentic quest in political philosophy, since, as Leo Strauss rightly said fifty years ago, "it is only when the Here and Now ceases to be the center of reference that a philosophic or scientific approach to politics can emerge."[6]

The thinker who escapes the Here and Now in order to gain some needed distance for a true philosophical evaluation risks being seen as an enemy of everything pertaining to the Spirit of the Age. This is especially true when he tries to scrutinize the assumptions of a dominant political regime. The very thought of such a query could arouse a citizen's suspicions that the philosopher does not share the principles of the current political regime. This suspicion of the political philosopher is as old as political philosophy itself. If someone says that a tolerant democracy is free from this type of suspicion, we have only to remind them of the American reception of Strauss's thought to prove the contrary.

Until now, American academics, or at least a large number of them, have not forgiven Strauss for having repeatedly and radically posed the question of the best regime. In the last fifty years, they could deal with various forms of Marxism, radical left ideas, Critical Theory, Neo-Nietzscheanism, Heideggerrianism and deconstructionism but they have rejected Strauss violently as a hidden enemy of all that is sacred in American political philosophy.

This tendentious reception of Strauss's thought in contemporary philosophy reminds us of the precarious situation of political philosophy in general when

---

[6] Strauss, *What is Political Philosophy? and Other Studies*, p. 16.

properly understood. If political philosophy is indeed the attempt, as Strauss stated, to "replace opinion about the nature of political things by a knowledge of the nature of political things,"[7] then political philosophers should keep their minds open to the possibility that the presuppositions and principles of any specific political regime could be inadequate or even untrue.

In his quest, a political philosopher should not presuppose that a particular regime is the final answer to the human problem, even though this particular regime seems the most decent and the most appropriate for the requirements of the present time. When political philosophy confuses its first task of answering the question of the best regime with the defense of a particular regime, it endangers the crucial distinction between opinion and truth. Paradoxically, this danger is especially sensitive in the case of a democracy which is the regime most favorable to philosophy and the closest imitation of the dialogical nature of philosophical quest.

It is therefore tempting for political philosophers to perceive in liberal democracy simply the embodiment of the best regime and thus to transform political philosophy into a kind of political science. The ultimate consequence of this transformation would be to erase the distance between opinions and truth, non-philosophers and philosophers. At the end of this process, the citizen will become the true philosopher and the philosopher will be no more than the ordinary citizen. Democracy will then prevail definitively over philosophy.

We think Strauss tried to avert this development. In his effort to revitalize the tradition of political philosophy, he wanted to keep philosophy separate from a too-strong identification with any specific political regime. This explains the central role played in his thought by the notion of the best regime *in words* instead of the best regime *in deed*. The best regime in words assumes a double function: first, it is a permanent standard from which we can evaluate the other regimes; second, this regime, at least theoretically, is tantamount to the regime where the philosophers are kings.

The best regime has never existed and could probably never be actualized. This is in fact the order of things. The concrete realization of the best regime would imply the sudden disappearance of the natural tensions between body and soul, opinion and truth, politics and philosophy, city and man. Unless a miraculous transformation of human nature occurs, these tensions are insuperable and even philosophy cannot eradicate them. For this specific reason, we dare say that the best regime is in Straussian parlance an "Idea," i.e., a "fundamental problem" which prompts us to adopt the general guideline proposed by Strauss: "Yet as long as there is no wisdom but only quest for wisdom, the evidence of all solutions is necessarily smaller than the evidence of the problems."[8] This proposal

---

[7] Ibid., pp. 11-12.

[8] Leo Strauss, *On Tyranny*, Victor Gourevitch and Michael S. Roth, eds. (New York: The Free Press, 1991), p. 196.

would seem unsatisfying for those who think that the task of political philosophy nowadays is to achieve modernity or to bring about universal justice and democracy on earth. In their eyes, political philosophy is more an active tool for transforming the world than a detached theoretical quest for the best regime.

We understand then why Strauss's willingness to keep open the question of the best regime, at least in theory, can awaken the worst suspicions among contemporary political philosophers. For them, Strauss's political philosophy is at best irrelevant because of its refusal of *the* evidence of our times. This already tendentious reception of Strauss's works has been rendered even more delicate by Strauss's very specific use in the American context. In the last decade, Strauss's questioning apparently became almost inaudible because the polemical tone surrounding his work was at its highest pitch. We can, however, hope that a more peaceful political situation in the United States will be conducive to a more detached and serene appreciation of Strauss's thought.

To grasp fully Strauss's eccentric position in contemporary political philosophy, it is useful to confront it with the position developed by Richard Rorty in an essay entitled "The Priority of Democracy to Philosophy."[9] This post-modern American philosopher epitomizes with an admirable frankness the intellectual and even the spiritual attitude that prevails in contemporary political philosophy and in the ethos of our regimes.

Rorty's intent is expressed in the title of his essay: he believes that democracy should take precedence over philosophy. Rorty makes two related claims: first, democracy has no need for strong philosophical justifications; second, any philosophical accounts contrary to democracy should be taken as private opinions and tolerated in so far as they do not intervene in the real political sphere. In other words, democracy and its institutions should take precedence over philosophical speculation. According to Rorty, philosophical speculation has the same status as the various religious opinions that exist in our democracies. They are matters for private opinion. Rorty therefore pleads for an extension of the Jeffersonian principle of tolerance. In the same manner that tolerance has neutralized the role of religious opinions in the political process, we must now dissociate the political from any philosophical justifications or opinions.

Rorty is well aware however that Jefferson and his peers had no intention of making such an extension. On the contrary, the American Constitution was founded on a very specific philosophical concept of rationality, the self and the world. According to this concept, reason must be the standard for public discussions and we can find a common morality in reason. Opposed to the rules of this universal morality discovered by reason are the various "prejudices" which come from traditions and often contradict the laws of reason. Modern natural right

---

[9] Richard Rorty, "The Priority of Democracy to Philosophy," in *Objectivity, Relativism, and Truth, Philosophical Papers*, vol. 1 (Cambridge: Cambridge University Press, 1991), pp. 175-196.

claims that we can deduce these laws from the consideration of human nature. It assumes the existence of an ahistorical idea of the human soul.

This is precisely the assumption which Rorty rejects: "Contemporary intellectuals have given up the Enlightenment assumption that religion, myth, and tradition can be opposed to something ahistorical, something common to all human beings qua human."[10] Rorty counts himself among these intellectuals: consequently he refuses any metaphysical attempts to justify such ideas as "human rights," "moral truth," "the modern concept of the self," "human nature" or "the human soul."

Following Dewey's argument, Rorty assumes that the validity of democracy is not the result of philosophical reasoning, but of the historical efficiency of democratic institutions. A given philosopher can very well desire to develop some theories of the human self to suit the democratic institutions, but, as Rorty states, "such a philosopher is not thereby justifying these institutions by reference to more fundamental premises, but the reverse: He or she is putting politics first and tailoring a philosophy to suit."[11] According to Rorty, the best regime is embodied in the institutions of liberal democracy, or more precisely in the institutions and "settled social habits" proper to the American experience. These institutions have been the result of a particular history and have produced also a specific kind of human, the "citizen" of liberal democracy.

Rorty could not help then to admit what a long tradition has constantly repeated: every regime produces a certain type of human being, encourages the practice of specific virtues and attempts to avoid the development of certain vices. In this spirit, Leo Strauss in accordance with Plato and Aristotle has maintained the idea that the question of the best regime is ultimately tantamount to the question, "What is the best life?" To answer this last question, we need to establish first an idea of what is human nature and then what is the hierarchy of needs and desires of human beings. In other words, we need to have some sort of philosophical anthropology. Rorty refuses precisely this claim: "No such discipline as 'philosophical anthropology' is required as a preface to politics, but only history and sociology."[12] Is he totally successful in this requirement? We do not think so. His whole argument is actually based on an implied concept of the best life and consequently of the essence of human beings.

This implied concept appears in Rorty's essay when he takes as imaginary interlocutors in a political debate Nietzsche and Loyola. Interpreting Rawls, Rorty argues that in a well-established liberal democracy the questions of a Nietzsche or a Loyola about the hierarchy of good and the link between religion and freedom of conscience must be rejected. Why? Here Rorty is perfectly consistent with his own historicism: they should be rejected, he claims, not because their views

---

[10] Ibid., p. 176.

[11] Ibid., p. 178.

[12] Ibid., p. 181.

are unintelligible or based on a false theory of the self but because "we heirs of the Enlightenment think of the enemies of liberal democracy like Nietzsche or Loyola as, to use Rawls's word, 'mad.' We do so because there is no way to see them as fellow citizens of our constitutional democracy, people whose life plan might, given ingenuity and good will, be fitted in with those of other citizens."[13] In Rorty's view, Nietzsche and Loyola are not crazy *per se*, but they are crazy as far as *we* are concerned. What defines the limits of sanity is in fact what *we*, as citizens of modern constitutional democracies, can take seriously. Our historical situation determines our judgment concerning the alternatives proposed by Nietzsche or Loyola.

But is not this dismissal contrary to the spirit of tolerance proper to liberal democrats? Should not a true democrat enter into discussion with the arguments of Nietzsche and Loyola concerning what human beings should be? And is not this willingness to commit himself in discussion the real proof that a liberal democrat can support a view about human nature according to which tolerance is superior to fanaticism? Again Rorty refutes this last possibility. For him, the idea of tolerance and the concept of humanity are sufficiently backed by the institutional arrangements and products of the particular history of constitutional democracies. He agrees that liberal democrats should engage in a debate with Nietzsche and Loyola, but only in a way that excludes a real discussion on the subject in dispute.

The liberal democrat would have two basic certitudes before entering the discussion: first, because we are essentially the products of history, there is no such thing as human nature, natural order or other similar metaphysical ideas and for that reason the primacy of justice over the quest for good should be defended only on the ground of its historical efficiency; second, this primacy of justice and democracy over "truth" and philosophy leads him to engage in a specific Rortian version of Socratic conversation, i.e., an open-minded conversation without the desire to reach any substantial truths.

It takes only one or two minutes of reflection to conclude that a Nietzsche or a Loyola has no chance to win the arguments in this discussion. First, their liberal opponent will assert the precedence of liberal political justice over philosophy; he will then refuse as a citizen of a modern liberal democracy to substantiate his claim with any philosophical arguments concerning human nature, while repeatedly referring to the historical and moral superiority of liberal democracy. In the end, he will declare his opponents crazy because they do not share his political views. However much "light-mindedness" the Liberal ironist will display in this conversation, one could not help thinking that he is in fact a dogmatist who is unaware of himself.

As a philosopher, Strauss was a great ironist. But he was certainly not a postmodern Liberal ironist. He invites us to take the challenges made by the visions

---

[13] Ibid., p. 266.

of human life embodied by Loyola or Nietzsche very seriously. According to Strauss, one must be especially attentive to Nietzsche's concerns about the destiny of "the noble" in the modern world, without being seduced by his powerful rhetoric. Nietzsche's violent rejection of democratic regimes arises from his concern that democracy has no sense of "the noble," and – even worse – will close the human soul to the ideal of "the noble" initiated by Christianity. There was therefore no doubt in Nietzsche's mind that the best regime would be one which could reverse this decline, i.e., an aristocratic regime dominated by free spirits. In such a regime, "the noble" would have precedence over justice to such an extent that justice will soon become the only expression of "the noble" and often a pure and arbitrary force. It is with regard to such possibilities that contemporary political philosophers insist on the absolute priority of justice over "the noble" in answering the question of the best regime. They repeat here the original alliance that most modern political philosophers contracted with the people against the proud and arrogant men of this world.

Ultimately, the alleged superiority of "the noble" over the just is based on an analysis of human nature. We can say the same thing for the modern assertion of the primacy of the just and of justice over other concerns. Every regime is thus founded on forgetting one aspect or the other of the human soul. Only political philosophy as properly understood can overcome by thought this political incompleteness of the soul. This task has been neglected by contemporary political philosophers. They refuse to consider seriously the various needs of the human soul as politically relevant. In reading the prominent works of contemporary political philosophers, one gets the impression that this variety can be reduced by a sophisticated system of procedures and norms. One would only have to adopt this system in order to harmonize the conflicting parts of the human soul. The underlying hope of this political philosophy is that these basic conflicts of the human soul will be dissolved by the convergent effects of good and just procedures, tolerance based on moral relativism, equality of opportunities and economic progress. There are still controversial issues among political philosophers, but they are technical in nature and are based on a fundamental agreement concerning the essence of human nature and the hierarchy of good.

The contemporary revival of political philosophy is then essentially ambiguous in its nature. On one hand, it seems that political philosophy has reasserted its autonomy with regards to the social and political sciences and is experiencing an unexpected renaissance. But, on the other, this resurrection of political philosophy from the Kingdom of the Dead Sciences comes at a price: political philosophy has forgotten the question of human nature. Or formulated more precisely, this question of human nature is always settled by the strength of prevailing opinions. In this sense, contemporary political philosophy tends to be dogmatic and unable to investigate its own prejudices on human nature.

One area for reflection where this lack of curiosity appears more blatant concerns the justification of the philosophic life as such. Strangely enough, contemporary political philosophers are not at all concerned with the defense of the philosophic life. It is true that in a democratic regime, since philosophy is protected by the general principles of freedom of speech and thought, such a defense or justification seems redundant.

Here is the primary difference between Strauss and the main proponents of contemporary political philosophy: Strauss thought that the difference between the philosophic life and political life was unbridgeable and therefore that the primary task of the political philosopher was to protect the freedom of the philosophical quest in justifying philosophy before the tribunal of the city. Strauss then appears to be mainly concerned with the necessity for political philosophers to preserve their autonomy towards any political regimes as good as they may be. He thought that political philosophers will better serve their political community if they maintain the difference between opinions and truth, an existing regime and the best regime.

Moreover, political philosophy is also and perhaps is essentially the political defense of the philosophic life as the best way of life. According to classical political philosophy as interpreted by Strauss, "the highest subject of political philosophy is the philosophic life" and, consequently, "'political philosophy' means primarily not the philosophic treatment of politics, but the political, or popular, treatment of philosophy, or the political introduction to philosophy – the attempt to lead qualified citizens, or rather their qualified children from the political life to the philosophic life."[14]

This appeal to the philosophic life beyond political life is certainly what distinguishes in the most radical way Strauss's approach to political life and philosophy from the contemporary one. It partly explains Strauss's strong desire to keep open the question of the best regime, since it prevents political philosophy falling prey to dogmatism and moralism. In this respect, a careful study of the major figures in contemporary political philosophy would show that Strauss has failed to restore political philosophy, at least in the sense he attributes to it.

Strauss was an "untimely" thinker and will remain so. But it is precisely for that reason that we who are often blinded by the mirages of the present must try to hear again the questions that he asked. He offers us a way to see our political cavern from an outside perspective and thus allow ourselves to enjoy a few brief moments of intellectual freedom. In the present state of political philosophy, this is not a worthless gift.

---

[14] Strauss, *What is Political Philosophy? and Other Studies*, p. 16.

Nathan Tarcov

PHILOSOPHY AS THE RIGHT WAY OF LIFE
IN *NATURAL RIGHT AND HISTORY* *

One theme in Leo Strauss's work is so salient that it seems almost too obvious to remark, yet its salience in his thought stands in sharp contrast with its near disappearance from so much of modern philosophy. That theme is the conception of philosophy as a way of life, and the related claims that the character of this way of life and its choice or justification as the right way of life are themselves major themes of philosophy, even *the* major themes of Socratic philosophy or, as Strauss would have it, classical political philosophy. This conception contrasts with the conventional contemporary academic conception of philosophy as a discipline (a discipline in the sense of a branch of research with its own methods and subject matters, rather than as *askesis* or formation of character).[1]

In *Natural Right and History* Strauss introduces "the idea of philosophy" in his discussion of conventionalism, a particular form of classical philosophy, early in the first chapter, "Natural Right and the Historical Approach." Following Plato's famous metaphor in Book VII of the *Republic*, Strauss writes that philosophizing means "to ascend from the cave to the light of the sun, that is to the truth," from "the world of opinion" to knowledge (11-12).[2] This distinction between the worlds of opinion and knowledge is not only epistemological but social or politi-

---

* This paper was originally prepared for and delivered at a conference on "Living Issues in the Thought of Leo Strauss" at the Carl Friedrich von Siemens Stiftung in Munich, June 20, 2002. [At a conference "Modernity and What Has Been Lost" at the Jagiellonian University in Krakow, June 5, 2009 Nathan Tarcov delivered a paper entitled "Machiavelli and the Origins of Modernity – *editors' note*].

[1] The conception of philosophy as a way of life (*manière de vivre, forme de vie, mode de vie*) especially with reference to ancient philosophy has been elucidated in recent decades by Pierre Hadot. See Pierre Hadot, *Philosophy as a Way of Life*, ed. Arnold I. Davidson, trans. Michael Chase (Oxford: Blackwell, 1995), and *What Is Ancient Philosophy?* trans. Michael Chase (Cambridge: Harvard University Press, 2002). On philosophy as *askesis* see Michel Foucault, *The Use of Pleasure*, trans. Robert Hurley (New York: Vintage Books, 1990).

[2] All parenthetical notes are to page numbers in Leo Strauss, *Natural Right and History* (Chicago: University of Chicago Press, 1953).

cal: the cave or world of opinion from which philosophy ascends is not private or individual opinion but public opinion, the authoritative opinion stabilized by the social fiat of a particular political community without which its members cannot live together.[3] "Philosophizing means, then, to ascend from public dogma to essentially private knowledge." Strauss's immediate restatement makes clear that "ascend to" does not mean "arrive at:" "the idea of philosophy" is only "the *attempt* to grasp the eternal" (12, emphasis added; see also 30). Shortly thereafter, he explains "the original meaning of political philosophy" in particular as "the *quest* for the natural or best political order" different from all actual orders, and therefore an *effort* "to transcend the actual" (15, emphasis added). Philosophy in general seems to be concerned with "the all-comprehensive truth" or "the eternal order," with "knowledge of the whole" (12, 30).[4] This truth seems to be not a single truth or proposition about the whole, but the answers to a number of persistent "fundamental questions," "fundamental issues," "fundamental problems," or even "fundamental riddles," questions such as whether science is essentially theoretical, whether technological progress is in need of strict moral or political control, or "the problem of justice" (23-24, 29-30, 32). Strauss makes clear in his response to radical historicism's critique of philosophy that philosophy "in its original, Socratic sense" is not knowledge of the answers to these questions or of the solutions to these problems, but only "knowledge of what one does not know, or awareness of the fundamental problems, and, therewith, of the fundamental alternatives regarding their solution that are coeval with human thought" (32). It is knowledge of the answers or solutions in the sense of awareness of what the alternative answers or solutions are, not in the sense of knowledge of which answer or solution is true or correct.

The first chapter of *Natural Right and History* concludes by contrasting the thorough politicization of philosophy into a weapon in the modern centuries with its original character as "the humanizing quest for the eternal order" and "a pure source of humane inspiration and aspiration" (34). It is not immediately clear what Strauss means here by "humanizing" and "humane," beyond the perhaps surprising contrast between the human, humane, or humanized and the political or politicized.[5] Philosophy as quest for the eternal order rather than politi-

---

[3] See "On Classical Political Philosophy," in Leo Strauss, *What Is Political Philosophy?* (Chicago: University of Chicago Press, 1959), p. 92: "philosophy, being an attempt to rise from opinion to science, is necessarily related to the sphere of opinion as its essential starting point, and hence to the political sphere."

[4] Strauss presents "the all-comprehensive truth" or "the eternal order" as the question that public dogma attempts to answer, but in a context that seems to suggest that this is also the aim of philosophy. This comprehensiveness is included in the provisional explanation of philosophy in "What Is Political Philosophy?," in *What Is Political Philosophy?*, p. 11.

[5] Strauss contrasts humanity with barbarism in the second chapter and declares Hobbes an enjoyable writer in part because of his "never failing humanity" in the fifth chapter of *Natural Right and History*, pp. 54, 166. He pairs humanity with human nature as the basis of a human

cal philosophy as quest for the best political order contrasts most clearly with politicized philosophy. Quest for or awareness of the eternal order may inspire humanity in the sense of kindness toward all human beings precisely by diluting or transcending attachment to one best present or future political order or type of political order in opposition to and sometimes at war with other political orders or types of political order. The natural or best political order for which the political philosophy of Plato and Aristotle was in quest was "meant to be, for the most part... beyond all actual orders" (15). Their political philosophy was not therefore meant to be a weapon in the service of actualizing the best order, and was therefore humanizing rather than politicized. The character of philosophy is further clarified when this contrast between modern politicized philosophy and original humanizing philosophy culminates in a reaffirmation of "the essential difference between intellectuals and philosophers," and a claim that the politicization of philosophy consists precisely in the blurring of that difference.[6] The difference between philosophers and intellectuals is clarified by being described as "formerly known" as the differences between philosophers and gentlemen and between philosophers and sophists or rhetoricians. Strauss does not explicitly say here what these differences consist in. Intellectuals, sophists, and rhetoricians may differ from philosophers insofar as they use thought or knowledge as weapons or instruments; intellectuals and gentlemen may differ from philosophers insofar as they use weapons and instruments other than thought or knowledge. Philosophy is thus a way of life that marks off philosophers as a class from such classes as intellectuals, gentlemen, sophists, and rhetoricians.

The second chapter of *Natural Right and History*, "Natural Right and the Distinction between Facts and Values," opens by invoking "philosophy in the full sense of the term," repeating, that is to say clarifying, the notion that "philosophy is possible only if man, while incapable of acquiring wisdom or full understanding of the whole, is capable of knowing what he does not know, that is to say, of grasping the fundamental problems and therewith the fundamental alternatives" (35). Whereas the explanations of philosophy in the first chapter seemed to hold open the possibility of ascending to the truth or knowledge of the whole, this explanation seems to concede that man is incapable of knowledge of the whole.[7] But this explanation adds that Socratic or political philosophy does answer "the question of how man ought to live" (36). It does so by giving the Socratic answer: "By realizing that we are ignorant of the most important things, we realize at the

---

life that is good because it is in accordance with nature in the third chapter, p. 95 and declares that "humanity itself is sociality," p. 129.

[6]   For the blurring of philosophy, see *Persecution and the Art of Writing* (Chicago: University of Chicago Press, 1952), p. 18.

[7]   The "while" preceding "incapable of acquiring wisdom or full understanding of the whole" could mean "as long as" rather than "whereas," still holding out the possibility of wisdom.

same time that the most important thing for us, or the one thing needful, is quest for knowledge of the most important things or quest for wisdom." Although philosophy does not have to answer all the fundamental questions, it has to answer the question of how to live because philosophy is a way of life. The Socratic answer to the question of how to live is in "perennial conflict" with "the anti-Socratic answer," the answer that wisdom is not the one thing needful, a conflict that must, contrary to the conclusion of Weberian social science, be resolved reasonably (36, 64, 67-76). Even when it is granted that only science or philosophy can lead to the truth which man can know, philosophy still must answer "the question of whether the search for knowable truth is good" (71-72). The anti-Socratic answer turns out to be that of divine revelation, that the one thing needful is "the opposite of that proclaimed by philosophy: a life of obedient love versus a life of free insight" (74).[8]

In what is avowedly only a "bird's-eye view" of the conflict between philosophy and theology or between reason and revelation toward the end of the second chapter, Strauss writes that "man is so built that he can find his satisfaction, his bliss, in free investigation, in articulating the riddle of being" (75). This affirmation attaches human satisfaction not to knowledge or wisdom but to the pursuit of knowledge, yet that pursuit answers the question of whether that search is good insofar as satisfaction or bliss seems undeniably good, and thereby carries with it "knowledge of the good" or at least of the good that man needs (74). Even though philosophy is good in the sense of being a source of human satisfaction or bliss, it still may not be evidently "*the* right life" if revelation offers a less limited kind of illumination, a more definite solution to the riddle of being, and another kind of bliss through a life of obedient love. In comparison, philosophy might then seem infinitely unimportant, which is not to say that philosophy otherwise claims to be infinitely important (75, 85). We may wonder whether the question of whether philosophy is "*the* right life" is a different, more demanding question than whether it is good, and if so why it is not good enough for philosophy to be good. Is it only because of the competing claims of revelation that a way of life that carries with it human satisfaction or happiness must also ask whether it is "right?"

The third chapter of *Natural Right and History*, "The Origin of the Idea of Natural Right," explains that philosophy came into being with the discovery of nature, above all in questioning the way of life of the community, which presents

---

[8] The phrase "one thing needful," as far as I am aware, alludes to Luke 10:42. According to the Introduction the liberal interpretation of natural right is that "the one thing needful is respect for diversity or individuality" (5). See also Strauss, *Jewish Philosophy and the Crisis of Modernity: Essays and Lectures in Modern Jewish Thought*, ed. Kenneth Hart Green (Albany: State University of New York Press, 1997), pp. 104, 327, and Strauss, "Reason and Revelation," in Heinrich Meier, *Leo Strauss and the Theologico-Political Problem* (Cambridge: Cambridge University Press, 2006), pp. 149-150, 175.

itself as the right way ultimately because it is a divine law (81-86).[9] The philosophic question of the right way to live and the Socratic answer to that question, philosophy as the right way of life, are first of all a questioning of the divine law as the answer. Philosophy distinguishes what is in truth from what is by law; philosophy questions the authority of the divine law or way of life of the community because it questions all authority (84-86, 91-93). According to Strauss, Socratic and conventionalist classical philosophy agreed that there is a human life that is "good because it is in accordance with nature," and that the philosophic life is that right life, though they disagreed as to whether that life requires justice or morality (95, 97, 110, 112, 113).

Toward the end of the third chapter Strauss returns to the difference between philosophers and sophists with which the first chapter ends, a difference that clarifies the character of philosophy as a way of life (115-117). Philosophers and sophists are distinguished not by the content or the truth of their teachings, but by their motives. Whereas the sophist is concerned with wisdom for the sake of the honor that attends a reputation for wisdom, the philosopher is "set in motion and kept in motion by the sting of the awareness of the fundamental difference between conviction or belief and genuine insight" (116). Whereas the sophist "knows better than most other men that wisdom or science is the highest excellence of man," the philosopher seems moved at least as much by the repulsiveness of mere belief as by the attractiveness of wisdom. The difference in their motives is manifest in the sophist's needing to display his (sham) wisdom and to conceal his (true) wisdom to gain prestige, but Strauss does not here explain how the philosopher may display or conceal his wisdom, or therefore exactly how the difference is manifest.

The fourth chapter of *Natural Right and History*, "Classic Natural Right," begins with a presentation of Socratic philosophy. The second chapter had already invoked the Socratic answer to the question of how man ought to live in its initial consideration of the possibility of philosophy in general and political philosophy in particular (35-36). "Like every other philosopher," Socrates identified wisdom or the goal of philosophy with the science of all the beings, but he deviated from his predecessors in identifying that science with understanding the nature of each of the beings or of each class of beings (122-123). He did not separate wisdom from moderation, which means primarily that whereas all philosophy consists in ascent from opinions to knowledge or truth, Socratic philosophy consists in such an ascent guided by opinions (123-124). The impression given is that the way of

---

9   The mentions of "the way of life" of the community are, as far as I am aware, the first mentions in the book of a "way of life," though philosophy has been characterized as a "life" (74-75). A "way of life" thus first appears in explaining "way" as the prephilosophic conception of the characteristic behaviors of things, which does not distinguish those of natural beings and those of the different human tribes, but gives paramount importance to the way of life of the community (82-83, 90).

life of Socratic philosophy therefore consists in conversation or friendly dispute based on the premise that all men always divine the truth, that the people who cherish any opinion about right are forced to go beyond it in the direction of truth provided a philosopher arises among them (124-125). The Socratic philosopher seems to depend on popular opinion to guide his quest, and the people seem to depend on the Socratic philosopher to force them to go beyond their opinion toward the truth (Strauss does not say how far they may go in its direction). There is no guaranty, he says, that philosophy itself will ever legitimately go beyond discussion or disputation to decision, at least about the whole, but Strauss does quickly remind us of "the fundamental Socratic thesis," presumably the Socratic answer to the question of how to live (126).

Strauss presents the answer of Socrates and his classic successors to the question of the good life for man as determined by "the hierarchic order of man's natural constitution" without mentioning philosophy (126-127; cf. 94-95). Indeed that good life involves not only understanding or the fulfillment of the natural inclination to pursue knowledge, but also "thoughtful action" or the fulfillment of man's natural inclinations "in the proper order to the highest possible degree" (127), of not only, one might say, intellectual but moral virtue (note "nobility" and "morally obtuse," 128). We are reminded of the earlier statement that Socratic philosophy disagreed with pre-Socratic or conventionalist philosophy about whether the life in accordance with human nature requires justice or morality (95). According to the classics, human nature is radically social and concern for the good of others is as natural as concern for one's own good (129), whereas for the conventionalists everyone by nature seeks nothing but his own good (106, 108, 109, 115). The Socratic or classic answer here seems to contrast with the conventionalists' conclusion that the good life, the life according to nature, is "the retired life of the philosopher who lives at the fringes of civil society" (113). Strauss's presentation here of the good life according to the classics leads away from philosophy to the life of the statesman, legislator, or founder (133).

The philosopher reappears in this presentation first only as the interpreter of the best regime for the guidance of the gentlemen (139). Then apparently only in response to the objection that the classic philosophers favored the rule of the gentlemen or urban patriciate because they belonged to that class, Strauss admits that as philosophers they possessed a "selfish or class interest," which "consists in being left alone" to devote themselves to investigation, and that they therefore favored the urban patriciate as the only class habitually sympathetic to philosophy and therefore most likely to cater to this interest (143). Their way of life seems thus very different from that presented earlier in the chapter as the good life, the life of thoughtful action of the statesman, legislator, or founder (126-134). Finally, apparently only in response to the blurring of the political character of classic natural right under the influence of biblical faith, which makes God-given natural law of "infinitely higher dignity" than the best regime, Strauss admits that for the classics too, political life is "essentially inferior in dignity" to the philosophic life (144-145).[10] In contrast to his earlier determination that the good life is the life of virtue on the basis of human nature (127), Strauss now admits that the definite character of the virtues cannot be deduced from human nature (145). In line with his strange suggestion that the classics "in a way anticipated" the crucial modi-fication of their teaching by the Christian identification of the best regime with the City of God (144-145), Strauss argues in his presentation of Socratic-Platonic natural right that the city (which he had earlier argued was necessary for human perfection and in accordance with justice and nature, 130-132) is necessarily un-just and so must transform itself into the "world-state," which in turn turns out to be unjust and so a divination of the cosmos ruled by God (148-150).[11] When Strauss says here that the "whole life" of "the wise" is devoted to something "ab-solutely higher in dignity than any human things," he seems again to be bringing out a classic anticipation of biblical faith.

Strauss apologizes that it is "not possible here to do more than barely to indi-cate" the reasons which force men "to seek beyond the political sphere for perfect justice or, more generally, for the life that is truly according to nature" (151). He explains that "the wise do not desire to rule" (151), but by speaking of philoso-phers here as if they were wise rather than merely in quest of wisdom, he omits and thereby silently raises the question whether they deserve to rule, whether they indeed know what is by nature good for others (140-141, 147).[12] They may know that their life is best for them; they may even know that it is the best life for man; but that is not to know what is best for those who cannot or will not lead that life. Nor does Strauss ask here explicitly whether it is just to compel the wise to rule, though he does say that it appears to be against nature to prefer the lower (ruling) to the higher (pursuit of truth).[13] By omitting both of these questions he makes it

---

[10]   The blurring invoked at the end of Chapter 1 may need to be understood in the light of this previous blurring.

[11]   The final argument about the cosmos ruled by God refers to such classic passages as the myths of Cronos in the *Statesman* and the *Laws*. The intermediate argument about the world state seems to originate oddly from a paragraph in Strauss's summary of Kojève's views omit-ted from the published "Restatement," which would have appeared between pp. 192 and 193 of *On Tyranny* (Chicago: University of Chicago Press, 1961, 2000).

[12]   Did he "surreptitiously substitute the wise man for the philosopher?" Cf. *On Tyranny*, p. 201.

[13]   Cf. *Republic* 519d8-520e3 and Strauss, *The City and Man* (Chicago: University of Chicago Press, 1964), pp. 127-128. Strauss notes the immediately preceding and succeeding passages from the *Republic* in the note to this paragraph in *Natural Right and History* (p. 152, n. 26); he notes this passage in a different context at the end of the third chapter (p. 119, n. 49). By calling philosophers "the wise," Strauss exaggerates and thereby highlights Plato's proce-dure of speaking of them as if they were wise rulers (e.g. *Republic* 484cd, 501b).

seem almost as if the rule of philosophers was unquestionably just and prevented only by the unwillingness or injustice of the philosophers. The question becomes less whether philosophy or the rule of philosophers is just as if justice were the standard, and more whether justice as "commonly understood," is "required for the sake of the philosophic life," that is to say, whether justice is good (cf. 146) as if the requirements of the philosophic life were the standard.[14] Insofar as justice and morality are understood to be required for the sake of the philosophic life, Socratic philosophy, as we recall, differs from conventionalist philosophy (95), but Strauss does not say how far that is and he raises the question whether such justice and morality are identical with justice and morality as commonly understood (e.g., acting according to law or benefiting others, 146-147).[15] He answers that question near the end of the chapter, when discussing Thomas Aquinas's having virtually contended that the end of man cannot consist in philosophical investigation, by remarking that "intellectual perfection or wisdom, as unassisted human reason knows it, does not require moral virtue" (163-164). This is not to deny that justice and morality are required for the philosophic life but to deny that "justice and morality as they are commonly understood" or "what Aristotle calls moral virtue" are identical with justice and morality insofar as they are required for the philosophic life (151).

Strauss goes on to argue that it is necessary for the philosopher to take care of the affairs of the city "whether in a direct or more remote manner" (152). "Direct" suggests holding political office like Cicero; "remote" suggests writing or teaching like Plato. Since philosophizing means ascent from the cave (11), this descent into the cave seems to be something other than philosophizing that it is necessary for philosophers to do. It is necessary because of both "the obvious dependence of the philosophic life on the city and the natural affection which men have for men." If the obvious dependence refers only to such matters as the need for economic support and physical security, then both reasons for this descent pertain not to philosophers specifically but to human beings generally. The dependence may, however, also include the guidance for Socratic philosophizing provided by the opinions of the city (124-125). Insofar as this descent is moved by affection rather dependence, it seems not to be a matter of mere necessity.[16] That natural affection is said to be "especially for their kin, regardless of whether or not these men

---

[14]   Cf. "On Classical Political Philosophy," in *What Is Political Philosophy?*, pp. 92-93 and *Persecution and the Art of Writing*, pp. 10, 20.

[15]   On this passage (151-152), see David Bolotin's unpublished paper, "On Chapters Three and Four of *Natural Right and History*," pp. 13-14.

[16]   Cf. *City and Man*, p. 128: "The clear distinction between the justice which is choice-worthy for its own sake wholly regardless of its consequences, and identical with philosophy, and the justice which is merely necessary, and identical in the highest imaginable case with the rule of the philosopher, is rendered possible by the abstraction from *eros* which is characteristic of the *Republic*... there is no reason why the philosopher should not engage in political activity out of that kind of love of one's own which is patriotism."

have 'good natures' or are potential philosophers." By saying that men as men have a generic affection especially for their kin, meaning presumably their blood relations, Strauss may lead us to wonder whether philosophers may not also have a specific affection for those who are their kin precisely in having "good natures" or being potential philosophers, which Strauss elsewhere calls "the love of the mature philosopher for the puppies of his race," an affection which may also motivate the descent into the cave.[17]

Strauss continues: "In descending into the cave, the philosopher admits that what is intrinsically or by nature the highest is not the most urgent for man" (152). This admission corrects the previous appearance that it is against nature to prefer the lower to the higher (151). This issue is addressed further when Strauss returns to Plato as well at the conclusion of his discussion of Aristotle. He explains as follows (though without explicit reference to the issue of the political engagement of the philosopher): "What is most urgent is legitimately preferred to what is less urgent, and the most urgent is in many cases lower in rank than the less urgent. But one cannot make a universal rule that urgency is a higher consideration than rank. For it is our duty to make the highest activity, as much as we can, the most urgent or the most needful thing. And the maximum effort which can be expected necessarily varies from individual to individual" (162-163). Here "the most needful thing" seems to be equated with the most urgent, which cannot always be the highest, cannot always be quest for wisdom or philosophizing.

Only when he turns to Aristotle later in this chapter does Strauss say that "Plato never discusses any subject – be it the city or the heavens or numbers – without keeping in view the elementary Socratic question, 'What is the right way of life?' And the simply right way of life proves to be the philosophic life" (156).[18] To say that philosophy is the right way of life seems to suggest that philosophy is a complete way of life, not merely a way to spend part of one's time, not a 9-to-5 job, not an activity to engage in after dinner after having spent the day trapping birds, gossiping, engaging in amorous fantasies and reminiscences, gambling, and quarreling, or hunting, fishing, and rearing cattle.[19] But man is essentially an "in-between" being (152), and philosophizing can be only part of the life of a philosopher, of the philosophic life. Does a philosopher gossip, fantasize, gamble,

---

[17]   *Persecution and the Art of Writing*, p. 36; cf. *On Tyranny*, pp. 199-202.

[18]   See David Janssens, *Between Athens and Jerusalem: Philosophy, Prophecy, and Politics in Leo Strauss's Early Thought* (Albany: State University of New York Press, 2008), especially pp. 99-101, 118-119, 190-192.

[19]   Cf. Plato, *Republic* 433a and 561cd to Marx, *The German Ideology* I A 1, in *The Marx-Engels Reader*, ed. Robert C. Tucker (New York: Norton, 1972) p. 160; see also Locke, "Labour," in *Political Essays*, ed. Mark Goldie (Cambridge: Cambridge University Press, 1997), pp. 326-328, and Machiavelli's letter to Francesco Vettori of December 10, 1513, in *The Prince*, trans. Harvey C. Mansfield, 2nd ed. (Chicago: University of Chicago Press, 1998), pp. 108-110.

quarrel, hunt, and fish philosophically? Most important, how far are justice and morality and concern for the good of others part of the philosophic way of life?

To say that philosophy is the right way of life is to say that it is not merely one of many equally eligible or equally created or equally given lifestyles. But it seems to imply that philosophy is one of several, not necessarily many, alternative ways of life, that there is a question as to how man ought to live, as to which way of life to choose, that one's way of life is not simply given, set, or fixed. It suggests even that the choice is not self-evident, that there are several plausible, eligible, competitive ways of life.

But do human beings, all human beings or any human beings, have a choice of ways of life? Is philosophy a choice rather than a necessity or compulsion; is it simply the way that philosophers are compelled to live by their natures? Must we speak of different natures and their characteristic ways of living, then, rather than a practical question of how man ought to live? Does philosophy claim to be the right way of life only in response to and in mimicry of the claim of way of life of the community?

Finally, we must ask what does all this have to do with us, we who "cannot be philosophers?"[20] What is the relevance for us of philosophy as the right way of life if it requires a nature so rare that we may be fortunate to have one philosopher living in our age? We should recall that "it is our duty to make the highest activity, as much as we can, the most urgent or the most needful thing. And the maximum effort which can be expected necessarily varies from individual to individual" (163).

---

[20] Strauss, *Liberalism Ancient and Modern* (Chicago: University of Chicago Press, 1968), p. 7.

David Janssens

THE PHILOSOPHER'S ANCIENT CLOTHES: LEO STRAUSS ON PHILOSOPHY AND POETRY

Underlying and animating Leo Strauss's work, three "quarrels" or tensions are often distinguished: 1) between Athens and Jerusalem, or reason and revelation; 2) between Ancients and Moderns; and 3) between philosophy and poetry.[1] The latter refers to a well-known passage in Plato's *Republic*, where Socrates criticizes poetry for its doubtful relationship to the truth, as well as for its deleterious effects on human life.[2] While most scholarship has focused on the first two quarrels, the third has received proportionally less attention. This is somewhat surprising, given what is often regarded as one of Strauss's most innovative and most controversial accomplishments: his rediscovery of the "art of writing" of pre-modern and early modern authors. When it comes to writing, it would seem that at least the relationship between philosophy and poetry merits closer scrutiny. In this paper, I will argue that understanding the philosophic ramifications of Strauss's rediscovery does indeed require us to be more attentive to the third quarrel in his work. The first part (sections 1 and 2) will argue that Strauss himself, from the very beginning, took it no less seriously than the other two quarrels. In the second part (sections 3 and 4), I will try to show that, as his understanding of the subject deepened, he became increasingly doubtful whether what Plato called the "ancient quarrel between poetry and philosophy" really is a *quarrel*. As he came to see it, ancient philosophy was fundamentally indebted to ancient poetry, not only as regards form, but also with regard to content. The philosophers, it seems, learned from the poets not only how to write, but also how to think. The third final part (section 5 and conclusion) explores some general ramifications of this view.

---

[1] Michael Platt, "Three Quarrels, Three Questions, One Life," in *The Crisis of Liberal Democracy: A Straussian Perspective* (New York: State University of New York Press, 1987), pp. 17-28.

[2] Plato, *Republic*, 607b-e.

1. Raider of the Lost Art

For those seeking to understand the significance of Strauss's rediscovery of the art of writing, the recent publication of his correspondence with Jacob Klein has provided a valuable additional resource.[3] In his letters to Klein, who was probably his oldest and closest friend, Strauss frequently reports on his progress in reading and understanding a number of authors, most notably Maimonides, Plato and Xenophon. Guided by Avicenna's seminal remark on prophecy, Strauss had already unearthed the Platonism of medieval Jewish and Islamic philosophers: their understanding of revelation within the framework of Plato's *Laws*, as well as their use of a specific mode of writing destined to remove suspicions of heterodoxy and to justify their philosophic activity. In the reports to Klein, Strauss develops the ramifications of these key findings in a series of dazzling bursts scattered throughout the letters. They offer compelling reading, not least because he is unusually candid about what he sees as the profound heterodoxy of the said authors. Thus, we learn that the *Guide of the Perplexed* is actually a subtle and critical parody of the Bible (GS3, p. 553), written by someone who, Strauss asserts, "simply was not a Jew in his faith" (GS3, p. 550). Similarly, speaking about Plato's political dialogues, Strauss tells Klein that "their actual theme is the relationship between *bios politikos* (the political life) and *bios philosophikos* (the philosophic life), and that it is devoted to a radical critique and rejection of political life" (GS3, p. 568). And, finally, Strauss repeatedly expresses his admiration for Xenophon, "the greatest rogue I know" (GS3, p. 567). In many ways, his observations prefigure the interpretations he started to publish at the end of the '30s.

One element that is no less conspicuous, however, is that Strauss's pursuit of the art of writing doesn't stop at *philosophic* authors. In 1938, in the midst of his explorations of Plato's *Laws*, he informs his friend that he has discovered Herodotus as an esoteric writer. The father of history, it turns out, was not primarily concerned with the factual reporting of speeches and deeds, but rather with guiding the most perceptive of his readers towards a critical, inquiring attitude with regard to their own laws and customs. Moreover, Herodotus points Strauss to the intimate and complex connection between critical inquiry and the need for an art of writing. To begin with, there is the question of persecution: as he tells Klein, the famous story of Gyges at the beginning of the *Inquiries* shows that whoever wishes to deviate with impunity from the traditional injunction to look exclusively to one's own must make sure he is hidden (GS3, p. p. 556).[4] However, no less important is the question of education: as Strauss also argues, recondite and enigmatic stories are the only way in which the thoughtful reader can be brought to question the authoritative stories in which he or she has been brought up and

---

    [3] Leo Strauss, *Gesammelte Schriften*, eds. Heinrich Meier, Wiebke Meier, vol. 3 (Stuttgart: Metzler, 2001), pp. 455-605. Henceforth cited within the text as "GS3."

    [4] Cf. Seth Benardete, *Herodotean Inquiries* (South Bend: St. Augustine's Press, 1999), pp. 13-16; Michael Davis, "The Tragedy of the Law: Gyges in Herodotus and Plato," *The Review of Metaphysics* 53 (2000), pp. 635-655.

embark on a genuine inquiry. If, as Strauss asserts, Herodotus's entertaining and instructive *logoi* contain an "antidote" against the traditional *logoi*, they can have this effect because they do not present themselves as such on first viewing, but only because they gradually arouse the attentive reader's interest on repeated readings (GS3, p. 557). In this respect, Strauss suggests, Herodotus's approach may well have been the model for Plato, whose *nomoi* – laws or songs – contain an antidote to the *nomoi* – laws or songs – in which the reader has grown up.

Soon after, it becomes apparent that this applies not only to the father of history, but also to his descendants, the Greek historians. As Strauss suggests to Klein, Thucydides and Xenophon were no more interested in merely recording a succession of events than Herodotus was. Their true aim was protreptic: to entice perceptive readers to liberate themselves from the spell of their authoritative opinions and to guide them towards a genuine education (*paideia*). However, the subterranean affinities between history and philosophy by no means mark the end point of Strauss's ruminations. In the same letter in which he reports his breakthrough on Herodotus, we find the following rumination: "But perhaps everything we have learned about the tragedians is completely wrong, too." (GS3, p. 557) A little later, once again discussing the practice of dissimulation (*eironeia*) that connects Herodotus, Thucydides and Plato, Strauss tentatively extends its horizon even further: "I'm curious to learn what is behind Sophocles, who according to tradition was a friend of Herodotus – I'm afraid it is also philosophy, and not *polis kai progonoi* (city and ancestors)." (GS3, p. 560) Thus, in addition to the historians, the poets must be taken into consideration if we wish to understand the art of writing of the philosophers. This applies no less – perhaps even more – to comedy than to tragedy: as Strauss indicates, Plato's general use of the dialogic-dramatic form, as well as his choice of particular settings, can be interpreted as a playful response to Aristophanes, who for his part was engaged in an ironic dialogue with tragedy (GS3, p. 562). Even this doesn't bring an end to Strauss's remarkable string of discoveries. Within the ambit of poetry, the origins of the art of writing prove to reach further back, beyond both tragedy and comedy, to the earliest Greek poets, Hesiod and Homer. Thus, in another letter to Klein, Strauss suggests that the *Theogony*, ostensibly the fountainhead of Greek mythology, actually contains a covert inquiry into the first things that is critical of the traditional account that prevails in the *polis* (GS3, p. 581-582). Similarly, the *Works and Days* are not merely an exhortation to a lazy brother, but a reflection, couched in "night speeches," on the tension between the wisdom accessible to the poet and the political perspective, which appears to foreclose that wisdom. The same tension informs the work of Homer, who like Hesiod chose to present his wisdom in the interstices of a carefully crafted diptych. Just as his account of the vicissitudes of Achilles and the Achaeans reveal the limits of *andreia* (courage) as the supreme political virtue, the self-identification of Odysseus as a cunning Nobody (*mètis - oùtis*) prefigures the philosophical wiles of Socrates (GS3, p. 574,

582). All this, Strauss asserts, seems to confirm Socrates's suggestion in Plato's *Theaetetus* that the old poets presented their wisdom by means of poetic artifacts.[5] At the same time, it points to a continuum in which the distinction between poets, historians and philosophers appears to dissolve. Starting with Homer and Hesiod, it stretches all the way to Socrates, Plato and Xenophon. According to Strauss, it even includes Parmenides, perhaps the philosopher-poet *par excellence*, and no stranger to duplicity either (GS3, p. 583).

2. Philosophers, Historians and Poets

In his letters to Klein, Strauss repeatedly suggests that studying the art of writing of the pre-Platonic poets and historians is indispensable for understanding that of Plato, not to mention Xenophon (GS3, p. 557, 560, 562, 581). When we turn to his published works, however, this acknowledgement is made much more implicitly. Of course, Strauss did publish extensive interpretations of two Greek historians and a Greek poet who were Plato's contemporaries: Thucydides, Xenophon and Aristophanes.[6] In addition, he wrote a long interpretive essay on Lucretius's poem *On Nature*, to which I will turn presently.[7] When it comes to pre-Platonic historians and poets, however, he is far less candid.

Still, a survey of Strauss's published works reveals that he does not always limit himself to dropping hints in footnotes. On a small number of occasions, he does discuss their writings at some length. Most of these occasions, it is true, appear to be quite marginal: they occur either in the context of interpretations of his cherished authors, or in reviews or discussions of the work of other contemporary scholars. Nevertheless, heeding Strauss's own warning that the views of an author are not necessarily those that are proffered in his most conspicuous and best-known writings, we do well to take them seriously. After all, the role of a reviewer, no less than that of the commentator, provides a specific immunity that allows one to critically engage their interpretations while offering the reader a glimpse – or something more than a glimpse – of one's own approach.

Thus, it may come as a small surprise to find a relatively extensive discussion of Hesiod in a lengthy – and acerbic – review of the classicist Eric Havelock's book *The Liberal Temper in Greek Politics*.[8] In the review, Strauss exposes the superficiality and conceitedness of Havelock's interpretation *ad oculos*, sim-

---

[5] Cf. Plato, *Theaetetus*, 180c-d; cf. *Republic*, 378d.

[6] Cf. Leo Strauss, *The City and Man* (Chicago: Rand McNally, 1964); *Socrates and Aristophanes* (New York: Basic Books, 1966); *Studies in Platonic Political Philosophy* (Chicago: The University of Chicago Press), pp. 89-104.

[7] Leo Strauss, "Notes on Lucretius," in *Liberalism Ancient and Modern* (New York: Basic Books, 1968), pp. 76-135.

[8] Strauss, "The Liberalism of Classical Political Philosophy," in *Liberalism Ancient and Modern*, pp. 26-64.

ply by contrasting it with an attentive, open-minded and charitable reading that brings to light questions and problems to which Havelock is altogether oblivious. Unsurprisingly, many of his remarks trace their origin to his initial discoveries of the '30s, and focus on the way Hesiod crafted his two major works, the *Theogony* and *Works and Days*. But this is not all. In the same review, Strauss drops enough hints to suggest that it is worthwhile to read other Greek poets with the same care: Aeschylus (*Prometheus, Agamemnon*), Sophocles (*Antigone*), Euripides (*Suppliants*) and Aristophanes (*Birds*), not to mention pre-Socratics like Anaxagoras, Anaximander, Xenophanes and Democritus, or sophists like Protagoras, Hippias or Antiphon. Viewed as a whole, the review tacitly sets standards for understanding ancient thought that are nothing short of revolutionary, precisely by pointing to the importance of the art of writing.[9]

Apart from the Havelock review, however, it is hard to find equally eloquent statements. Even in Strauss's most famous statement on the subject, *Persecution and the Art of Writing*, almost no reference is made to ancient historians or poets. The single and notable exception is Parmenides, who is mentioned in the context of a particularly enigmatic disquisition on *logica equina* and horses. However, a reader of the book will soon discover another name that is curiously missing from the index. In the essay that supplies the title of the whole book, Strauss discusses the difficulty for the censor of determining whether an author writes esoterically. He concludes with a seemingly rhetorical question: "But how can that be proved, if even *Homer* nods from time to time?"[10]

It is well worth tracing this expression to its source. In *The Art of Poetry*, Horace writes that "he is offended whenever the good Homer falls asleep (*indignor quandoquo bonus dormitat Homerus*)."[11] But Horace doesn't say whether he ever has had occasion to become indignant at his illustrious predecessor. Moreover, the line that follows leaves undecided whether the problem lies with the poet or the reader: "but it is allowed that sleep creeps up to a long work (*verum operi longo fas est obrepere somnum*)."[12] Without doubt, Strauss was also thinking of that other reader of Homer and Horace who questions Homer's somnolescence and puts the problem squarely and exclusively with the reader. In his *Essay on Criticism*, Alexander Pope asserts: "Those oft are Stratagems which Errors seem/

---

[9]   Conspicuously absent in the review is Parmenides. This absence, however, is remedied elsewhere in the margins of Strauss's writings, to wit in his *in memoriam* for Kurt Riezler (Leo Strauss, *What is Political Philosophy?* [Glencoe: The Free Press, 1959], pp. 233-260). This text is somewhat better known because it contains important observations on the meaning and significance of the new thinking of Heidegger (and, to a lesser extent, Rosenzweig). However, when discussing Riezler's book on Parmenides, Strauss also makes sure to provide some pointers as to how, in his view, the philosopher-poet should be read.

[10]   Leo Strauss, *Persecution and the Art of Writing* (Glencoe: The Free Press, 1952), p. 26 (emphasis added).

[11]   Horace, *The Art of Poetry*, 358-359.

[12]   Ibid., 360.

Nor is it Homer Nods, but We that Dream."[13] Moreover, Pope, counseling the amateur of Homer's works to "read them by day and meditate by night," indicates that it is difficult to distinguish between the poetic and the philosophic art of writing. Referring to the young Vergil's hesitation to model his *Aeneid* on Homer's work, instead drawing his poetry "from nature's fountain," he continues: "But when to examine every part he came/Nature and Homer were he found the same/ Convinced, amazed, he checks the bold design/And rules as strict his labored work confine/As if the Stagirite o'erlooked each line/Learn hence for ancient rules a just esteem/To copy nature is to copy them."[14] The appeal to the *philosopher* Aristotle as a judge of poetic works echoes the words of Horace, who tells his reader that "wisdom is the principle and source of correct writing," while adding the curious advice that "the Socratic papers (*chartae Socraticae*) can provide you with the subject matter."[15]

While there is little doubt that Strauss was aware of his sources, the connection between philosophy and poetry is intimated only later in the essay, when he turns from the perspective of the censor to that of the artful writer and points to the inevitability of noble lies. It is worth quoting the section in full:

> ... [an able writer] would defeat his purpose if he indicated clearly which of his statements expressed a noble lie, and which the still more noble truth. For philosophic readers he would do almost more than enough by drawing their attention to the fact that he did not object to telling lies which were noble, or tales which were merely similar to truth. From the point of view of the literary historian at least, there is no more noteworthy difference between the typical pre-modern philosopher (*who is hard to distinguish from the premodern poet*) and the typical modern philosopher than that of their attitudes toward "noble (or just) lies," "pious frauds," the "ductus obliquus" or "economy of the truth." Every decent modern reader is bound to be shocked by the mere suggestion that a great man might have deliberately deceived the large majority of his readers. And yet, as a liberal theologian once remarked, these imitators of the resourceful Odysseus were perhaps more sincere than we when they called "lying nobly" what we would call "considering one's social responsibilities."[16]

It is no accident that Strauss refers both to the Platonic notion of "noble lies" and to the Hesiodic and Homeric concept of "tales similar to the truth," just as he suggests that both pre-modern philosophers and poets are imitators of the resourceful Odysseus.[17] Taken as a whole, this passage suggests that philosophy and poetry are "hard to distinguish." Of course, Strauss does not say that it is impossible to make the distinction: there may be important differences between

---

[13]   Alexander Pope, *Essay on Criticism*, 1.178-179.

[14]   Ibid., 1.30-140

[15]   Horace, *The Art of Poetry*, 308-309.

[16]   Strauss, *Persecution and the Art of Writing*, 35-36 (emphasis added).

[17]   Hesiod, *Theogony*, 27; Homer, *Odyssey*, 19.203; Leo Strauss, *Xenophon's Socrates* (Ithaca: Cornell University Press, 1972), pp. 19-20; Leo Strauss, *On Tyranny* (Glencoe: The Free Press, 1948), pp. 47-48.

the philosopher and the poet that, although difficult to perceive, are nevertheless essential. But at least when viewed from the perspective of the art of writing, the similarities seem to outweigh the differences. For this reason, I submit, any attempt to assess the meaning of Strauss's thesis on the subject must take this indication into account.

3. Lies like the Truth

What did Strauss learn from the pre-Platonic poets and historians with regard to the art of writing? Given his reticence on this point, any attempt to answer this question must proceed carefully and with caution. Nevertheless, a few general observations can be made. To begin with, the ancient poets showed Strauss that the art of writing is a matter of *action* at least as much as of reflection. Differently stated, the poets' wisdom becomes apparent not so much in what they *say* as they write, but rather in what they *do* as they write. More specifically, their action becomes visible in and through the choices that they make with regard to both form and substance of their work.[18] This applies to even to the most basic of elements, such as the mere number or variety of writings. As Strauss observes, it is no accident that both Homer and Hesiod chose to present their teaching not in a single work, but in at least *two* distinct works, respectively the *Iliad* and the *Odyssey* and the *Theogony* and *Works and Days*. This act of division or *diairesis* (making one into two or more) introduces multiplicity and, at the same time, complementarity: it allows the poet to make all kinds of explicit and implicit cross-references that induce the reader to explore how the various parts are interrelated and fit together into a whole like a puzzle. Thus, *diairesis* invites us to compare the opening and the theme of the *Iliad* with that of the *Odyssey*, or to wonder why the *Theogony* tells of the origins of the gods, while *Works and Days* recounts the origins of man.

However, poetry also displays the opposite action: making two (or more) into one, or *synthesis*. Both Homer and Hesiod make extensive use of images and myths, which bring together separate and heterogeneous elements into a seemingly homogeneous whole. On the most general level, Strauss notes, poetry presents an artificial unity of the universal and the particular: it only allows its wisdom, its knowledge of the universal, to become apparent in and through the particular, which is usually a combination of speeches and deeds.[19] Here again, it is up to the reader to trace the artificiality and reconstruct the implicit reasoning. As Strauss notes, the truth "is located in the space between the deeds and

---

[18] Thus, in *Persecution and the Art of Writing* he quotes both Blackstone's saying *scribere est agere* and Milton's assertion in *Areopagitica* that "reason is but choosing" (*Persecution and the Art of Writing*, 22-23). Cf. Strauss, *Gesammelte Schriften*, vol. 2 (Stuttgart: Metzler), p. 558.

[19] Leo Strauss, *The Rebirth of Classical Political Rationalism* (Chicago: The University of Chicago Press, 1989), p. 80.

the speeches. The full truth is pointed *to* by the dualism of the deeds and the speeches. It is not pointed *out*."[20]

As such, dividing and collecting are general characteristics, not only of ancient poetry, but of classical history and philosophy as well. They govern the perplexing diversity of Heraclitus's aphorisms and of Herodotus's *Inquiries*, the two poems of Empedocles (*Purifications* and *On Nature*), the two parts of Parmenides' single poem *On Nature* ("The Way of Truth" and "The Way of Opinion"), the trilogies of the tragedians, and even the hologram of the Platonic dialogues, which combine epic, history, tragedy and comedy within a whole novel form.[21] In each case, Strauss indicates, it does not suffice to merely look at the argument that is made in these writings: one must read and interpret it in light of the action, which contains an argument in its own right.

A second aspect of ancient poetry, intimately related to the first, is the emphasis it puts on concealing and revealing, or revealing by concealing. Already in his letters to Klein, Strauss shows how the poets indicate, not only that subject matter and design are inextricably bound up, but also that their connection remains hidden. Thus, he suggests, turning the very title of the *Works and Days* into its opposite brings to light Hesiod's strategy of concealment, just as the story of Gyges reveals Herodotus's strategy in the *Histories*. However, even more characteristic of poetic dissimulation is the fact that both Homer and Hesiod invoke the Muses as the divine inspiration of their song, while indicating that they are intractable and not very reliable sources. Thus, at the beginning of the *Odyssey*, Homer enjoins the Muse: "Of these things, goddess, daughter of Zeus, *beginning where you will*, tell even us." (*Odyssey*, 1.10, emphasis added.) Likewise, at the beginning of the *Theogony*, Hesiod has the Muses say: "we know how to tell many *lies like the truth*; but we know, *when we will*, to sing the truth." (*Theogony*, 27-28, emphasis added.) Hesiod's expression "lies like the truth" (*pseudea etumoisin homoia*) echoes Homer's own comment on the story that Odysseus tells Penelope in order to hide his identity (*Odyssey*, 19.203). In this way, they point us back to the human and political dimension of dissimulation. After all, we shouldn't forget that Odysseus wants to avoid the fate of Agamemnon and tests the mood in Ithaca before making his presence known.

This brings is to a third element. Arguably, the figure of Odysseus plays a key role in Strauss's understanding of the relationship between poetry and philosophy. For in many respects, Odysseus epitomizes and integrates a number of elements that Strauss regards as eminently characteristic of philosophy and the philosopher. To begin with, he is the privileged witness and narrator of the first manifestation known to us of *phusis* or nature. In order to help Odysseus in resisting the charms of Circe, the god Hermes digs up a plant called *moly* and shows him its nature (*Odyssey*, 10.302-306). A careful reader of Homer, Strauss

[20]   Ibid., p. 96 (emphasis added).
[21]   Cf. Strauss, *The City and Man*, p. 57.

points out that the passage implies that nature in fact poses limitations on the divine omnipotence that is professed in the same passage.[22] *Phusis* adumbrates a necessity that even the gods cannot change, and which is intelligible to human beings. As Strauss argues in *Natural Right and History*, the discovery of *phusis* has momentous consequences, as it leads to a distinction between things that are by nature and things that are conventional: "The distinction between nature and convention, between physis and nomos, is therefore coeval with the discovery of nature and hence with philosophy."[23] However, Strauss immediately adds: "Nature would not have to be discovered if it were not hidden." (Ibid.) This is no less an echo of Homer, who intimates in the same passage that digging up *moly* is difficult for mortal men. However, it is even more difficult to understand its nature, which consists in the hidden unity of its seemingly contrary parts, its black root and white flower.[24]

Still, we should not forget that the story of Hermes's revealing the nature of *moly* is told by Odysseus himself, and this brings us to a fourth point. Compared to Achilles, who cannot be dissociated from his lineage, Odysseus possesses a peculiar strangeness, a conspicuous distance and independence with regard to his own background and ancestry. Thus, Homer alternately calls him by a number of epithets that show the complexity and profundity of his character, his experience and flexibility, as well as his resourcefulness and his deceitfulness: "of many turns" (*polytropos*), "of many designs" (*polymètis*), "of many wiles" (*polymechanos*), "of many sufferings" (*polytlos*) and so on. These qualities become apparent in a variety of ways. As Homer indicates, Odysseus is a skilled speaker: he knows what to say, when and to whom, and thus also knows how to say different things to different people as well as how to appear differently to different people, much like a con artist (cf. *Iliad*, 3.220-224). Thus, in his famous encounter with the Cyclops Polyphemus, he conceals his identity by calling himself *Outis*, "no-one" (*Odyssey*, 9.366), which subsequently is explicitly related to *mètis*, "shrewdness" or "mind" (*Odyssey*, 9.405-406). In this way, Odysseus's various characteristics – his experience, his practical and rhetorical talents, but also his knowledge of nature – converge in the anonymity of mind. Wisdom as knowledge of nature, Homer seems to indicate, is bound up with detachment from one's self and one's background.

---

[22]   Cf. Strauss, *The Rebirth of Classical Political Rationalism*, p. 252

[23]   Leo Strauss, *Natural Right and History* (Chicago: The University of Chicago Press, 1953), p. 90.

[24]   Homer, *Odyssey*. 10, 302-306. In fact, the very description of *moly* is intriguing: while its flower is "white like milk," its root is black. If, as Rémi Brague suggests, its *phusis* is what unites these two aspects, Homer's image almost reads as an emblem of poetic dividing and collecting. An oblique image is used to show up oblique nature (Rémi Brague, *Aristote et la question du monde* [Paris: Presses Universitaires de France, 1988], p. 20). Likewise, when Hesiod says in *Works and Days* that "the gods keep the means of living hidden from human beings" (WD, 42) the poem as a whole seems to show a way out of that predicament.

Doubtless, Strauss was aware of the affinities between Odysseus and Socrates. Already in the letters to Klein, he shows himself to be guided by Xenophon, who draws an explicit parallel between their talents as "safe speakers."[25] Very likely, he was also aware at an early stage of the way in which the Socratic quest for *phusis* is connected with his oddness (*atopia*) and his dissimulation (*eironeia*), just as the obliqueness of the Platonic dialogues echoes and imitates the hiddenness of nature. Moreover, there is some evidence that Strauss's understanding of Homer also made him aware of the importance of the political dimension of the Socratic pursuit of nature. Odysseus, the man who "saw the cities and knew the minds of many human beings" (*Odyssey*, 1.3) may have shown Socrates and Plato that the former is a condition of the latter: one has to see the city in order to know the minds of its citizens. At the same time, it reveals a tension between the two: the anonymity of mind is at odds with the self-understanding of the city, its laws and its virtues. In a letter to Klein, Strauss refers to the diatribe of Thersites, who criticizes Agamemnon's greed and his unjust treatment of Achilles, as well as the womanlike softness of the Achaeans (*Iliad*, 2.225-242). It is curious, Strauss comments, "that Thersites *says* the truth." (GS 3, 582). As he points out in *Persecution and the Art of Writing*, careful writers may occasionally state the truth, but they most likely will do so by putting it in the mouth of some disreputable character.[26]

At the same time, Strauss probably noticed Homer's ironic action, not only of choosing the crooked Thersites as an advocate for manliness and courage (along with the cuckold Menelaus, who echoes Thersites's words at *Iliad*, 7.96), but also of hinting at the underlying affinities between Thersites and Odysseus. In the letter to Klein, Strauss suggests that the tacit critique of the ideal of *andreia* (courage or manliness) is in fact a *Leitmotiv* that connects Homer *via* Parmenides (and perhaps Thucydides) with Plato and Xenophon. As he construes it, the playful allusions to the effeminacy of the philosophers indicate that they saw the ideal of *andreia* as a major obstacle and even as a threat to the pursuit of wisdom. The cult of manliness not only leads us away from the condition of peace that is a prerequisite for philosophy, but carried to its extreme it produces a tyrannical disorder of the soul that makes philosophizing altogether impossible.[27] In most of his published work, Strauss chose to remain reticent on this element of ancient thought, although his interpretations of Xenophon's *Oeconomicus* or Plato's *Republic* allow it to transpire nevertheless. Like his ancient models, he probably realized that a radical and explicit critique of courage – such as it was undertaken and disseminated by modern philosophy – would compromise the political framework on which poet and philosopher alike depend.

---

[25]   Xenophon, *Memorabilia*, 4.6.15. Cf. Strauss, *What is Political Philosophy?*, p. 93.

[26]   Cf. Strauss, *Persecution and the Art of Writing*, p. 36.

[27]   Leo Strauss, *The Political Philosophy of Hobbes: Its Basis and Its Genesis* (Oxford: Clarendon Press, 1936), pp. 146-147.

However this may be, the critique of manliness leads us to a more general issue: the tension between thought or wisdom and politics. In his preliminary comments on Hesiod to Klein, Strauss refers to the story of the hawk and the nightingale in the *Works and Days*. As he interprets it, the story is an allegory for the relationship between the singer-poet and the king (*Works and Days*, 198-212). In his review of Havelock, he elaborates this as follows: the king has the power to do as he pleases with the singer, without a title other than sheer force, the natural right of the stronger that also underlies *andreia*. However, Hesiod qualifies this view in the *Theogony*: the singer surpasses the king because he has the ability to sing "the glorious deeds of the human beings of old and of the gods" (*Theogony*, 100). In this respect, the king seems to depend on the poet for fame and recognition. Without song, political deeds remain devoid of meaning and authority. Moreover, Hesiod also leaves no doubt that song involves dissimulation: singing glorious deeds makes men "forget their cares and not remember their sorrow" (*Theogony*, 102-103). Strauss points out that Forgetfulness is the brother of Work, while the Muses are the daughters of Memory: singing glorious deeds is itself a deed that makes some forget while it reminds others.[28] And whereas the farmer must strip naked to do his work, the singer's work requires him to clothe himself, just as the Muses who inspire him go about in a thick mist (*Works and Days*, 391-392, 730-734; *Theogony*, 9). Thus, it seems that when the philosopher prepares to sing his songs (*nomoi*), he dons a garb that is quite ancient.

4. Poetry and Philosophy: What Quarrel?

The discussion above will, I hope, bear witness to the importance of ancient poetry for Strauss's understanding of the art of writing of the classical philosophers. Of course, the question remains whether philosophy and poetry, even if they are hard to distinguish, do not remain fundamentally different. In the last of his five lectures on "The Problem of Socrates," Strauss offers what may well be his most comprehensive statement on the "ancient quarrel between philosophy and poetry." There, his "final word" seems to assert the essential difference between philosophy and poetry, as well the superiority of the former over the latter:

> Poetry presents human life as human life appears if it is not seen to be directed toward philosophy. Autonomous poetry presents nonphilosophic life as autonomous. Yet by articulating the cardinal problem of human life as it comes to sight within the nonphilosophic life, poetry prepares for the philosophic life. Poetry is legitimate only as ministerial to the Platonic dialogue, which in its turn is ministerial to the life of understanding. Autonomous poetry is blind in the decisive respect.[29]

According to Strauss, the poets ultimately remain the valets of morality and theology: although they are critically aware of the defects of reigning opinion

---

[28] Strauss, *Liberalism Ancient and Modern*, p. 27.

[29] Strauss, *The Rebirth of Classical Political Rationalism*, p. 183.

and thus concerned with truth, they nevertheless remain trapped within the cave of the city and its laws. Philosophy, by contrast, is concerned with knowledge of nature and thus superior to poetry. In view of our discussion above, however, we may wonder whether ancient poetry, even on Strauss's own understanding, ever was truly autonomous and thus blind in the decisive respect. Earlier on in the same lecture, he grants that "in principle the poets do exactly the same thing as Plato himself," and that "neither the Platonic dialogue nor the poetic work is autonomous; both are ministerial, both serve to lead men to the understanding of the human soul."[30] In this respect, we should not forget that poetry not only points to the understanding of the soul, but also to the understanding of nature, as becomes apparent in and through the *Odyssey*, to say nothing about the *physiologia* of Aristophanes or Lucretius.

The work of the latter, in fact, shows that the dependence also points the other way. In his interpretation of Lucretius's *De Rerum Natura* (*On the Nature of Things*), Strauss suggests that the poet has a better understanding than the philosopher of man's profound attachment to the world, which underlies both religion and poetry. Because of this understanding, and as distinguished from religion, poetry shows itself to be the ally of philosophy in its relationship to religion: "Because poetry is rooted in the prephilosophic attachment, because it enhances and deepens that attachment, the philosophic poet is the perfect mediator between the attachment to the world and the attachment to detachment from the world."[31] In fact, Strauss even speaks of a *union* between poetry and philosophy that one could not abandon without compromising philosophy itself:

> Yet in surpassing Empedocles, Democritus and Epicurus had separated philosophy entirely from poetry. Poetry became at best the handmaid of philosophy. Yet the poet possesses insights which Epicurus may have lacked, above all the understanding of men's attachment to the world and what this implies. By restoring the union of philosophy and poetry, by presenting the true and final teaching poetically, Lucretius may be said to surpass Epicurus; the Lucretian presentation of the truth is superior to the Epicurean presentation. Yet if we consider the crucial importance of the Epicurean gods in the Epicurean presentation of the truth, are we not driven to say that in the decisive respect Epicurus too is a poet? Do the Epicurean gods not magnify or embellish the whole?[32]

The Lucretian restoration shows, in other words, that only a philosophical poet or a poetic philosopher is able to recognize that the quest for nature cannot dispense with taking into account and studying human nature. In this respect, Lucretius appears to repeat the Socratic turn, which according to Cicero consisted in calling philosophy down from heaven, setting it up in the cities, introducing it into the houses and summoning it to examine life and customs, as well as good

---

[30] Ibid., pp. 179-180.

[31] Strauss, *Liberalism Ancient and Modern*, p. 85.

[32] Ibid., p. 134.

and evil.[33] As we will see, it is worth considering whether even the original turn would have been possible without poetry.

Thus, it is not clear whether Strauss is altogether serious when he asserts that Plato presents the philosophic life in order to guide us to the life of thought, while "poetry does not present poetry in order to induce its hearers to become themselves poets."[34] If poetry, like philosophy, serves to lead to the understanding of nature and the human soul, it must induce at least some of its hearers to become more than just hearers. At least in Homer's case, his poetry did entice at least some of its hearers to become accomplished poets in their own right. From Hesiod to Heraclitus, from Aeschylus to Sophocles and Euripides, from Thucydides and Herodotus to Plato, from Lucretius and Vergil to Horace and Ovid, almost every post-Homeric poet and philosopher felt drawn to engage in a subtle contest or conversation with the blind bard.

For this reason, I am inclined to concur with Seth Benardete when he suggests that Strauss's reading of Plato eventually caused him to reconsider the distinction between philosophy and poetry, and to reckon with the possibility that "the Socratic revolution in philosophy seems to be coeval with Greek poetry, which had realized from the start, with its principle of telling lies like the truth, the relation of argument and action. Homer and Hesiod, then would have to be recognized as already within the orbit of philosophy."[35] Notice the nuance that Benardete introduces: Homeric and Hesiodic poetry are within the orbit of philosophy, but do not for that matter coincide with it. At least, this implies that poetry doesn't constitute a solar system entirely different from that of philosophy. But doesn't Benardete's remark equally apply to a considerable number of ancient *philosophic* works? With regard to the poems of Empedocles and Parmenides, not to mention the Platonic dialogues, couldn't one argue that they too remain in the orbit of philosophy, to the extent that they always leave it to the reader to discover the ways and means to land?

Going even further, one could ask to what extent the Socratic turn, with its descent into the cities and its interest in the human things, doesn't also involve magnifying and embellishing the whole. This may be the reason why Stanley Rosen, in his interpretation of Plato's *Republic*, suggests that, "in the last analysis, there is no quarrel between poetry and philosophy." As Rosen points out, in the *Republic* the quarrel, as well as the subjection of poetry to philosophy, figure within a *poetic* work in which philosophy is subjected to a *political* project, thereby subverting the hierarchy ostensibly propounded by the work. In any case, if Benardete's estimation is correct, the philosopher's clothes are more ancient than

---

[33]   Cicero, *Tusculan Disputations*, V.10.

[34]   Strauss, *The Rebirth of Classical Political Rationalism*, p. 182.

[35]   Seth Benardete, *The Argument of the Action: Essays on Greek Poetry and Philosophy* (Chicago: The University of Chicago Press, 2000), p. 416.

one would suppose. But what does this teach us with regard to the questions that were raised previously? To conclude, I will formulate some general observations.

5. The Second Sailing

To begin with, the pedigree of esoteric writing seems to suggest that its possibility and even its necessity are not only – and perhaps not primarily – a matter of political conditions, but perhaps of the *human* condition. As Strauss observes in his critique of Havelock, "most men read more with their 'imagination' than with open-minded care and are therefore much more benefited by salutary myths than by the naked truth."[36] This utterance may strike us as vintage Strauss, pressing the divide between the few wise and the many unwise. However, when we pay closer attention, there is much to ponder. The observation that begins the sentence is undoubtedly true. If few people read with "open-minded care," that is because this is extremely difficult, both because of the circumstances and because of the disposition of the reader. The ancient poets and philosophers doubtless were aware of what contemporary sociological and psychological research presents as a major discovery: that most of us, when reading, consciously or subconsciously seek confirmation of our views and opinions, and pay no heed to anything that contradicts them. By the same token, we tend to go through a text too fast, passing over what doesn't square with or might render questionable our prejudices. To counter this tendency requires considerable effort, if only because it requires us to slow down considerably. Whoever has tried his hand at reading Plato, Xenophon or Thucydides guided by Strauss's commentaries will be familiar with the experience: the exhilaration and admiration that attends the discovery of how well crafted the text is, but at the same time the irritation and frustration at having missed so much, because we allowed ourselves to be fooled by our prejudiced imagination.

At the same time, the question is whether this experience of failure is not part and parcel of the esoteric writer's design. For that design never becomes apparent at a first reading, but only after repeatedly revisiting the text. And this brings us to the second part of Strauss's observation, to wit that careless readers are "much more benefited by salutary myths than by the naked truth." In fact, given the context, the choice of words is odd: in his succinct but telling discussion of Hesiod, Strauss has just indicated that in esoteric writing – Hesiod's as much as Plato's – the truth is rarely if ever naked, but almost always clothed in myths, salutary or not. What is more, setting aside the question how and where the naked truth can be found in a world of appearances, our only access to it is by studying the colorful attire in which poets, historians and philosophers have arrayed it.

---

[36] Strauss, *Liberalism Ancient and Modern*, p. 40. Cf. Strauss, *Persecution and the Art of Writing*, p. 24.

Perhaps, then, we should not take Strauss's rhetorical flourish too seriously. After all, we shouldn't forget his important caution in *Thoughts on Machiavelli*: "The problem inherent in the surface of things, and only in the surface of things, is the heart of things."[37] This intriguing sentence also provides us with a clue as to what Strauss understands "the naked truth" to be. Far removed from any absolutism or "foundationalism," it seems that the only truth he is prepared to acknowledge is the permanence of certain fundamental problems. As he asserts in response to Alexandre Kojève, a "zetetic" or querying approach to truth is the only possible justification of philosophy: "Philosophy as such is nothing but genuine awareness of the problems, i.e., of the fundamental and comprehensive problems."[38] As such, philosophy understood in this way finds its most pointed expression in the Socratic knowledge of ignorance:

> Knowledge of ignorance is not ignorance. It is knowledge of the elusive character of the truth, of the whole. Socrates, then, viewed man in the light of the mysterious character of the whole. (…) We may also say that he viewed man in the light of the unchangeable ideas, i.e., of the fundamental problems. For to articulate the situation of man means to articulate man's openness to the whole. This understanding of the situation of man which includes, then, the quest for cosmology rather than a solution to the cosmological problem, was the foundation of classical political philosophy. (WPP 139)

But if truth consists in the persistence of certain fundamental problems, and if philosophy consists in becoming aware of these problems, we must wonder whether the primary objective of the art of writing is not instrumental in triggering and fostering this awareness. Consider what Strauss says about the overall character of the Platonic dialogues:

> Plato's work consists of many dialogues because it imitates the manyness, the variety, the heterogeneity of being. The many dialogues form a *kosmos* which mysteriously imitates the *kosmos*. The Platonic *kosmos* imitates or reproduces its model in order to awaken us to the mystery of the model and to assist us in articulating that mystery.[39]

It is important to note that Strauss says that we can learn to articulate the *mystery* of the model, not the model itself. In the light of what we have learned about the ancient pedigree of the philosophers' art of writing, the question arises whether this general characterization cannot be extended, *mutatis mutandis*, to the works of the ancient poets and historians. In the case of Homer and Hesiod, it could be argued that their writings serves a similar purpose: they offer a cryptic

---

[37] Leo Strauss, *Thoughts on Machiavelli* (Chicago: The University of Chicago Press, 1958), p. 13.

[38] Strauss, *What is Political Philosophy?*, p. 116. See also "On a Forgotten Kind of Writing," which is a reply to some criticisms of *Persecution and the Art of Writing*: "History of philosophy necessarily presupposes the persistence of the same fundamental problems. This and this alone, is the trans-temporal truth which must be admitted, if there is to be history of philosophy." (*What is Political Philosophy?*, p. 229)

[39] Strauss, *The City and Man*, p. 62.

imitation of a hidden order – nature or the means of living – in order to rouse the reader's awareness, not so much of the order, but of its hiddenness. Phenomeno-logically speaking, one might say that they imitate the strangeness of appearances in order to make us aware, not of what lies beyond them, but of the strangeness itself. This ties in with a point that was made earlier about the experience of failure: by offering a cryptic imitation, the esoteric writer ensures that the reader necessarily begins in the element of misunderstanding and thus of estrangement. This failure to understand, however, is the only possible incentive for a subse-quent attempt at genuine understanding: under the impression that he has missed something, the reader is enticed to revisit the surface of the text. When she finds he has indeed missed something, she is brought to realize that what she has failed to perceive in fact points to numerous other omissions on his part.

In this way, the art of writing imitates the well-known "second sailing" that Socrates describes in the *Phaedo*: having started to philosophize as a "physiolo-gist" and having failed, he abandoned the direct study of nature in order to turn to people's speeches. According to Benardete, this means that philosophy can only emerge from a failed attempt to philosophize: "The false start of philosophy can alone jumpstart philosophy."[40] The art of writing of the ancient poets, historians and philosophers may be said to deliberately provoking this false start. By offer-ing an enigmatic imitation, by telling lies like the truth, the artful writer ensures that the reader necessarily begins in the element of misunderstanding. This failure to understand, however, is the only possible incentive for a subsequent attempt at genuine understanding: guided to perplexity, the reader is enticed to revisit the surface of the text, and thus to undertake a "second sailing" on her own account. As Benardete points out, the "second sailing" is already prefigured in the *Odys-sey*. In the tenth book, king Aeolus gives Odysseus a bag of winds to speed his journey home. However, his mutinous crew opens the bag and his ship is blown right back to their point of departure, the island of the Aeolians. When Odysseus asks Aeolus for help again, the latter angrily rebuffs him, telling him that he can no longer count on the support of the gods. After this episode, Odysseus and his crew can only rely on themselves, their strength and their oars to complete their journey: they have to row nonstop for six days and nights (*Odyssey*, 10.78). How-ever, it is within this new predicament that, soon after, Odysseus discovers the togetherness of what is seemingly disparate, or *phusis*.[41]

Moreover, both with regard to the model and to its imitation, hiddenness is perhaps as much a result of our defective perception as it is a result of the esoteric writer's talent. In this sense, it is not all that difficult for us to be "benefited by salutary myths:" the art of writing does not so much point us to what is hidden,

---

[40]   Plato, Phaedo, 96a-102a; Benardete, *The Argument of the Action: Essays on Greek Poetry and Philosophy*, p. 408.

[41]   Seth Benardete, *The Bow and the Lyre: A Platonic Reading of the* Odyssey (Lanham: Rowman & Littlefield, 1997), p. 82.

but to what is in fact right in front of us even though we fail to see it. For this reason, the difference between the esoteric and the exoteric meaning of a text is equally relative to the reader: there is only one text, and to penetrate "deeper" into the heart of it only means that we become more aware of what always was on the surface though we didn't observe it.[42] This may explain why Strauss, when speaking of the fact that writings are accessible to all, notes of an esoteric writer, both that "all of his writings would have to be, strictly speaking, exoteric" and that "no written exposition can be, strictly speaking, esoteric."[43]

Our failure to perceive may be related to the fact that we are thumotic beings. As Strauss points out, Plato resuscitated the Homeric notion of *thumos* from the desuetude in which it had fallen: both poet and philosopher understood how spirited anger, which lies at the basis of our imagination as well as of our thirst for justice, order and meaning, shapes and determines the way in which we perceive reality, to the point of making us ascribe intentionality to lifeless objects.[44] Perhaps, then, *thumos* may also be instrumental in the way we read texts, making us read what we want to and ignore what we don't want to read. If this is the case, the art of writing of poets, historians and philosophers may well be designed to counteract and redirect the operation of *thumos*: by perplexing us, it invites us to slow down and check our imagination as we try to make sense of the scattered traces of authorial intentionality. This may also explain why philosophy was viewed as "passive" and even "feminine" from the thumotic perspective of the city.

At the same time, Strauss cautions us to beware from positing or imagining intentionality where there is none: "Reading between the lines is strictly prohibited in all cases where it would be less exact than not doing so."[45] Of course, this is no final guarantee that the reader's interpretation is not just a thumotic projection or *Hineininterpretieren*. Indeed, Strauss admits that reading between the lines can never lead to certainty. But, as he retorts, neither do alternative methods of reading, which have the additional drawback that they generally ignore even the few instances where authors clearly indicate they wish to be read between the lines: "I would be happy if there were suspicion of crime where up to now there has only been implicit faith in perfect innocence."[46] At the very least, reading between the lines makes us suspicious of the ostensible moral clarity exhibited by the author and become aware of the moral complexity that underlies it. Reading the ancient poets carefully is an antidote to facile and superficial moralism, just as reading Plato carefully is a powerful antidote to our congenital Platonism,

---

[42]   As Sherlock Holmes rebukes his friend Dr. Watson, "You see, but you do not observe." (Arthur Conan Doyle, *A Scandal in Bohemia*, 1892).

[43]   Strauss, *Persecution and the Art of Writing*, pp. 35 and 187.

[44]   Strauss, *The Rebirth of Classical Political Rationalism*, pp. 165, 169.

[45]   Strauss, *Persecution and the Art of Writing*, p. 30.

[46]   Strauss, *What is Political Philosophy?*, pp. 231-232.

which causes us to rashly reify the things we value.[47] This does not mean that the art of writing leads us to depreciate or even destroy what we hold dear: rather, the poetic-philosophic fabric invites us to examine *sine ira et studio* the web of our own opinions.

With *thumos*, we also touch upon the question of the political dimension of the art of writing. If this art is primarily geared to the human condition as such, it would seem that it remains possible and relevant regardless of the political context in which it is practiced. Even in contemporary democracy, where slow, patient and attentive reading has become more rare than ever before, philosophic poetry or poetic philosophy retains its capacity to draw our attention to the mysteriousness and heterogeneity of being. The political ramifications of this capacity, I think, are the following. Becoming aware of the mysteriousness of being through the art of writing is attended by the recognition that freedom of thought is much harder to attain than we are willing to admit: not only and not primarily because of specific political circumstances, but because we rarely realize how strong the hold is that our views, opinions and prejudices exercise on us.[48] This, I think, is one of the dimensions of Strauss's assertion that "society will always try to tyrannize thought:" more than just the rule of one man without laws, tyranny denotes the absence of care, attention and openness that prevents the human soul from perceiving the mysteriousness of being.[49]

6. Conclusion

While there is an undeniable element of elitism involved in this view, it doesn't amount to more than an elitism of the mind, based on natural differences in capacity of being attentive and resisting the charms of one's thumotic imagination. In nurturing these qualities, the effect of the art of writing is rather to pull us away from politics, not to induce us to any political action. Hence, I tend to agree with recent interpretations of Strauss's work arguing that his political thought is a-political at its core.[50] As Strauss himself indicates, rediscovering pre-modern philosophy also invites us to recover the primacy of theoretical reason, while at the same time it invites us to question the predominance of practical reason in modernity.[51] That same predominance may have made it difficult to perceive

---

[47] Michael Davis, "Making Something from Nothing: On Plato's Hipparchus," *The Review of Politics* 68 (2006), pp. 547-563.

[48] Strauss, *The Political Philosophy of Hobbes*, p. xvi.

[49] Strauss, *On Tyranny*, p. 27. Cf. Plato, *Republic*, 619a-c.

[50] Cf. Heinrich Meier, *Leo Strauss and the Theologico-Political Problem* (Cambridge: Cambridge University Press, 2006), pp. xvii-xviii; Harald Bluhm, *Die Ordnung der Ordnung: Das politische Philosophieren von Leo Strauss* (Berlin: Akadmie Verlag, 2002), p. 22.

[51] Leo Strauss, *Philosophy and Law: Contributions to the Understanding of Maimonides and His Predecessors*, trans. E. Adler (New York: State University of New York Press, 1995), p. 103.

how radically unpolitical or transpolitical Strauss's conception of philosophy is at heart. Still, he does drop a hint near the end of the chapter on "Persecution and the Art of Writing" by pointing out that the ultimate goal of the art of writing is not political but *pedagogical*:

> The works of the great writers of the past are very beautiful even from without. And yet their visible beauty is sheer ugliness, compared with the beauty of those hidden treasures which disclose themselves only after very long, never easy, but always pleasant work. This always difficult but always pleasant work is, I believe, what the philosophers had in mind when they recommended education. Education, they felt, is the only answer to the always pressing question, to the political question par excellence, of how to reconcile order which is not oppression with freedom which is not license.[52]

The answer to the political question par excellence is not political action, but education.[53] It is not far-fetched to surmise that Strauss was thinking of the Platonic echo in the Latin root of the word: *e-ducere*, "to lead out or away from." After all, Plato may have taught him that the cave only becomes visible as a cave upon the attempt to leave it. Of course, according to Strauss we moderns have embedded ourselves in a cave underneath the Platonic cave, rendering the philosophic ascent more difficult than ever. However, this does not preclude the splendor of the poetico-philosophic attire from continuing to attract, surprise and alert us. It suffices to refer to Lessing, the modern-ancient poet-philosopher whom Strauss repeatedly praised as his *maître à penser*. As this statement, which Strauss cites approvingly, makes clear, ancient philosophy and poetry teach us the art of *seeing*:

> We see more than the Ancients; and yet our eyes may perhaps be inferior to the eyes of the Ancients: the Ancients saw less than we do; but their eyes, generally speaking, may have been slightly sharper than ours – I'm afraid that the entire comparison between the Ancients and the Moderns might come down to this.[54]

---

[52] Strauss, *Persecution and the Art of Writing*, p. 37.

[53] Cf. Arthur Melzer, "On the Pedagogical Motive for Esoteric Writing," *The Journal of Politics*, Vol. 69, no. 4, p. 1015-1031.

[54] Gotthold E. Lessing, *Briefe Antiquarischen Inhalts*, 45.

Paweł Armada

LEO STRAUSS AS ERZIEHER: THE DEFENSE OF THE PHILOSOPHICAL LIFE OR THE DEFENSE OF LIFE AGAINST PHILOSOPHY?

As we have all experienced it there is a growing interest in the legacy of Leo Strauss. This is partly due to some political matters. Especially since the beginning of the so-called War on Terror, when the intellectual as well as personal background of the American foreign policy was being meticulously investigated, many significant books have been published in order to explain the core of the Straussian thought or reveal a putative scale of Leo Strauss's influence on academic and also political discourse. At the same time the author of the *Natural Right and History* had been recognized as a godfather of the neo-conservative movement and this meant a despicable figure from the point of view of most of those who found themselves in opposition to some decisions coming from Washington. There was even a kind of accusation leveled against Leo Strauss that he was a nihilist, or someone akin to the Grand Inquisitor, who deliberately concealed his real face of an extremely modern thinker, and who denied any standards of judgment concerning political life preparing, instead, a set of "noble lies" addressed to the masses. In response to this, there has emerged a powerful defense of a Straussian position, especially on the part of those who identify themselves with a school of political thinking of which Strauss was a founder, telling now what they consider to be the truth about his work, that it was animated by a steady adherence to liberal democracy accompanied by a constant effort to revive the political philosophy of the classics.

However, there remains a deep controversy regarding the most basic tenets of Straussian thinking which may be gradually explained thanks to the job that was also started not many years ago and concerns a detailed research into the writings of Leo Strauss, including many texts published in his youth and the prolific correspondence with some other renowned thinkers. The question that seems to underlie his oeuvre is the question of an inevitable conflict between politics and philosophy. Yet, what must be emphasized is his specific manner of understanding these two terms as the two ways of life. As for politics, he stated in his first commentary explicitly devoted to an ancient writer that "political life, if taken seriously, meant belief in the gods of the city, and philosophy is the denial of the gods of the city."[1] But what does seriousness mean in such a context? What can be seen as a criterion for taking something to be a serious thing? Should seriousness be connected with sacredness or even, more precisely, with steadfast defense of what is sacred ("first") to us, and probably unsacred, if not contemptible, to our enemies? Should seriousness be related to divine command regarded as the basis for a particular mode of living together in a community? If so, the faith would be necessary for a citizen. One believes in gods and this faith is a basis for his being a member of one of many communities existing in the world. Should we assume that a relation to the highest authority, certainly perceived as the ultimate source of law by which any political community exists, is in fact indispensable for the very existence of a community? So if there is a natural order of political things, does it not depend on the "ancient idea of law,"[2] the law of not human origin, preceding any philosophical discourse concerning the idea of "natural right" that Strauss considered advisable to explore in his mature work written under some specific conditions, namely the confrontation with the totalitarian regimes and the increasing weakness of the Western spirit?

The fundamental conflict between politics and philosophy can be also depicted in classical terms as a problem of relation between "the cave," which means the political community, on the one hand, and the struggle to ascend from the cave, led by Socratic philosophers, on the other hand. We may thus say that the *conditio sine qua non* of the philosophy is the cave itself. If so, the defense of the philosophic way of life should be primarily understood as the defense of a necessary ground for any possible philosophical enterprise or, to put it in other words, of the commonsensical perception of political things which has something to do with the faith mentioned above; the state of perception where political philosophy, i.e., conscious living a philosophical life, begins. He who is predestined to understand "the cave" philosophically cannot dispense with prior, i.e., prephilosophic, understanding of the faith that enables living together in the cave; I think that this can plausibly be described as the task of political science. And what the philosopher has to think about, most and above all, begins in "the cave," but first that cave must have occurred to him as simply "the world." These concluding words of Strauss put forward after he has presented what he calls Thucydides' "'common sense' understanding of political things," are most instructive:

> Philosophy is the ascent from what is first for us to what is first by nature. This ascent requires that what is first for us be understood as adequately as possible in the manner in which it comes to sight prior to the ascent. In other words, political understanding or

---

[1] Leo Strauss, "The Spirit of Sparta or the Taste of Xenophon," *Social Research* 6, no. 4 (November 1939): p. 531.

[2] Cf. Leo Strauss, *Philosophie und Gesetz*, in Leo Strauss, Heinrich Meier ed., *Philosophie und Gesetz - Frühe Schriften* (Stuttgart: Metzler, 1997), p. 61.

political science cannot start from seeing the city as the Cave but it must start from seeing the city as a world, as the highest in the world; it must start from seeing man as completely immersed in political life...

For what is "first for us" is not the philosophic understanding of the city but that under-standing which is inherent in the city as such, in the prephilosophic city, according to which the city sees itself as subject and subservient to the divine in the ordinary under-standing of the divine or looks up to it. Only by beginning at this point will we be open to the full impact of the all-important question which is coeval with philosophy although the philosophers do not frequently pronounce it – the question *quid sit deus.*[3]

Having taken this all into consideration, we can ask a simple question: What is to be learnt from Leo Strauss, especially for someone trying to reflect upon the fundamental issues concerning the proper meaning of the politics or political life? Here I mean someone who was not lucky enough to become one of his pupils, so unable to take any conversation with him; I mean a reader. Thus the question may be stated as follows: Are we allowed to think that some findings of his may provide us with a philosophic concept of the transcendental or transcontextual standards of political judgment or a theoretical solution, in a strict sense, to the most urgent problems of our age that we see as political scientists? This question suits a scholar who is wondering about some cure for an overwhelming, if not easily expressed in the language of scholarship, lack of seriousness or a strong feeling of senselessness that appears to pervade political life in the society which has finally "replaced virtue by trade." A half a century ago Strauss wrote about the mass culture that had been flourishing under liberal democracies of the West: "If we contrast the present day usage of 'culture' with the original meaning, it is as if someone would say that the cultivation of a garden may consist of the garden's being littered with empty tin cans and whisky bottles and used papers of various descriptions thrown around the garden at random."[4] It is quite safe to say that his appraisal of the current state of affairs would be even worse or that the problem of modernity in the sense of "lowering the standards" of human life (a subject he treated so famously) remains plaguing the society we live in. But does there, we ask him, exist any kind of remedy stemming from philosophi-cal enterprise, or apt to be discovered on the way of the philosopher, to serve the purpose of recovering "the original meaning of culture," so to say? Can we imagine any form of education developed against our present situation? Would it be education towards philosophy or in favor of philosophy as the way of life transcending the borders of political communities? Can Straussian reflection on the philosophic ascent help us to improve or restore the cave?

---

[3] Leo Strauss, *On Thucydides' War of the Peloponnesians and the Athenians*, in *The City and Man* (Chicago: The University of Chicago Press, 1964), pp. 240-241.

[4] Leo Strauss, *What is Liberal Education?*, in *Liberalism Ancient and Modern* (Ithaca: Cornell University Press, 1968), p. 4.

This question of Leo Strauss as an *Erzieher*, a teacher or educator, especially
of those who practice political science, and so come across his name, is what
I have been striving to deal with since I started my investigation into his books
(and what must be taken for granted is that I, living whole my life in Poland, never met either Leo Strauss himself or anyone who studied with him so my knowledge stands or falls on what I learned from the books). When I started translating
Strauss's *On Tyranny* into Polish I wondered about a dedication I found in the
opening paragraph of the *Introduction* to this book. It reads: "It is proper that
I should indicate my reasons for submitting this detailed analysis of a forgotten dialogue on tyranny to the consideration of political scientists." And he adds
at the end of the *Introduction*: "Still, I believe that I have not dotted all the i's.
One can only hope that the time will again come when Xenophon's art will be
understood by a generation which, properly trained in their youth, will no longer
need cumbersome introductions like the present study."[5] So it seems that Strauss
claims to reveal to us something that we are not able immediately to grasp when
we read the text of Xenophon on our own, something probably forgotten because
of the basic direction of modern thought affecting our way of understanding or
misunderstanding such profound political phenomena as the tyranny we must
face. At the same time, there is a hint given to us that not everything has been
fully explicated. At any rate, we find ourselves compelled to wonder about the
gains we make as attentive readers of a carefully written dialogue that we are
encouraged to read through the lenses we are provided with by an interpreter
capable of inspiring our confidence in his job. We may promptly observe that
"Socratic rhetoric" or "a forgotten kind of writing" we are urged to learn of is
principally connected with classical virtue, prudence or moderation, "animated
by the spirit of social responsibility."[6] Not everything should be voiced. There
are harmful claims or corrupting pictures as well as there are readers fond of run-
ning after their fellow-citizens suspected cherishing unorthodox beliefs. Unlike
Machiavelli, who indeed referred to Xenophon as to no other ancient authority,
Socrates' pupil used to make use of silence rather than sophisticated blasphemy
or merely shocking statements. As Strauss wrote in another text, "Xenophon's
moral universe has two poles, the one pointed by the great political man, say,
by Cyrus, and the other pointed to by Xenophon's revered master, Socrates. But
there is no place for Socrates in Machiavelli's moral universe."[7]

What is to be called a radical break from the whole Great Tradition of Socratic philosophy, a break that is said to have its ultimate consequence "in ex-

---

[5] Leo Strauss, *On Tyranny. Revised and Enlarged* (Ithaca: Cornell University Press,
1963), pp. 21, 27.

[6] Ibid., p. 26.

[7] Leo Strauss, "Machiavelli and Classical Literature," *Review of National Literatures*,
no. 1 (Spring 1970), p. 13.

plicitly condemning to oblivion the notion of eternity"[8] (hence the very horizon of philosophizing) but, first of all, in a political context, a break with the art of liberal education that seems to be the proper result of the philosopher's attitude towards his fellow-citizens (or just the best of them, namely the same who must have justifiably been regarded as inclined to become "passionately opposed to philosophy"), this break was made by a man who seems to be driven by the so-called anti-theological passion or ire. The passion in question induced Machiavelli "to take an extreme step of questioning the supremacy of contemplation."[9] Before Machiavelli, "the contemplative life," we must remember the fact, "had found its home in monasteries"[10] as there had emerged Christianity which recognized philosophy in its specific way therefore making it "subject to ecclesiastical supervision."[11] We must ask, however, what should be thought the source of the anti-theological passion or ire? Or, in other words, what should be claimed responsible for modern fantastic political hopes or "the modern utopianism of the social engineer"[12] that has its trace in the prophetic work of Machiavelli, for the "modern solution" whose actualization is to be considered, indeed, impossible?

The problem with philosophy is that, in short, it is a special kind of activity that is meant to transcend the limits of any political community, thus questioning the law the community depends on. At the same time, philosophy cannot be practiced outside the walls of the city, so to speak. Philosophical life consists in contemplation that is an "asocial perfection" that "normally presupposes a political community, the city."[13] However, insofar as the claims of philosophy could be put into synthesis with the claims of a revealed religion, namely of that religion which "could parade itself as the true philosophy"[14] based on a "set of dogmas," the result seems to be nothing else than the opening of the gates for some universal tyranny, if not the "universal and homogeneous state" (with "homogeneity" having probably been derived from the Christian notion of charity). It is extolled, although perhaps in an ambivalent manner, by one of Strauss's philosophical adversaries (and lifetime friends), Alexandre Kojève, the correspondence with

---

[8] Leo Strauss, *What is Political Philosophy?*, in *Introduction to Political Philosophy: Ten Essays* (Detroit: Wayne State University Press, 1989), p. 57.

[9] Leo Strauss, *Marsilius of Padua*, in *Liberalism Ancient and Modern*, p. 201.

[10] Strauss, *What is Political Philosophy*, p. 43.

[11] Leo Strauss, *Introduction*, in *Persecution and the Art of Writing* (Chicago: The University of Chicago Press, 1988), p. 21.

[12] Leo Strauss, "What Can We Learn From Political Theory?," *The Review of Politics* 69 (2007), p. 523.

[13] Leo Strauss, *Progress or Return?*, in Leo Strauss, K.H. Green ed., *Jewish Philosophy and the Crisis of Modernity: Essays and Lectures in Modern Jewish Thought* (Albany: State University of New York Press, 1997), p. 109.

[14] Laurence Lampert, *Leo Strauss and Nietzsche* (Chicago: The University of Chicago Press, 1996), p. 140.

whom we can find in *On Tyranny*. For Strauss, the emergence of the "Final State" marks the "end of philosophy on earth."[15]

This final appraisal of the "Final State" fulfilling "the modern solution" may seem obvious for any devoted reader of Strauss. Yet the basic problem remains. From a certain point of view, a Straussian depiction of what philosophy originally was, of the way of life as led by Socrates, may be construed as embarrassingly idealistic. To be sure, Strauss devotes a great many disarming lines to acquaint his readers with the beauty and nobleness "of what a philosopher is,"[16] apparently presenting an attitude that he ascribed to Nietzsche. Strauss said of him as follows: "If I understand him correctly, his deepest concern was with philosophy, and not with politics... philosophy, in order to be really philosophy, and not some sort of dogmatism, is the sake of *natural* men, of men capable and willing to live 'under the sky,' of men who do not need the shelter of the cave, of *any* cave."[17] Can we suspect that Strauss, in principle, shares this view? Certainly, following his classic models, he wrote of philosophy as the highest human activity or even the peak of human excellence. Philosophy is then described as "the highest form of the mating of courage" and moderation that is "necessarily accompanied, sustained, and elevated by *eros*" and hence "graced by nature's grace."[18] In *On Tyranny* there is also a mention of "the highest form of justice" that refers to "the preserve of those who have the greatest self-sufficiency which is humanly possible."[19] In response to Kojève, who wants to see the philosopher as a political participant in a truly universal goal concerning preparing of the coming of the "Final State," Strauss depicts the Socratic philosopher as "radically detached from human concerns," disinterested as well as benign or a simply harmless person, however, one who has to make his "radical detachment" "compatible with an attachment to human beings"[20] as he is fed by them and he finds the souls of potential philosophers, "the puppies of his race,"[21] when talking to them. By another occasion Strauss emphasized that "however profound the difference, or the antagonism, between Socrates and the non-philosophic citizens may be, in grave situations he identifies himself completely, as far as his body is concerned, with

---

[15]   Leo Strauss, *Restatement on Xenophon's Hiero*, in *On Tyranny*, p. 226.

[16]   Leo Strauss, *An Introduction to Heideggerian Existentialism*, in *The Rebirth of Classical Political Rationalism: An Introduction to the Thought of Leo Strauss* (Chicago: The University of Chicago Press, 1989), p. 40.

[17]   Leo Strauss, *The Living Issues of German Postwar Philosophy*, in Heinrich Meier, *Leo Strauss and the Theologico-Political Problem*, trans. Marcus Brainard (Cambridge: Cambridge University Press, 2006), p. 137.

[18]   Strauss, *What is Political Philosophy?*, p. 39.

[19]   Strauss, *On Tyranny*, p. 94.

[20]   Strauss, *Restatement on Xenophon's Hiero*, p. 213.

[21]   Leo Strauss, *Persecution and the Art of Writing*, in Strauss, *Persecution and the Art of Writing*, p. 36.

the city, with 'his people.'"[22] Furthermore, the philosophy, although presented as the way of life "side by side with the city," "has necessarily a humanizing or civilizing effect" so that a political community would need "philosophy, but mediately or indirectly, not to say in diluted form."[23] Thus it seems we circle back to the forgotten art of Xenophon Strauss helped us to understand by what he calls, ironically or not, the "cumbersome introductions."

But what must be added here is that the Straussian notion of philosophy is a specific one as regards notable effects of the philosophic enterprise. We learn that philosophy, however noble or excellent, "could appear as Sisyphean or ugly, when one contrasts its achievement with its goal."[24] Philosophers are those who engage in the never-stopping enterprise of raising the weightiest questions and reflecting on possible or liable solutions. If they are to remain philosophers, not changing into sectarians or ideologists, they must think zetetically. It means they should find themselves becoming much more certain of the persistence of problems they face than any convincing solutions which are supposed to be reached by them. They share awareness that their striving for wisdom, or knowledge of the whole, is never to be completed so they can never offer anyone the truth as such to be implemented. Yet they must be aware, too, of the political consequences of their enterprise and hence inherent limitations of what they do. It means also, as Strauss wrote, that while "in the case of gentlemen" (the best of the philosophers' fellow-citizens) "one can make a simple distinction between the playful education of the potential gentleman and the earnest work of the gentleman proper, in the case of the philosopher this simple distinction between the playful and the serious no longer holds" and this is precisely because of the latter's "need of being acquired again from the start."[25] So we feel obliged to accept that no real Socratic philosopher could deliver to us the certain basis of the most serious law that a particular society we live in is essentially in need of. The philosopher is not the prophet (i.e., the lawgiver) even if he is capable of the rational understanding of the prophet's task on his own terms. This, of course, was not accepted by the modern thinkers from Machiavelli on.

We learn, moreover, that philosophy is something that we can love through reading the "Great Books," love by recollecting the grandeur bequeathed to us, but we cannot be philosophers ourselves.[26] We cannot be astonished, indeed, by the fact that those who deserve being depicted as the philosophers, those able to think through their situation as the human beings trying to know who they really

---

[22] Leo Strauss, *Plato's* Apology of Socrates *and* Crito, in Leo Strauss, *Studies in Platonic Political Philosophy* (Chicago: The University of Chicago Press, 1983), p. 51.

[23] Leo Strauss, *Liberal Education and Responsibility*, in Strauss, *Liberalism Ancient and Modern*, p. 15.

[24] Strauss, *What is Political Philosophy?*, p. 39.

[25] Strauss, *Liberal Education and Responsibility*, p. 14.

[26] Cf. Strauss, *What is Liberal Education?*, p. 7.

are, those asking about "the mysterious nature of the whole," are "extremely rare natures." It appears quite unreasonable to hold that there are many such seekers for wisdom living at the same time and just in the city one lives in. It is, accordingly, hard to expect Socrates to be met, e.g., as a teacher at the same university where one studies. To be sure, Strauss did not assert that there are many philosophers around. Contrary to Allan Bloom's statement of this (made in the obituary speech[27]), he does not seem to regard himself as one equal to Plato or Nietzsche and while talking about the importance of Heidegger he underlines his being merely a scholar putting all his efforts into understanding the thought of the great, if mistaken, German thinker.[28] In fact, being faced with the brilliant interpretation of the past is not the same as having encounter with the past itself.

According to Strauss, as he wrote in his remarkable letter to Karl Löwith, we should consider ourselves as "natural beings living and thinking under unnatural conditions."[29] If this is the case, another simple question immediately occurs: What can be the natural conditions of human living? There is an answer given by Strauss, one very troublesome. In another great letter he says that he really believes "that the political order, as Plato and Aristotle have sketched it, is the perfect political order," while "the modern solution" is *contra naturam*. The natural conditions are to be found only within closed societies, not a world-state, and "one can show from political considerations that a small city-state is in principle superior to the large state or the territorial-feudal state." At the same time, he admits that this natural order cannot be simply restored "in the *extremely unfavorable situation*" that we experience today.[30] However, just pondering over such a possibility, one is to be reminded that a closed society or a particular community in the classical sense may be described as "totalitarian" insofar as "it embraced and regulated morals, divine worship, tragedy and comedy."[31] It is the community of law that concerns every aspect of the human life, provided it is a life of one who at the same time belongs to a political whole and believes in its particular foundation. It is a community of Plato and Alfarabi and not of Thomas Aquinas, to say nothing about the moderns. It is the community where the life of the philosopher resembles the life of the hermit much more than the life of the intellectual playing his role as a celebrity.

When talking about the liberal education, Strauss points to an explanation of the essential difficulty met by a serious teacher, even if serious just with regard

[27] Cf. Allan Bloom, *Leo Strauss: September 10, 1899 – October 18, 1973*, in *Giants and Dwarfs: Essays 1960-1990* (New York: Touchstone Books, 1991), p. 239.

[28] Cf. Strauss, *An Introduction to Heideggerian Existentialism*, p. 29.

[29] *Korrespondenz Leo Strauss – Karl Löwith* (letter from June 23, 1935), in Leo Strauss, Heinrich Meier, Wiebke Meier eds., *Gesammelte Schriften*, vol. 3: *Hobbes' politische Wissenschaft und zugehörige Schriften – Briefe* (Stuttgart: Metzler, 2008), p. 650.

[30] *Korrespondenz Leo Strauss – Karl Löwith* (letter from August 15, 1946), in *Gesammelte Schriften*, vol. 3, p. 662-663.

[31] Strauss, *Persecution and the Art of Writing*, p. 21.

to his students, that "the cause of this situation is that we have lost all simply authoritative traditions in which we could trust, the *nomos* which gave us authoritative guidance, because our immediate teachers and teachers' teachers believed in the possibility of a simply rational society."[32] Hence, it seems that the "simply rational society" is a fatal idea that contaminated modern minds, depriving people of the commonsensical understanding of the law or the necessity of the law. Yet such an understanding is a prerequisite not only for political life, namely for living one's life in a serious and sensible way within his community, but also for the way of life as the philosopher. And one essential thing we cannot focus on here is that the law as derived from the divine authority of the omnipotent God forms a constant challenge to any philosophical enterprise from the outset to its end. We can probably say that from the political perspective what is most important, however, is the seriousness and sensibleness of the very foundation the political community relies upon.

The most famous and influential book of Strauss's, *Natural Right and History*, begins with quoting two short passages from the Bible that seem to prove that we still have something like a sound feeling of justice, and then the question is given whether the American people "in its maturity still cherish the faith in which it was conceived and raised,"[33] the very faith that the Americans owe the power and prosperity of their nation to. It is clear that such faith in the nation's foundation is distinct from possessing philosophical or scientific evidence of, say, necessity of that particular foundation.[34] However, we can think of the young people, as impetuous as Plato's Glaucon, who demand being taught about the idea of justice, the idea that could be perceived by them as a rational justification of their obedience to laws. This is a peculiar situation in the natural world of man when there arises a significant "doubt of authority." Strauss showed us by his manner of reading that, e.g., "in the *Republic* the discussion of natural right starts long after the aged Cephalus, the father, the head of the house, has left to take care of the sacred offering to the gods: the absence of Cephalus, or of what he stands for, is indispensable from the quest for natural right," namely for the conversation dealing with the political meaning of philosophy. Strauss says to us that "men like Cephalus do not need to know of natural right"[35] and this would imply that men who need the philosophic concept of natural right are precisely those prone to ignore "a torch race in honor of a goddess" or any celebration like this.

What must be emphasized, in my opinion, is that a philosopher or a man who loves philosophy is able to help political men in understanding what is just and

---

[32] Strauss, *What Is Liberal Education?*, p. 8.

[33] Leo Strauss, *Natural Right and History* (Chicago: The University of Chicago Press, 1953), p. 1.

[34] Cf. Leora Batnitzky, *Leo Strauss and Emmanuel Levinas: Philosophy and the Politics of Revelation* (Cambridge: Cambridge University Press, 2006), pp. 117-139.

[35] Strauss, *Natural Right and History*, p. 84.

that finally what is just as particular as enabling or conditioning the activity of the philosopher who transcends the particular or goes beyond the cave.

My conclusion, I hope a somewhat provocative one, is that the figure of the Socratic philosopher by Strauss as an *Erzieher* is deliberately idealized in order to redeem the claims of politics or political life or maybe human life as such (since every man is thought to be a fundamentally political man and this assertion regards the philosopher as well; there must be something to ascend from). Then, in a sense, the Straussian concern about politics, politics being threatened by someone's careless exposing the philosopher's mode of being, is substantially preceding the concern about the philosophic life as ascribed to Nietzsche. In other words, living in the cave comes before living "under the sky." And even with the highest estimation for the philosophy as it might be, as prudent as detached or concerning about the eternal, we still need a prophet or a faith in the law given by the prophet of our city. We cannot dispense with a need for political truth, the truth of a particular community, however moderated by a rational enterprise of the Socratic philosophy. This is the natural horizon of politics comprising a common sense of right and wrong that we have lost.

Jürgen Gebhardt

MODERN CHALLENGES – PLATONIC RESPONSES: STRAUSS, ARENDT, VOEGELIN

This conference is devoted to the work of Leo Strauss. It raises the question of the meaning and relevance of his legacy today. The wording of the general conference theme implies that a consideration of this legacy involves the notion of the inherently flawed character of modernity. In the course of the last centuries the omnipresent albeit elusive term "modernity" has acquired many meanings. From its origins in the famous "Querelle des Anciens et des Modernes" the multifaceted meaning of "modern" developed through various intellectual and aesthetic discourses; but it was not until the 20th century that it crystallized into the collective singular "modernity," a term intended to designate the present historical era as whole, and the (global) civilization which the ascendancy of the West has brought about.

Why this brief note on the semantics of the term? It was occasioned by my rethinking the title of the talk that I had suggested to the conference organizers. For, first, Leo Strauss figures prominently as a critic of modernity, and secondly he is rightly viewed as a partner in a more general crisis discourse, the particular nature of which is suggested by the names of Eric Voegelin, Hannah Arendt and Michael Oakeshott. Thus, in order to bring this legacy of political thought into focus, I think it is useful to look at this one particular thinker in the legacy's broader context. All of these thinkers reacted to what they thought was a fundamental crisis that had engulfed the European world. The crisis had reached an extreme expression in totalitarianism, but in their view it was much older and had emerged in the course of the Western civilization well before the catastrophes of the 20th century. These thinkers focused on a critical understanding of the disorder of the times in terms of a reflexive understanding of the human predicament itself, a reflection that emerged for the first time in classical antiquity. The crucial point of the argument I wish to develop concerns this reflexive grounding of a critical theoretical position: The classical experiences and their symbolic explications are cardinal aspects of a theoretical reformulation of the quest for human order in the present.

I suggest that we look at a theoretical discourse carried on by a group of thinkers whose quest for an understanding of the political differs essentially from other varieties of political theorizing. As far as a principled exploration of, and a critical probing into, the political phenomena of the 20th century is concerned, Strauss, Voegelin, Arendt and Oakeshott share a common ground. I do not mean to suggest theoretical identity. These thinkers differ considerably in their respective approach to human affairs – last but not least, on account of their different personal life stories and particular intellectual backgrounds. What they represent is a plurimorphic political theory that moves within the purview of the concrete historical situation of their age and submits the age to critical investigation; it does not yield to the prevalent climate of opinion but searches instead for the essential in human affairs which it articulates in terms of a comprehensive understanding of human existence in society and history. The above mentioned conscious recourse to the foundational experiences of the theoretical enterprise is not a return to sterile classicism or the cultivation of dogmatic traditionalism. This fact is demonstrated by the extremely diverse ways in which these thinkers became involved with classical Greek thought and experience. Whatever specific shape the encounter with Athens took, its impact on the respective work of these theorists was decisive for their understanding of the meaning of political theory as a "peri ta anthropina philosophia."[*]

It may be asked why I speak of "platonic responses" instead of using terms like classical or ancient. One might think this term suitable to express the conscious Platonic stance of Strauss and Voegelin but not for expressing the positions of Arendt and Oakeshott. At closer inspection however it turns out that, first, these latter two were engaged in a continuous argument with Plato, even if they kept a critical distance to central tenets of his thought. But under "platonic responses" I refer to something else: namely that each thinker's response constitutes a paradigm of order grounded on a conception of representative humanity in the sense of the reflexive paradigm of the platonic city. I will return to this point in the concluding section of these remarks.

The core ideas that add up to what Oakeshott called the ideal character of political philosophy, or – framed in a different idiom – to a discursive paradigm, permit us to speak of distinct voices engaged in a discourse based on a common understanding of what is of substantial importance. I readily admit that a thorough exploration of the subject would have to include a nuanced and detailed study of the works and intellectual biographies of, at least, Strauss, Voegelin, Arendt, Oakeshott, and some other kindred minds of their generation, for example Jouvenal. Carefully carried out this study would result in an intellectual group portrait. Naturally, every true philosopher stands alone and his work and thought crystallize in a symbolic form of its own. Therefore, the common features that are my theme are found woven into the complex intellectual fabric of each thinker's

---

[*] Philosophy of the human things [*editors' note*]

work, and cannot be easily isolated. Today, in the confines of this lecture, I cannot offer such a group portrait. For this broader picture I must refer you to the plethora of interpretive literature, and my own studies, on the subject. What I will attempt here is to identify the essential in the various theoretical texts and to distinguish it from its specific modal forms of expression.

But first permit me a short digression in order to illustrate the gulf that separated these four political theorists from their intellectual environment in academia, an environment that conferred upon them the status of intellectual extraterritoriality from their first appearance in the post-war era. In some ways it was – and still is – a reenactment of the classical conflict between the philosopher and the city. I refer here, of course, to the debate on the so-called decline or even death of political theory that began in the 1950s – and was said to have ended with the publication of Rawls's *A Theory of Justice* in 1971. The debate was carried on by eminent social scientists and philosophers at a time when the seminal works of Strauss, Voegelin, Arendt and Oakeshott began to appear. How does one account for this remarkable discrepancy between, on the one hand, an imagined decline of political theory and, on the other, the obvious presence of a thriving political philosophy? In 1994 Bhikhu Parekh examined this debate. Adding Berlin and some others to the list of distinguished thinkers of this period he called the declaration of the death of theory an intellectual blunder and blamed it on the intellectual inertia that accepted such a dubious thesis on trust due to plain ignorance. He wrote that those who heralded the death of political philosophy "simply did not know the full range of works that were appearing at the time in the discipline."[1] This is a devastating judgment, but, in my view, there was even more involved here. These political theorists confronted the dominant intellectual culture within and outside of academia with a theoretical counter-position that claimed authority in matters of reason and spirit. The academy, engaged in the so-called behavioral revolution, reacted to this challenge energetically, resisting it and, in part, trying to negate it by silence. There is another interpretation of the academy's response, made from the vantage point of a kind of academic nativism. Thus in 1979 John G. Gunnell traced the root of the conflict within political theory, and between political theory and political science, to "the intrusion of ideas promulgated by the German émigrés of the 1930s...." In the perspective of the Americans these thinkers appeared to be political scientists, "but their ideas had been formed in the context of German philosophy and in confrontation with the practical experience of totalitarianism. Whether left or right in their ideological leanings, many of these individuals represented a position and orientation that threatened some of the basic premises of American political science and political theory."[2] Without

---

[1] Bhikhu Parekh, "Some Reflections on Contemporary Political Philosophy," Paper presented to the IPSA World Congress in Berlin (1994), p. 10.

[2] John G. Gunnell, *Between Philosophy and Politics: The Alienation of Political Theory* (Amherst: The University of Massachusetts Press, 1986), pp. 13-14.

mentioning Oakeshott, an Englishman, and therefore not fitting the argumentative framework, Gunnell denounced in particular Strauss, Voegelin and Arendt as the producers of a myth of a Western political tradition – a myth that in the 1960s was transformed into the canonized history of ideas. Within this mythical matrix these thinkers diagnosed "the big underlying crisis" of the West as being caused by the onslaught of the forces of modernity. Gunnell immunized himself and his readers against philosophical theorizing by making its proponents into "historians of political theory" who invented a "historical tradition" that was a rationalized version of the past.[3]

I might note in passing that the canonized history of political thought – from Plato to the present – is of Anglo-phone making since it originated with Dunnings's influential *History of Political Theories* in the early 20th century – something which Gunnell knew very well.[4]

Returning from this excurse, let us focus on the intent of our thinkers' theoretical approach. It is of course true that the notion of a general crisis of Western civilization – a world in disarray – was the overriding motive for a principled search for order. This implies that the political philosopher is by definition the diagnostician of a critical state of public affairs. After all political philosophy came into being in response to the deadly crisis of the Greek polis. Nor were the 20th century crisis-discourses abstract exercises in cultural pessimism. But not everybody was prepared to translate his immediate personal experience into a radical questioning of the ruling cultural, spiritual, and intellectual forces of the time in order to 1) get to the roots of the crisis, and 2) to engage in the search for standards of human agency that reflect man's experience of his humanity.

"The crucial issue," Strauss pointed out, "concerns the status of those permanent characteristics of humanity, such as the distinction between the noble and the base...."

> It was the contempt for these permanencies which permitted the most radical historicist in 1933 to submit to, or rather to welcome, as a dispensation of fate, the verdict of the least wise and the least moderate part of his nation [...] and, at the same time to speak of wisdom and moderation. The biggest event of 1933 would rather seem to have proved, if such proof was necessary, that man cannot abandon the question of the good society, and that he cannot free himself from the responsibility for answering it by deferring to History or any other power different from his own reason.[5]

> The crisis of modernity reveals itself in the fact, or consists in the fact, that modern western man no longer knows what he wants – that he no longer believes that he can know what is good and bad, what is right and wrong. Until a few generations ago, it was generally

---

[3]   Ibid., p. 20, pp. 116-117.

[4]   John G. Gunnell, *Political Theory: Tradition and Interpretation* (Cambridge, MA: Winthrop Publishers, Inc., 1979), p. 16.

[5]   Leo Strauss, *What is Political Philosophy?* (Glencoe, Ill.: The Free Press, 1959), pp. 26-27.

taken for granted that man can know what is right and wrong, what is the just or the good or the best order of society – in a word that political philosophy is possible and necessary.[6]

This adumbrates the cultural condition characterized by Hannah Arendt as

a chaos of mass-perplexities on the political scene and of mass-opinions in the spiritual sphere which the totalitarian movements, through terror and ideology, crystallized into a new form of government and domination. Totalitarian domination as an established fact, which in its unprecedentedness cannot be comprehended through the usual categories of political thought, and whose 'crimes' cannot be judged by traditional moral standards.[7]

In his introduction to *The Political Religions* (already published in 1938) Eric Voegelin states:

I do not wish to say that the fight against National Socialism should not be an ethical one as well. In my view, it is simply not carried out radically; and it is not carried out radically because it lacks its radix, its religious roots. Rather than participating in this rootless and hence questionable defensive ethical fight, it seems to me more essential to discuss the fundamental issues of our time and to describe the phenomenon of evil that must be combated.[8]

I present these quotes less for philosophical reasons than in order to uncover the spiritual and emotional impulses that are behind the radical questioning of the present age. From this point of view the breakdown of European civility under the onslaught of totalitarianism did indeed signal the fact that the aspirations of what Strauss called the "modern project" had miscarried. European self-understanding prided itself on being the epitome of historical modernity – in the same sense singularly and collectively the ideological mass-movements and the various forms of totalitarianism claimed to be the avant-garde of modernity. It was this obvious fundamental disorder at the root of European modernity that had contaminated in different degrees the Euro-Asian continent and threatened to assume global proportions. The post-war I generation of intellectuals was deeply troubled by an unprecedented upheaval that shattered the all certainties of the past and multifaceted crisis discourse emerged all over Europe. In this respect a probing into the historical genesis of the illness of the present age became a necessity in order to understand the nature of the crisis.

This historical crisis discourse carried on by the political philosophers was informed by the conviction that the present crisis was foremost induced by cultural and spiritual determinants. Their crisis-analysis differed in form and substance

---

[6] Leo Strauss, Hilail Gildin ed., *An Introduction to Political Philosophy: Ten Essays* (Detroit: Wayne State UP, 1989), p. 81.

[7] Hannah Arendt, *Between Past and Future: Six Exercises in Political Thought* (New York: Viking Press, 1963), p. 26.

[8] Eric Voegelin, William Petropulos and Gilbert Weiss eds., *The Drama of Humanity and other Miscellaneous Papers 1939-1985 – The Collected Works of Eric Voegelin*, vol. 33 (Columbia, Missouri: University of Missouri Press, 2004), p. 23.

but again one can discern a certain agreement. Strauss's analysis of the three waves of modernity focuses on the radical modification of a pre-modern political philosophy since Machiavelli that reshaped the whole intellectual and spiritual landscape and prepared the ground for the modern ideologies. "The crisis of our time has its core in the doubt of what we can call the 'modern project.'"[9] Voegelin started with a history of political ideas that, as he worked on it, grew into "a comprehensive systematic critique of politics and the modern civilization" that presented itself as a civilizational drama whose last act was the totalitarian execution of an inner-worldly eschatology that had emerged from sectarian Christianity – the famous thesis of the Gnostic character of modernity is derived from this analysis.[10] Arendt, for reasons of her own, suspected "that the crisis of the present world is primarily political, and that the famous 'decline of the West' consists primarily in the decline of the roman trinity of religion, tradition, and authority, with the concomitant undermining of the specific foundations of the political realm." [11] Oakeshott's study of the rise of rationalism and the emerging politics of faith overlapped with Strauss's and Voegelin's crisis-analysis but was mitigated by his English traditionalism.

These few references must suffice for the purpose at hand. In retrospect we might discern certain single-mindedness at work. But recent narratives on the making of the modern Western world by authors like Taylor, Gillespie and Lilla do not essentially contradict the findings of their predecessors – and, after all, the symptoms of the crisis are still with us.

Does the critical clarification of the historical forces that crystallized in our totalitarian past, as "a revolt against modernity" – so named by McAllister in recent book devoted to Strauss and Voegelin – convince us? The argument lives primarily on the conservative reception of these thinkers and less on their theoretical intentions and results. McAllister translates these results and intentions into "beliefs" and concludes that Strauss and Voegelin "believed that they lived in an age of crisis."[12] McAllister, like Gunnell, seems to argue that these theorists fabricated a crisis scenario of their own as if the breakdown of Western civilization under the impact of European totalitarianism in the "age of catastrophe" (Hobsbawm) had never occurred. Here we have a case of an eclipsing of the very reality that the true theorist was to confront head on.

---

[9]   Leo Strauss, "Political Philosophy and the Crisis of Our Time," in George J. Graham and George W. Carey eds., *The Post-Behavioral Era: Perspectives On Political Science* (New York: David McKay Co. Inc., 1972), pp. 217-242, 217.

[10]   Eric Voegelin, "Letter to Henry B. McCurdy" from October 8, 1945, in Jürgen Gebhardt ed., *Selected Correspondence, 1924-1949 – The Collected Works of Eric Voegelin*, vol. 29 (Columbia, Missouri: University of Missouri Press, 2009), p. 450.

[11]   Arendt, *Between Past and Present*, p. 140.

[12]   Ted V. McAllister, *Revolt Against Modernity: Leo Strauss, Eric Voegelin, and the Search for a Postliberal Order* (Lawrence, Kansas: University Press of Kansas, 1996), p. 279.

The meaning of the critical assessment of this reality for a philosophical enterprise is not to recreate the past but to revive a paradigm of order that restates human dignity in modern terms. This modernity within modernity is revealed in the self-understanding of one's own vocation: theirs is the vocation of the scholar who philosophizes and theorizes in the pursuit of scholarship ("Wissenschaft" in the German sense). They shared a vision of scholarship which defined higher learning in terms of the search for truth and philosophical self-cultivation. According to Strauss

> The scholar is radically dependent on the work of the great thinkers, of men who faced the problems without being overpowered by any authority. The scholar is cautious; methodological not bold. He does not become lost to our sight in, to us, inaccessible heights and mists, as the great thinkers do.... The scholar becomes possible through the fact that the great thinkers disagree.[13]

The scholar, as Voegelin noted, has the duty to undertake the critical analysis of the phenomena of disorder according to the state of science for his own sake as a man, and to make the results accessible to his fellow men.[14] Again I have to limit myself to what I think are the essentials. Arendt admits that the truth-teller standing outside of the political realm acts in the tradition of the ancient academy as a guardian of a truth that it may prevail in the public sphere. "The historical sciences and the humanities which ... stand guard over, and interpret factual truth and human documents, are politically of greatest relevance."[15] The political philosopher practices a scholarship that, in terms of its systematic conceptual approach and methodology, is committed to the principles of modern hermeneutics. These scholars represent a reflective modernity within modernity. The argument may stand as such since I have to limit myself to what I think are the essentials of this theoretical concern with the past. It can be illustrated by a well known quote from Leo Strauss. He affirms the obvious fact that the principles of the classics are not directly applicable to present day societal situations.

> Only we living today can possibly find solutions to the problems of today. But an adequate understanding of the principles as elaborated by the classics may be the indispensable starting point for an adequate analysis, to be achieved by us, of present-day society in its peculiar character, and for the wise application to be achieved by us, of these principles to our tasks.

---

[13] Leo Strauss, Thomas L. Pangle ed., *The Rebirth of Classical Political Rationalism: An Introduction to the Thought of Leo Strauss* (Chicago: The University of Chicago Press, 1989), pp. 29-30.

[14] Eric Voegelin, Maurice P. Hogan ed., *Order and History, Volume 1: Israel and Revelation – The Collected Works of Eric Voegelin*, vol. 14 (Columbia, Missouri: University of Missouri Press, 2001), p. 24.

[15] Hannah Arendt, "Truth and Politics," Paper prepared for the Annual Meeting of the American Political Science Association (1966), p. 22. The wording differs from the published version: Hannah Arendt, "Truth and Politics," *The New Yorker* (February 25, 1967).

Political philosophy embodies the standards of a good that is humane order and for this reason the citizen or statesman and the philosopher are mutually interdependent.[16]

In the same vein Eric Voegelin argues that "(m)uch can be learned ... from earlier philosophers concerning the range of problems, as well as concerning their theoretical treatment; but the very historicity of human existence, that is, the unfolding of the typical in meaningful concreteness, precludes a valid reformulation of principles through return to former concreteness...." And this precludes a "literary renaissance of philosophical achievements of the past; the principles must be regained by a work of theoretization which starts from the concrete, historical situation of the age, taking into account the full amplitude of our empirical knowledge."[17] And here a rather positive understanding of the modern intellectual situation comes into play: "Today we stand on the threshold of the beginning of great philosophical developments, through the development of a philosophy of history, which for the first time must explore the realm of phenomena in its global breadth and temporal depth"[18] – a perspective that Strauss might have critically commented on.

Hannah Arendt is also interesting in this respect because she differed from Voegelin and Strauss in explicitly distinguishing between ancient philosophy, in particular Plato, and the quasi transhistorical paradigm of ancient politics. The latter is identified with and modeled upon the polis defined in terms of a plurality of human beings living in the community of mutual understanding, interlocution, and interaction. But she aims for more than just setting up the ancient model as the regulative principle of all true politics that displays after all the characteristics of an Aristotelian polis. Distancing herself from what she called Plato's a-politism she in fact argued from a philosophical position in resorting to Aristotle's science of politics. In her concluding consideration of "Philosophy and Politics" she points out that "the breakdown of common sense in the present world signals that philosophy and politics, their old conflict notwithstanding, have suffered the same fate. And that means that the problem of philosophy and politics, or the necessity for a new political philosophy from which could come a new political science, is once more on the agenda." If philosophers "were ever to arrive at a true political philosophy they would have the plurality of man, out of

[16] Leo Strauss, *The City and Man* (Chicago: The University of Chicago Press, 1964), p. 11.

[17] Eric Voegelin, Manfred Henningsen ed., *Modernity without Restraint – The Collected Works of Eric Voegelin*, vol. 5 (Columbia, Missouri: University of Missouri Press, 1999), p. 89.

[18] E. Voegelin, David Walsh ed., *Anamnesis: On the Theory of History and Politics – The Collected Works of Eric Voegelin*, vol. 6 (Columbia, Missouri: University of Missouri Press, 2002), p. 335.

which arises the realm of human affairs – in its grandeur and misery – the object of their thaumazein.* "[19]

Let me add a brief word here on Oakeshott. He develops his own paradigm of order in his *Civil Condition*. It is "as a mode of human intercourse... an ideal character glimpsed here and there in the features of human goings on."[20] The defining properties have emerged in the course of Western political philosophy from its Socratic beginnings to Aristotle, Cicero, Thomas and Montesquieu. Integrated into a paradigm of the civil condition this paradigm may serve as the regulative idea of a true human form of political existence.

Am I right to designate the reflective enterprise and the ensuing various paradigms of order created by political philosophers for modern society as being fundamentally Platonic? This question does not refer to the particular reading of Plato but it concerns a basic agreement on the contemplative disposition of a philosophical life committed to the quest for a true understanding of human affairs and devoted to the reflexive discourse on the perennial issues of the human predicament. Strauss spoke of the mutual interdependence of the philosopher and the citizen: the philosopher sets the critical standards of an order in accordance with the requirements of human excellence, but he is compelled to transcend the limits of political life by pursuing the true happiness of a contemplative life of reason. In this sense the philosopher is in the world but not of the world.

None of these thinkers considered his work to be an ideal, a blueprint, or a utopia to be realized in modern politics. They relied only on the educative persuasion and their personal authority – in other words they were by definition not public intellectuals. They followed the classical example of Plato and Aristotle in detaching themselves from the exigencies of normal politics. Even Arendt who quite often took a stand on public issues stated "that thinking and acting are not the same, and, to the extent that I wish to think, I have to withdraw from the world."[21] The public mission of the philosopher-scholar is, in my understanding, informed by a theoretical vision modeled upon Plato's image of the city. This city – founded in reflexive discourse – is, according to Plato, perhaps

> a paradigm laid up in heaven for him who wishes to contemplate it and so beholding to constitute a city in himself. Whether it exists now or ever will come into being makes no difference. The politics of this city only will be his and of none other.[22]

---

*   wonder [*editors' note*]

[19]   Hannah Arendt, "Philosophy and Politics," *Social Research* 57, no. 1 (Spring 1990), pp. 73-103, 102-103.

[20]   Michael Oakeshott, *On Human Conduct* (Oxford: Oxford University Press, 1991), p. 180.

[21]   Quoted in Melvyn A. Hill ed., *Hannah Arendt: The Recovery of the Public World* (New York: St. Martin's Press, 1972), p. 308.

[22]   Plato, *Republic* 592 b.

Such a paradigm does not provide us with a concept of order to be put into effect by political action. Rather it evokes the unseen measure that operates as an ordering force in the minds and hearts of those citizens who take seriously their responsibility for the life that they share in common with their fellow-citizens.

Arkadiusz Górnisiewicz

KARL LÖWITH AND LEO STRAUSS ON MODERNITY, SECULARIZATION, AND NIHILISM

Karl Löwith and Leo Strauss are thinkers who have not been reckoned with together too frequently. This state of things seems to be the more striking since at a first glance they appear to agree on some crucial points regarding the situation of the modern man. In this article I will try to explore their respective views on modernity with a particular emphasis on its political consequences. The first impression is that both Löwith and Strauss share a negative view of modernity and their writings provide a deeply insightful account of that dissatisfaction. But there are some other reasons that seem to encourage an attempt to compare their thought and life. They came to know each other during the tumultuous Weimar era and to some extent followed similar life paths by sharing the fates of émigrés. Given the footnotes, reviews and explicit quotations, Strauss and Löwith read each other's works, and maintained lifelong correspondence. It is not a completely negligible fact that in a letter from April 28, 1954 to Alexandre Kojève Strauss asked him to send a copy of *On Tyranny* to Karl Löwith saying that he would have an understanding of the issue controversial between him and the Frenchman.[1]

However, one should not forget that in the final analysis Leo Strauss came to be seen as a political philosopher who had attempted something very ambitious, namely, a thoroughgoing critique of the modern historical malady, the revival of classical political philosophy, and establishment of a school of political thinking. Compared to that Karl Löwith may seem to be a more restrained and introverted personality. He was a philosopher who may be referred to as a chronicler of European nihilism and explorer of continuity and change in modern historical consciousness. This difference becomes visible in their respective ways of writing. Strauss usually disguised his views in the form of dense commentary on philosophical texts; however, his moderation was scattered from time to time by the outbursts of a truly passionate prose, as in his debate with Alexandre Kojève. Löwith preferred a characteristic melancholy style and his mode of proceeding

---

[1] Leo Strauss, *On Tyranny.* Revised and Expanded Edition, Victor Gourevitch and Michael S. Roth, eds. (Chicago: The University of Chicago Press, 2000), p. 263.

was perfectly captured by Strauss himself in his review of Löwith's seminal work *From Hegel to Nietzsche*: "It is written *sine ira et studio*, without sentimentality or vagueness, and with competence and a natural grace. The treatment is narrative and meditative rather than disputative or analytical. At times (…) the author (…) seems to draw rather than speak."[2]

Before taking a closer view at the picture of modernity they draw it may be profitable to recall a few basic historical facts that lie in the background of their encounter.[3] Strauss was born to an Orthodox Jewish family in a small city in northern Germany, but he relatively quickly emancipated himself from the Jewish tradition owing to his *Gymnasium* education. Löwith was born in Munich to a Protestant family of Jewish origin and grew up in a rather well-established world of the pre-war bourgeoisie. These different backgrounds seem to account for the fact that the problem of Jewish faith and the Jewish fate had always remained a strong presence in Strauss's thought. Correspondingly, Karl Löwith explored the meaning of Protestantism for German philosophy and was even mistakenly taken by some readers to be a Protestant theologian. In 1965, in the autobiographical Preface to *Spinoza's Critique of Religion*, Strauss wrote that he was "a young Jew born and raised in Germany who found himself in the grips of the theologico-political predicament."[4] In fact, the theologico-political problem had remained his lifelong challenge and may be regarded as the foreground of his concern.[5] In turn, Karl Löwith in his account of the situation in Germany written in 1940, entitled *My Life in Germany Before and After 1933*, claimed that he had never emphasized his Jewishness before Hitler's seizure of power and perceived himself as a German whose life was based firmly and completely on "emancipation."[6] But regardless of these differences they both had to leave Germany when the Nazis came to power. They both witnessed the turmoil and upheaval of European civilization, belonging to a generation which had very strong feelings of decay, crisis and hitherto unknown demise of belief in almost everything that had been previously deemed sacred or indispensible. In other words, they belonged to a generation that – in Löwith's own words – "had been cheated of any sign of homecoming."[7] Their confrontation with modernity must be seen against the backdrop of the imminent crisis of the European spirit which may be labeled as the crisis of modernity. One may rightly say that the experience

---

[2] Leo Strauss, "Review of Von Hegel bis Nietzsche," *Social Research*, 8:4 (Nov. 1941), p. 513.

[3] I draw the biographical data from Wiebrecht Ries, *Karl Löwith* (Stuttgart: J.B. Metzlersche Verlagsbuchhandlung, 1992).

[4] Leo Strauss, *Spinoza's Critique of Religion* (New York: Schocken Books, 1965), p. 224.

[5] Heinrich Meier, *Leo Strauss and the Theologico-Political Problem*, trans. M. Brainard (Cambridge: Cambridge University Press, 2007), pp. 3-28.

[6] Karl Löwith, *My Life in Germany Before and After 1933*, trans. E. King (London: The Athlone Press, 1994), p. 57.

[7] Ibid., p. 16.

of political and cultural upheavals prompted them to undertake the philosophical investigation of the basic tenets of the modern world. Both Löwith and Strauss approached the problem of modernity by posing and exploring in a profound way the problem of its legitimacy. One of the most fundamental questions was the question of "whether our task is to push down what is falling, i.e., a disintegrating world, or whether it is the more responsible task of reforming and renewing our tradition."[8] As we will see, they ultimately decided in favor of the latter alternative. One may say that they both experienced a remarkable change of philosophical orientation. In case of Leo Strauss that change occurred around 1932 in the form of his rejection of his previously held "prejudice" that the return to pre-modern philosophy is impossible and was accompanied by his rediscovery of the art of writing practiced by philosophers of earlier ages.[9] In Karl Löwith that change of orientation seems to have occurred circa 1935 when he started subjecting the "historicist-relativist" point of view to criticism and defending the notion of philosophy as a "force of integral knowledge which gives rise to an order of human affairs" rather than committing itself to the demands of the time.[10]

In 1949, a few years after World War II, Löwith published in Chicago one of his most influential and discussed books, *Meaning in History. The Theological Implications of the Philosophy of History* (the date of publication coincides with Strauss's Walgreen lectures, published later on as *Natural Right and History*), where he advances the so-called secularization thesis. The book's subtitle proved somewhat misleading since Löwith's main aim lies primarily not in showing the theological implications of history but, on the contrary, the theological presuppositions or theological background of modern philosophies of history, and our historical consciousness as such. In his study Löwith elaborates the problem of modernity on the plane of philosophy of history by which he understands "a systematic interpretation of universal history in accordance with a principle by which historical events and successions are unified and directed toward an ulti-

---

[8]   Karl Löwith, "Review of 'What Nietzsche Means' by George Allen Morgan," *Philosophy and Phenomenological Research*, vol. 2, no. 2 (Dec. 1941), p. 242.

[9]   Strauss, *Spinoza's Critique of Religion*, p. 31. Cf. Meier, *Leo Strauss and the Theologico-Political Problem*, pp. 64-65: "The grounds that induced the philosophers to write exoteric-esoterically, however, go far beyond political considerations of censorship and persecution. They arise from the insight into the insuperable tension that exists between the political community and philosophy. The exoteric-esoteric double-face is the attempt to protect philosophers from society and nonphilosophers from philosophy. It is destined to take account of the necessities of politics on the one hand and of the requirements of the philosophical life on the other. The art of careful writing is therefore the expression of an equally fundamental and comprehensible reflection on politics, philosophy, and the nature of the philosopher."

[10]   Berthold Riesterer, *Karl Löwith's View of History: A Critical Appraisal of Historicism* (Hague: Martinus Nijhoff, 1969), pp. 33-34.

mate end."[11] His point of departure is the claim that we find ourselves more or less at the end of the modern rope which "has worn too thin to give hopeful support." We encounter a situation in which "to ask earnestly the question of the ultimate meaning of history takes one's breath away; it transports us into a vacuum which only hope and faith can fill."[12] In other words, the ability of the modern philosophy of history to provide a meaningful account of human history has almost disappeared. Once a spell-binding and fruitful intellectual endeavor, now philosophy of history loses its credentials in the wake of the dissolution of the belief in progress and reason. Löwith tries to explain the current demise of philosophy of history as well as the more fundamental problem regarding the very possibility of raising the question about the ultimate meaning of history. As he put it, "it is the very absence of meaning in the events themselves that motivates the quest."[13] He claims that philosophy of history is dependent on theology of history, namely on the theological concept of history as a history of fulfillment and salvation. One can find the genuine source of philosophy of history in the Jewish and Christian faith. In this way he dismisses the prejudice that proper historical thinking begins only in modern times. In his study he reverses the historical presentation on the assumption that readers belonging to "a generation that is just awakening from the secular dream of progress" would have a better understanding of his thesis if they were shown the theological background of these trains of thought that are not completely unfamiliar, i.e., the belief in progress, and not as distant as the religious belief in providence. This explains why he starts from Burckhardt's renunciation of philosophy of history, which is closer to our mode of thinking than anything else, and goes back through the ages to the original Biblical story of salvation.[14] Löwith presents his arguments by contrasting the Greeks and the Bible. The Ancients did not look for the ultimate meaning of history; they were mesmerized by the beauty of the universe; they were concerned not with the *Lord of History*, but with the *logos* of the cosmos.[15] The Greeks believed in the rationality of the natural cosmos that was governed by the cyclical or periodical law of growth and decay. According to this law "everything moves within recurrences, like the eternal recurrence of sunrise and sunset, of summer and winter, of

---

[11] Karl Löwith, *Meaning in History. The Theological Implications of History* (Chicago: The University of Chicago Press, 1949), p. 1.

[12] Ibid., p. 3.

[13] Ibid., p. 4.

[14] The "turning points" in Löwith's book are linked with the names of Marx, Hegel, Comte, Voltaire, Bossuet, Vico, Joachim, Augustine, and Orosius.

[15] Ibid., p. 6: "To the Greeks (...) historical events and destinies were certainly not simply meaningless – they were full of import and sense, but they were not meaningful in the sense of being directed toward an ultimate end (...) they supposed that it is possible to foretell the future; to the Old Testament writers only the Lord himself could reveal, through his prophets, a future which is independent of all that has happened in the past and which cannot be inferred from the past as a natural consequence."

generation and corruption."[16] This cosmic law set also the pattern for their understanding of history and, as Löwith contends, there was no room for the universal significance of a unique historical event like the incarnation of God. The eminent ancient historians like Thucydides, Herodotus or Polybius were concerned almost completely with political history, and – Löwith concludes – "that history, like a magnifying mirror reveals also the nature of man, but not as ever-changing, but rather constantly the same."[17] The Bible brings about the claim that history has an ultimate meaning which transcends the actual historical events; it accounts for the setting of eschatology as the basic pattern of Western historical consciousness. Thus Löwith contends that the Biblical faith brings into the world something of a tremendous importance:

> the significance of this vision [history as a story of salvation - AG], as both *finis* and *telos*, is that it provides a scheme of progressive order and meaning, a scheme which has been capable of overcoming the ancient fear of fate and fortune. Not only does the *eschaton* delimit the process of history by an end, it also articulates and fulfills it by a definite goal. The bearing of the eschatological thought on the historical consciousness of the Occident is that it conquers the flux of historical time, which wastes away and devours its own creations unless it is defined by an ultimate goal. Comparable to the compass which gives us orientation in space, and thus enables us to conquer it, the eschatological compass gives orientation in time by pointing to the Kingdom of God as the ultimate end and purpose.[18]

In other words, the historical process is rendered comprehensible on the ground of the theological principle consisting of man's sin against God and God's willingness to redeem man from the state into which he has fallen.[19]

Löwith writes that the moderns are neither ancient Ancients nor ancient Christians, but a mélange of both; we still live on the Christian and classical capital

---

[16]   Ibid. When Löwith refers to the cosmos in the Greek thought he means a specific constitution of the natural world, "an orderly totality as distinct from a disorderly, chaotic totality of the same beings which, as cosmos, are *kata kosmon*, cosmos-like" (Karl Löwith, "Heidegger: Problem and Background of Existentialism," *Social Research*, 15:1/4, 1948, p. 353). It is the notion of an orderly cosmos which was known earlier, but its usage was firmly established only in Plato's *Timaeus*. But one should not forget that there is, to use Rémi Brague's expression, "the other Greece," e.g., Epicureanism which considers the sky not the source of repose and order, but the "primary source of terror," and which confronts Plato with a view of the world as a perishable arrangement of atoms that might have been completely different. Platonic "imitation of the world" is thus rendered impossible: "The fact that our world is only one exemplar prevents it from being an example." (Cf. Rémi Brague, *The Wisdom of the World. The Human Experience of the Universe in Western Thought*, trans. T. Lavender Fagan, Chicago: The University of Chicago Press, 2003, pp. 29-43).

[17]   Karl Löwith, *Permanence and Change. Lectures on the Philosophy of History* (Cape Town: Haum, 1969), p. 12.

[18]   Löwith, *Meaning in History*, p. 18.

[19]   Ibid., p. 183.

even if we are reluctant to think of ourselves in those terms. This ambiguity becomes perfectly visible in the philosophy of history of Alexis de Tocqueville, Oswald Spengler, and Arnold Toynbee. The author of *Democracy in America* perceives the progress democracy has made worldwide as something ordained by Providence and yet he believes that this process ought to be moderated by human efforts lest it take on dangerous and unwished-for consequences. In Spengler's view of the declining West the inescapable fate ought to be willed, which reminds one about Nietzsche's *amor fati* and not necessarily the classical writers. And finally, Toynbee no longer accepts the Christian reckoning of time and yet he tries to secure the claim that Christianity is still the greatest new event in history as seen from the "astronomical" perspective (i.e., time that has elapsed since the world's beginning). He avers that the movement of civilizations is cyclical, but the movement of religion is on a single track that goes continuously upward and will end up in establishment of Christianity as the world religion. Löwith dismisses his philosophy as a product of someone who is "neither an empirical historian nor good theologian," and who fell prey to modern naturalistic and secularized thinking.[20] These three examples may serve as an additional illustration of Löwith's secularization thesis which may be summarized as follows:

> The Greek historians wrote pragmatic history centered around a great political event; the Church Fathers developed from Hebrew prophecy and Christian eschatology a theology of history focused on the supra-historical events of creation, incarnation, and consummation; the moderns elaborate a philosophy of history by secularizing theological principles and applying them to an ever increasing number of empirical facts. It seems as if the two great conceptions of antiquity and Christianity, cyclic motion and eschatological direction, have exhausted the basic approaches to understanding history.[21]

It becomes clear that Löwith conceives modernity not in terms of a radical break with the preceding tradition; on the contrary, he underlines the persistence of the eschatological pattern in shaping our modern consciousness. In this sense he denies modernity's claim to radical autonomy, originality or legitimacy. One may wonder whether Löwith's account of the secularization of the Biblical faith does not blur the difference between the Middle Ages and modernity if, regardless of all differences, they share the same basic eschatological pattern, even if the latter has secularized it. However, this objection is qualified by the fact that Löwith's view of modernity is much more intricate. The already discussed eschatological pattern is only one of the essential "components" of modernity. The other, which is of utmost importance, refers to the demise of the vision of the world as an orderly *cosmos* as the consequence of the birth of modern natural science. In other words, modernity actually begins with "the dissolution of natural and social *order* in which man was supposed to have a definite *nature* and *place*, while modern man 'exists', displaced and out of place, in extreme situations on

---

[20] Ibid., pp. 14-15.

[21] Ibid., p. 19.

the edge of chaos."[22] Philosophers of early modernity, such as Francis Bacon and Descartes, declared that the goal of science is to make man the master of nature: "the better man succeeded in this the more could the natural science be serviceable to man's historical purposes and projects."[23] Löwith contends that the historical movements of modernity owe their intensity to modern natural science: "In consequence of this modern tendency to think and act in terms of purposes, the quest for meaning has become focused in history, because only as history can the world be related directly to man and his purposes."[24] The birth of historicism and existentialism is due to the modern scientific outlook which, by making the earth more "serviceable" to man, bears responsibility for our ever increasing estrangement from it. He writes:

> The exclusive emphasis on our human existence and on the world as a historical one has a concomitant in the lack of sense for that which is natural. The denaturation of human life to a historical existence did not, however, arise with modern historicism and existentialism, but with modern natural science. It is against the background of nature as conceived by modern natural science that existentialism itself comes into existence, for its basic experience is not of historicity but the contingency of human existence within the whole of natural world.[25]

This rise of the experience of "contingency" of man's being in the world is understood by Löwith as the reverse side of the destruction of the vision of an orderly cosmos, the experience one can find expressed in the writings of such various philosophers and poets as Pascal, John Donne, Kant, Kierkegaard, and Nietzsche. In other words, modernity is marked by the demise of the natural theology and cosmology of antiquity and supernatural theology of Christianity: "If the universe is neither eternal and divine (Aristotle) nor contingent but created (Augustine), if man has no definite place in the hierarchy of an eternal or created cosmos, then, and only then, does man begin to 'exist', ecstatically and historically."[26] Löwith concludes that there are discernible connections between this "cosmological nihilism of modern subjectivity" and the political implications of modern thinking. More specifically, he focuses on the 19th century process of dissolution of the Hegelian philosophy of spirit and the shift in the very notion of philosophy which now becomes a "world-view" or "interpretation of life."[27] Löwith claims that the political consequences of existentialism become visible in the proximity between Martin Heidegger's existentialist philosophy and Carl

---

[22] Löwith, "Heidegger: Problem and Background of Existentialism," p. 347.

[23] Karl Löwith, "Nature, History, and Existentialism," *Social Research*, 19:1/4 (1952), p. 83.

[24] Ibid., p. 84.

[25] Ibid., p. 88.

[26] Löwith, "Nature, History, and Existentialism," p. 94.

[27] Karl Löwith, *From Hegel to Nietzsche. The Revolution in Nineteenth Century Thought*, trans. D.E. Green (New York: Columbia University Press, 1991), p. 64.

Schmitt's political "decisionism." According to him, Heidegger's affirmation of the authentic *Dasein* corresponds to Schmitt's affirmation of the political; "freedom for death" to "sacrifice of life." He believes that in both cases the principle is the same, i.e., naked "facticity" or all that remains when one has disposed of all life content.[28] And, as we have learnt from Löwith's narrative of the development of Western thought, "there is an intimate relation between the experience of a naked, factual, absurd existence, and the anonymity of the world itself in which we happen to exist."[29]

Strauss and Löwith agree as to the essential aim of modern natural science. Strauss in the Introduction to *City and Man* expresses a thought that he has advocated in many places, i.e., that the modern project was originated by philosophers who viewed nature as something to be conquered for the sake of man and his natural needs.[30] To some extent Strauss acknowledges that it is possible to consider modernity in terms of the secularization thesis.[31] Nonetheless, he claims that the common notion of secularization, i.e., the becoming of what is transcendent and other-worldly, immanent and this-worldly, needs to be qualified. First, the secularization thesis attempts to integrate the eternal into a temporal context, so the former is no longer understood as eternal. In this way secularization presupposes a radical change of thought, and according to him that change occurred primarily not within theology itself but came into being with the emergence of modern natural and political philosophy or science. In the final analysis secularization is an accommodation of theology to that new intellectual climate and it ends up in the conceited contention that the providential order can be known to the enlightened men. Strauss claims that:

> The theological tradition recognized the mysterious character of Providence especially by the fact that God uses or permits evil for his good ends. It asserted, therefore, that man cannot take his bearings by God's providence but only by God's law, which simply forbids man to do evil. In proportion as the providential order came to be regarded as intelligible to man, and therefore evil came to be regarded as evidently necessary or useful, the prohibition against doing evil lost its evidence. Hence various ways of action which were previously condemned as evil could now be regarded as good. The goals of human action were

---

[28] Karl Löwith, *The Political Implications of Heidegger's Existentialism*, in *The Heidegger Controversy*, ed. Richard Wolin (Cambridge, Ma.-London, Eng.: The MIT Press, 1993), pp. 173-174. Cf. Karl Löwith, "Der okkasionelle Dezisionismus von C. Schmitt," in Karl Löwith, *Sämtliche Schriften*, vol. 8, ed. K. Stichweh (Stuttgart: J.B. Metzlersche Verlagsbuchhandlung, 1984), pp. 61-62.

[29] Löwith, "Nature, History, and Existentialism," p. 89.

[30] Leo Strauss, *The City and Man* (Chicago: The University of Chicago Press, 1978), p. 7.

[31] Cf. Nathan Tarcov, "Preface to the Japanese translation of *On Tyranny*," *Perspectives on Political Science*, vol. 33, no. 4 (Fall 2004), p. 225: "Strauss ultimately leaves open the question of 'how far the epoch-making change that was effected by Machiavelli is due to the indirect influence of the Biblical tradition' and, therefore, also the question of the truth of Kojève's view that modern philosophy is the secularized form of Christianity."

lowered. But it is precisely a lowering of these goals which modern political philosophy consciously intended from its very beginning.[32]

Second, Strauss points out that the secularization thesis may have too general a character: "Secularization means the preservation of thoughts, feelings, or habits of biblical origin after the loss or atrophy of biblical faith (...) [It] does not tell us anything as to what kind of ingredients are preserved in secularizations."[33] Yet modernity, as understood by Strauss, was conceived as a positive project which at the same time may be characterized in a most general way as a radical modification, or rather rejection, of premodern political philosophy. This shortcoming on the part of the explanatory force of the secularization thesis prevents Strauss from embracing it as the main interpretive tool in his explanation of the origins of modernity; nevertheless, secularization of the Christian legacy, as we will see, will play an important role in Strauss's explanation of some characteristic features of modernity.

Strauss explains the project of modernity as comprising three waves of modernity. The first wave began with Machiavelli and was completed by Bacon and Hobbes; the second is connected with Rousseau; the third with Nietzsche. According to Strauss, the author of the *Prince* rejected the entire philosophical and political tradition by lowering the standards, by taking his bearings not by how men ought to live, but how men actually live. Classical political philosophy was concerned with the search for the best political order, i.e., the political order which gives support to the practice of virtue. Its basic premise is that the good life is the life according to nature, and nature is conceived as providing man with the standard that is independent of his will. Strauss dismisses the accusation exerted by some contemporary thinkers that Plato was a utopist (i.e., in Popper's *The Open Society and Its Enemies*) with the remark that the classical philosophers were perfectly aware that the best city is a city in speech, not in deed; that the bringing of the best city into existence is so demanding that it ultimately depends on improbably favorable circumstances.[34] Machiavelli is more modest but at the same time he is more ambitious as well; he claims that chance can be controlled

---

[32]   Leo Strauss, *Natural Right and History* (Chicago: The University of Chicago Press, 1965), p. 317. According to Hans Blumenberg, "Leibniz's theodicy characterizes the bad things in the world no longer in moral terms but rather in instrumental ones. Leo Strauss saw the element of 'secularization' precisely in this that not only has providence lost its mysteriousness for reason, but at the same time the claim to absoluteness of the divine laws has been overlaid by the justification of evil means by the grandeur of the overall end. The *Theodicy* paves the way for the modern concept of history to the extent that it demonstrates the rationality of absolute ends by the model of divine action." (Hans Blumenberg, *The Legitimacy of Modernity*, trans. R. Wallace, Cambridge, Ma.- London, Eng.: The MIT Press, 1985, p. 55).

[33]   Leo Strauss, "The Three Waves of Modernity," in *Political Philosophy. Six Essays*, ed. Hilail Gildin (Indianapolis-New York: Pegasus-Bobbs-Merill, 1975), p. 83.

[34]   Ibid., p. 84: "The establishment of the best regime depends necessarily on uncontrollable, elusive fortuna or chance (...) According to Plato's *Republic*, e.g., the coming into being

and the human matter transformed. Hence the moral or political problem becomes a technical problem, and nature as a standard gets overlaid by the ideal of civilization. The conquest of nature is conducted in order to relieve man's estate and to make man's life easier and safer. In Strauss's narrative each wave of modernity ends up in crisis, and each consecutive wave may be essentially understood as a response to the previous crisis, though it always brings about the radicalization of modernity. When Machiavelli destroyed the connection between politics and natural law, Hobbes restored it in such a way that it no longer accorded with the classical notion of natural law but with the modern theory of the state of nature which presents nature not as a standard of good life, but as hostile to human wellbeing. Strauss understands Hobbes's state of nature in which war of all against all is a real threat and constant possibility as essentially polemical; in other words, the state of nature has been conceived in such a way that men cannot help but want to get out of it; they must embark on a civilizing mission aimed at establishing a civil state that will let them live relatively peacefully and safely under the power of that mortal god Leviathan.[35] Hobbes replaces natural law, understood in terms of duties and obligations, with the rights of man (e.g., the right to self-preservation) which makes him the true founder of liberalism. Rousseau's intention to restore the classical notion of virtue dismissed by Hobbes marks the second wave of modernity. However, his attempt failed due to the fact that he was unable to extricate himself from the modern concept of the state of nature; in Rousseau man's humanity is a product of the historical process which is not teleological; in Strauss' words, "man becomes human without intending it."[36] The discovery of history which has taken place between the times of Rousseau and Nietzsche is crucial to the third wave of modernity. In the course of the 19th century Hegel's belief in the absolute moment in history became shattered and replaced with the belief that the historical process is either unfinished or unfinishable, though the belief in rationality and progress survived. The thoroughgoing critique of rationality and progress is the product of the third wave of modernity, namely Nietzsche. He draws the final and radical conclusion that the historical insight uprooted the claim on the part of all known ideals to be grounded in nature, God, or reason. Nietzsche teaches us that reason builds upon irrationalities and that all hitherto known ideals are merely of human invention.

Strauss's stance on modernity may be briefly summarized as follows. Modernity not only lowers the goal of man and seeks actualization of the best social order complying with it, but it promises a universal reconciliation between citi-

---

of the best regime depends on the coincidence, the unlikely coming together, of philosophy and political power."

[35]   Leo Strauss, "Notes on Carl Schmitt, *The Concept of the Political*," in Heinrich Meier, *Carl Schmitt and Leo Strauss. The Hidden Dialogue*, trans. J.H. Lomax (Chicago: The University of Chicago Press, 2006), p. 99.

[36]   Strauss, "Three Waves of Modernity," p. 90.

zens.[37] Contrary to the classical thought, modernity presupposes that that there are no insurmountable differences between men; in other words, if universal Enlightenment is possible, the efforts of philosophy and politics can go hand in hand. Strauss engaged in the debate with Kojève because he regarded him to be exemplary representative of the "modern solution" (i.e., the replacement of the moral virtue by universal recognition[38]). The nature of the modern solution implies that the esoteric-exoteric distinction no longer needs to be upheld.[39] The crisis of modernity springs from its unfulfilled promises; as Strauss put it, "the classical solution is utopian in the sense that its actualization is improbable" while "the modern solution is utopian in the sense that its actualization is impossible."[40]

But there is much more to Strauss' view of modernity than the three wave hypothesis. It is important to add that the Christian legacy plays an important role in Strauss's understanding of the development of Western thought. In contrast to Löwith he points towards the difference within so-called Judeo-Christian tradition by discussing an agreement between the Jewish and Muslim thought on the one hand and ancient thought on the other:

> it is not the Bible and the Koran, but perhaps the New Testament, and certainly the Reformation and modern philosophy, which brought about the break with ancient thought. The guiding idea upon which the Greeks and the Jews agree is precisely the idea of the divine law as a single and total law which is at the same time religious law, civil law, and moral

---

[37] Robert Pippin, "The Modern World of Leo Strauss," *Political Theory*, vol. 20, no. 3 (Aug., 1992), p. 451: "The 'ancient' position by contrast (…) is easy to state: no reconciliation. The city or the public world is a permanent cave. Even if the philosopher in the *Republic* can be persuaded (perhaps by the force of the argument that he owes the city a debt) or, paradoxically, can persuade the many to compel him to return, it is clear that he must rule in the dark. He cannot bring the outside light in, and it never seems to enter his mind to attempt to bring those inside out (apart from a select few)."

[38] Strauss, *On Tyranny*, p. 210.

[39] David Janssens underlines the importance of the difference between esotericism and exotericism for understanding the difference between classical and modern philosophy: "The philosopher as such transcends the political realm, as a human being he owes obedience to the laws of the polis and respect to its opinions. For this reason, Plato subjects the philosopher to the divine law of the best regime, which compels him to devote his wisdom to justice and the care of his fellow men. In this way, he exoterically preserves the primacy of justice and courage, while esoterically crowning wisdom as the highest virtue. We should not forget, however, that wisdom is understood here in the Socratic sense, as the awareness of ignorance regarding the good and the just. The distinction between an esoteric and an exoteric dimension allows Plato to mediate between the political power of opinion and the philosophic pursuit of the truth, without detracting from either. In contrast, Hobbes's radical critique of courage starts from a passion that is equally developed in all human beings, and ultimately aims at eradicating the difference between esotericism and exotericism." (David Janssens, *Between Athens and Jerusalem. Philosophy, Prophecy, and Politics in Leo Strauss's Early Thought*, Albany: State University of New York Press, 2008, p. 162).

[40] Strauss, *On Tyranny*, p. 210.

law. And it is indeed a Greek philosophy of the divine law which is the basis of the Jewish and Muslim philosophy of the Torah or the Shari'a; according to Avicenna, Plato's *Laws* is the classic work on prophecy and the Shari'a. The prophet occupies in this medieval politics the same place the philosopher-kings occupy in Platonic politics: by fulfilling the essential conditions of the philosopher-kings, enumerated by Plato, he founds the perfect city, i.e., the ideal Platonic city.[41]

Strauss claims that Christianity seems to account not only for the "Christianization" of Plato, but also for the radical character of the modern critique of religion. On this point both Strauss and Löwith remain in fundamental agreement with Nietzsche: modern atheism has little in common with the age-old Epicurean motif and is descendant of Biblical morality.[42] This new atheism from "intellectual probity" fights religion not because of its allegedly disturbing character but because it is a delusion.[43]

One may also wonder whether in fact there is in Strauss the fourth wave of modernity, which would belong to Heidegger. This seems to be justified at least by the importance Strauss gave to Heidegger's radicalization of modernity, i.e., his existentialism.[44] Here it suffices to remark that Strauss's appraisal of the significance of Christian legacy for the modern thought reveals itself again in his judgment that Heidegger and the "new thinking" have failed to extricate them-

---

[41]   Leo Strauss, "Some Remarks on the Political Science of Maimonides and Farabi," trans. R. Bartlett, *Interpretation*, vol. 18, no. 1 (Fall 1990), pp. 4-5.

[42]   Strauss, *Spinoza's Critique of Religion*, p. 29. Cf. Löwith, *Meaning in History*, p. 7: "Nietzsche was right when he said that to look upon nature as if it were a proof of the goodness and care of God and to interpret history as a constant testimony to a moral order and purpose – that all this is now past because it has conscience against it." Both Strauss and Löwith refer to fragment 357 of *Gay Science* where Nietzsche says that that what really triumphed over the Christian God is Christian morality itself, "the concept of truthfulness that was understood ever more rigorously, the father confessor's refinement of the Christian conscience, translated and sublimated into a scientific conscience, into intellectual cleanliness at any price." (in *The Nietzsche Reader*, eds. K. A. Pearson, D. Large, Malden-Oxford-Carlton: Blackwell Publishing, 2006, pp. 371-372).

[43]   According to Leo Strauss this new atheism, contrary to the Epicurean critique of religion, is bold and active, and it accords with the general outline of the "modern solution:" "Liberated from the religious delusion, awakened to sober awareness of his real situation, taught by bad experiences that he is threatened by a stingy, hostile nature, man recognizes as his sole salvation and duty, not so much 'to cultivate his garden' as in the first place to plant a garden by making himself the master and owner of nature. But this whole enterprise requires, above all, political action, revolution" (Strauss, *Spinoza's Critique of Religion*, p. 29).

[44]   Cf. Leo Strauss, "An Introduction to Heideggerian Existentialism," in Leo Strauss, *The Rebirth of Classical Political Rationalism*, ed. Thomas L. Pangle (Chicago: The University of Chicago Press, 1989).

selves from the Christian presuppositions and represent awareness that is in the fundamental sense "a secularized version of the Biblical faith."[45]

All differences regarding the understanding of the origins of modernity aside, both Strauss and Löwith conclude that modernity ended up in crisis which proper name seems to be nihilism. While Löwith speaks about existence in existentialist ontology as "blind and deaf to any light that does not burn in its own sphere and to any voice that does not sound from itself," existence that is "a cave-dweller who knows neither Platonic sun nor the Christian regeneration, nor the Jewish waiting till the day of redemption,"[46] Strauss goes even further and employs the highly suggestive picture of the "second cave" with regard to modernity in general. Strauss's attempt to reopen the quarrel between the Ancients and the Moderns, as well as his defense of the claims of Revelation against the assault of modern rationalism (i.e., his critique of Spinoza's refutation of the Revelation), and rejuvenation of the notion of natural right may be seen in the light of his task to undermine the predominant historical consciousness of our times and return to philosophy in its original Socratic sense. As he reflected, "philosophy in the original meaning of the word presupposes the liberation from historicism (…) liberation from it, and not merely refutation (…) the liberation from historicism requires that historical consciousness be seen to be, not a self-evident premise, but a *problem*."[47] In turn, Löwith describes his efforts as a correction of our obsession with temporality or history and its vicissitudes.[48] He wants to regain an attitude toward the world that is theoretical in the classical sense, i.e., free of historical consciousness and elevated above practice and pragmatic restrictions.[49] This attitude is less anthropocentric since, as he reminded us, the world and the human world are not equivalent; one can imagine the natural world without a reference to man, but man cannot be imagined without the existence of the world:

---

[45] Strauss, *Spinoza's Critique of Religion*, pp. 12-13: "Heidegger wishes to expel from philosophy the last relics of Christian theology like the notions of 'eternal truths' and 'the idealized absolute subject.' But the understanding of man which he opposes to the Greek understanding of man as the rational animal is, as he emphasizes, primarily the Biblical understanding of man as created in the image of God. Accordingly, he interprets human life in the light of 'being towards death,' 'anguish,' 'conscience,' and 'guilt'; in this most important respect he is much more Christian than Nietzsche." Cf. Karl Löwith, "Heidegger: Thinker in a Destitute Time," in Karl Löwith, *Martin Heidegger. European Nihilism*, ed. Richard Wolin, trans. G. Steiner (New York: Columbia University Press, 1995), p. 116.

[46] Karl Löwith, "M. Heidegger and F. Rosenzweig or Temporality and Eternity," *Philosophy and Phenomenological Research*, vol. 3, no. 1 (Sep., 1942), pp. 60-61.

[47] Leo Strauss, "Living Issues of German Postwar Philosophy," in Meier, *Leo Strauss and the Theologico-Political Problem* (Cambridge: Cambridge University Press, 2007), p. 133.

[48] K. Löwith, *Permanence and Change*, p. 8.

[49] Jürgen Habermas, "Karl Löwith: Stoic Retreat from Historical Consciousness," in *Philosophical-Political Profiles* (Cambridge, Ma.-London, Eng.: The MIT Press, 1990), p. 84.

"We come into the world – he does not come to us – and we separate from it while he outlives us."[50]

The recognition of the crisis of modernity led them to reflect on whether there might be any possibility of return. For Strauss the problem of return is ambiguous at the very outset since the Western tradition consists of the two major elements that oppose each other: the Bible and Greek philosophy, Jerusalem and Athens. This disagreement, this battle for minds and hearts has been increasingly neglected though it is the crucial element of the vitality of the Western civilization. In turn, for Löwith the problem of return emerged above all in the form of two interpretations of nihilism delivered by Kierkegaard and Nietzsche.[51] Their philosophies may be understood as returns – the former as the return to the uncorrupted purity of early Christianity, and the latter as the return to the ancient vision of the cosmos in the form of the doctrine of the eternal recurrence of the same. They shared the insight that men need eternity in order to withstand the flux of time and aimed to restore the right place to eternity, which has come into oblivion[52]. Kierkegaard's "eternal instant" and Nietzsche's paradox of "the eternal recurrence" are the means by which they attempted in a distinctly different ways at the overcoming of nihilism. But while for the Danish philosopher nihilism is the product of our estrangement from the ideals of the first Christians, for the German philosopher it is the consequence of our being Christians for two millennia. Löwith was deeply concerned with both authors in his writings; however, he had chosen Nietzsche as one of his major themes because he seemed to be a touchstone of the present and at the same time the sharpest negation of his own time. "In contrast to this timely or untimely use" Löwith "tried to establish the idea of eternity as the central focus of his philosophy."[53] Löwith's book on Nietzsche published in 1935 as *Nietzsches Philosophie der ewigen Wiederkunft des Gleichen* was acclaimed by Strauss himself; in one of his letters to Löwith he acknowledges his debt to his book by saying that it enabled him to understand the relation between nihilism and the doctrine of the eternal recurrence of the same.[54] Nietzsche seems to have formulated at the early age the key alternative which he reiterated during his life and expressed it in words that sound both beautiful and dramatic: "Thus man outgrows everything that once embraced him; he has no need to break the shackles – they fall away unforeseen when a god commands

---

[50]   Karl Löwith, "Mensch und Geschichte," in Karl Löwith, *Sämtliche Schriften*, vol. 2, eds. K. Stichweh and M.B. de Launay (Stuttgart: J.B. Metzlersche Verlagsbuchhandlung, 1983), p. 346.

[51]   Karl Löwith, "Kierkegaard und Nietzsche oder philosophische und theologische Überwindung des Nihilismus," in Löwith, *Sämtliche Schriften*, vol. 6 (Stuttgart: J.B. Metzlersche Verlagsbuchhandlung, 1987), pp. 53-74.

[52]   Löwith, "M. Heidegger and F. Rosenzweig or Temporality and Eternity," p. 77.

[53]   Löwith, *My Life in Germany Before and After 1933*, p. 83.

[54]   Leo Strauss, *Gesammelte Schriften*, vol. 3, eds. Heinrich Meier, Wiebke Meier (Stuttgart-Weimar: J.B. Metzler Verlag, 2008), p. 648.

them; and where is the ring that in the end still encircles him? Is it the world? Is it God?"[55] Löwith sees in Nietzsche's decision in favor of the latter the most crucial part of his thought. According to him Nietzsche's attempt is "the attempt to tie the existence of modern man, which has become eccentric, back into the natural whole of the world."[56] Though sympathetic to Nietzsche's goal, Löwith claims that his attempt failed. The reason is that Nietzsche was too modern and thus unable to free himself from not only modern presuppositions and a way of feeling, but the Christian one as well. It may be said that he attempted something great, i.e., he attempted to re-marry the modern man to the ancient vision of the world at the peak of modernity. Yet the means at his disposal in the 19th century could not be other than the means of the post-Copernican world. In this historical situation the age-old idea of the eternal recurrence of the same remerged in a deeply flawed modernized form. According to Löwith, Nietzsche sang his song to the "innocence" of existence with a broken voice because he sang it on the ground of Christian experience:[57]

> For the Greek understanding of man, being a man means in effect being a 'mortal,' whereas Nietzsche wanted to 'eternalize' the fleeting existence of finite man. For the Greeks the eternal recurrence of emergence and decline explained the constant change in nature and history; for Nietzsche the recognition of an eternal recurrence demands an extreme and ecstatic point of view. The Greeks felt fear and reverence before inexorable fate; Nietzsche made the superhuman effort to will and to love fate (…). Nothing else is so striking in Nietzsche's thought as the emphasis on our creative essence, creative through the act of will, as with the God of the Old Testament. (…) Nietzsche lived and thought to the end the metamorphosis of the biblical 'Thou shalt' into the modern 'I will,' but he did not accomplish the decisive step from the 'I will' to the 'I am' of the cosmic child of the world, which is innocence and forgetting. As a modern man, he was so hopelessly separated from an original 'loyalty to the earth' and from the feeling of an eternal security under the vault of heaven, that his effort to 'translate' man 'back' into nature was condemned to failure from the outset. His teaching breaks apart into two pieces because the will to eternalize the existence of the modern ego (an existence it is thrown into) does not harmonize with the beholding of an eternal cycle of the natural world.[58]

In Nietzsche's definition of nihilism ("since Copernicus man rolls from the center toward an unknown place X") Löwith found the compelling expression of his own concern with the demise of cosmological thought. In turn, Strauss employs the term nihilism in different contexts, but it seems plausible to speak about its two major applications. The first one is connected with the three waves

---

[55] Friedrich Nietzsche, "Mein Leben," in *Werke in drei Bänden*, vol. 3 (Munich: Carl Hauser Verlag, 1954), p. 110.

[56] Karl Löwith, *Nietzsche's Philosophy of the Eternal Recurrence of the Same*, trans. J. Harvey Lomax (Berkeley-Los Angeles-London: The University of California Press, 1997), p. 94.

[57] Ibid., p. 120.

[58] Ibid., p. 121.

of modernity, or their outcome – historical malady, relativism, and the crisis of political philosophy, i.e., the situation of the modern individual who knows only the Weberian wars between rivaling gods or ideals. The second use is developed by Strauss in his text on German nihilism where he says that "nihilism is the rejection of the principles of civilization as such."[59] Strauss conceives German nihilism in terms of a protest against the ideal of modern civilization we have learnt while discussing the origins of modernity. In this view nihilism is born out of a moral protest at the root of which one can find the hatred for the vision of the world in which everyone would be satisfied and pacified; in other words, against the world which permits no place for seriousness. The basic demands of the moral life are connected with the so-called closed society, i.e., society that is permanently confronted with the possibility of *Ernstfall* or war, with seriousness as such. Strauss claims that this very passion or conviction is not contemptible in itself, although it took on the basest form of nihilism known as the National Socialism. It would not be a misappropriation were we to defend the view that Strauss remained favorably disposed to that conviction; one of the most visible places where he dwells on this "conviction" is his passionate debate with Alexandre Kojève. He launched a powerful attack on what came to be known as the universal and homogenous state using arguments familiar to that of young "German nihilists:"

> If the universal and homogenous state is the goal of History, History is absolutely 'tragic' (…) For centuries and centuries men have unconsciously done nothing but work their way through infinite labors and struggles and agonies, yet ever again catching hope, toward the universal and homogenous state, and as soon as they have arrived at the end of their journey, they realize that through arriving at it they have destroyed they humanity and thus returned, as in a cycle, to the prehuman beginnings of History. *Vanitas vanitatum. Recognitio recognitionum.*[60]

Strauss wonders whether the nihilistic revolt against the universal and homogeneous state may not be the only possible action on behalf of man's humanity, even if it will lead to the repetition of the entire historical process "from the horde to the final state." That kind of "new lease on life" is for Strauss more preferable than the "indefinite continuation of the inhuman end." After all, Strauss asks rather rhetorically, "Do we not enjoy every spring although we know the cycle of the seasons, although we know that winter will come again?"[61]

Coming to the conclusion: At the beginning of these remarks it was said that Strauss regarded Löwith as someone with whom he shared understanding of some most important issues, e.g., the problem of the universal and homogeneous state. Having briefly compared their views on modernity one can understand that there

---

[59] Leo Strauss, "German Nihilism," eds. David Janssens and Daniel Tanguay, *Interpretation*, 29:3 (Spring 1999), p. 364.

[60] Strauss, *On Tyranny*, pp. 208-209.

[61] Ibid., p. 209.

are insights in their thoughts that seem to draw their reflection upon modernity close to each other. This proximity becomes particularly visible in their rejection of the universal and homogenous state. However, the ground of that rejection is slightly different. Strauss rejects it in the name of a truly human life which has become increasingly endangered by the tyranny of universality and homogeneity. One may say that his rejection is based primarily on his adherence to the ideal of a morally serious political community, which he found formulated most compellingly in the writings of the ancient political philosophers, and embodied in the life of Greek *polis*.[62] Löwith's rejection would not be apolitical, but rather "transpolitical." His adherence to the ideal of being loyal to the earth or being citizens of the world rather than of the universal and homogeneous state seems to be of Stoic origin albeit blended with Nietzschean attempts. In this way he reminds us about the perspective that transcends both the small political community and the inhuman community of universal and homogenous state. In our times, when the seriousness of life and the very prospects of life on earth are at stake, Strauss' and Löwith's perspectives seem to be all the more worthy of consideration.

---

[62] Strauss, *Gesammelte Schriften*, vol. 3, p. 662.

Emmanuel Patard

REMARKS ON THE STRAUSS-KOJÈVE DIALOGUE AND ITS PRESUPPOSITIONS

One of the most prevailing modern prejudices consists of the belief in the superiority of the achievements enabled by the development of modern thought, over all previous forms of thought. This belief has been put today into question: the mortal threats for humanity and its world engendered by technical progress, the doubts about the possibility of universal enlightenment, of universal and perpetual peace, call into question dramatically the self-confidence of Western civilization. The modern project aimed at establishing paradise on earth; however, it may be no intolerable exaggeration to say that in some of its latest attempts at accomplishment, it came not so far from establishing hell on earth. Leaving aside various short-lived attempts to restore traditional positions or to elaborate eclectic syntheses, we notice that this situation prompts many present-day thinkers to try to trace back, through historical studies, the genealogy of modern thought, in order to understand the source and conditions of such a failure.

Alexandre Kojève, the famous commentator of Hegel, still stood for the modern project, the aim of which he called "universal and homogeneous State," the End-State which is supposed to fulfill the fundamental aspirations of Man, to solve all contradictions and conflicts in human thought and action. Kojève challenged *On Tyranny*, Leo Strauss's defense and illustration of the classical view of the fundamental problems through a commentary on Xenophon's *Hiero*. This dialogue was "the only writing of the classical period which is explicitly devoted to the discussion of tyranny and its implications" and a writing which marks the point of closest contact between premodern science (which rests on the foundations laid by Socrates) and modern political science (which rests on the foundations laid by Machiavelli).[1] Kojève's critical review[2] was for Strauss a fitting

---

[1] Leo Strauss, *On Tyranny*. Revised and Expanded Edition, Victor Gourevitch and Michael S. Roth, eds. (2nd ed., Chicago: The University of Chicago Press, 2000), pp. 24, 23, and 25.

[2] "L'action politique des philosophes," *Critique*, Vol. 6, no. 41 (Oct. 1950), pp. 46-55, and no. 42 (Nov. 1950), pp. 138-155; longer version with the title "Tyrannie et Sagesse," in *De la Tyrannie* (Paris: Gallimard, 1954), pp. 215-280.

opportunity to confront the philosophical quarrel between Ancients and Moderns, in a "Restatement" which appears to be the most extensive and the deepest reply to the critiques which have been addressed to his achievement. Strauss described Kojève as "one [of] the three people who will have a full understanding of what I am driving at."[3] He agreed with Kojève in the rejection of contemporary intellectualism, positivist political and social science, and of all the other degraded forms of theoretical inquiry.[4] They agreed that, despite the prevailing relativism, the genuine possibility and necessity of philosophy nevertheless remained.[5] A dialogue between them was therefore possible and meaningful.

In the famous concluding paragraph of his "Restatement," Strauss stated the conflicting presuppositions of his discussion with Kojève: "Philosophy in the strict and classical sense is quest for the eternal order or for the eternal cause or causes of all things. It presupposes then that there is an eternal and unchangeable order within which History takes place and which is not in any way affected by History" and Kojève's rejection of it "in favor of the view that 'Being creates itself in the course of History,' or that the highest being is Society and History, or that eternity is nothing but the totality of historical, i.e., finite time." Having just received and read the "Restatement," Kojève wrote to Strauss: "I am in full agreement with the conclusion."[6] We are then entitled to consider it as an adequate start-point in order to understand the full meaning of their discussion as they understood it themselves. The final, well-known sentence from Strauss's concluding paragraph clearly alludes to Heidegger's revival of the question of Being (*Seinsfrage*), and it implies that a common agreement between Strauss and Kojève against Heidegger is crucial in their debate. This agreement implies in its turn that Heidegger's way of thinking is involved, however implicitly, in the discussion.

---

[3] Strauss to Kojève, December 6, 1948, trans. Victor Gourevitch, in *OT* (2000), p. 239.

[4] See, e.g., Kojève, *Essai d'une histoire raisonnée de la philosophie païenne*, vol. 1 (Paris: Gallimard, 1968), pp. 34 ff. "I am glad to see, once again, that we agree about what the genuine problems are, problems which are nowadays on all sides either denied (Existentialism) or trivialized (Marxism and Thomism)." (Strauss to Kojève, September 4, 1949, in *OT*, p. 244.)

[5] See "Restatement," in *Interpretation: A Journal of Political Philosophy*, Vol. 36, no. 1 (Fall 2008), p. 41; "The Last Letter," *ibid.*, p. 92. Kojève's Introduction to his *Essai* (pp. 20 ff.) is mainly meant to *show* the possibility of philosophy: "(...) doing philosophy is also (and perhaps even: only) answering the question whether one must do it or not. But as long as one does it, one has already answered this question? [...] Such a proof is probative only if what one wants to prove is *possible*." (p. 21 – All translations are mine, except of the letters from Strauss.)

[6] Kojève to Strauss, September 19, 1950, in *OT*, p. 255.

1. Alexandre Kojève's neo-Hegelianism: from "Geist ist Zeit" to the End of History

According to Kojève, the contemporary confusion in thought come from the attempts, doomed to failure, to regress from Hegel or to go past him; but these attempts still remained situated in Hegelianism, however unconscious: "(...) being the first wise man, he is the last philosopher in general and the last 'historical man' in the proper meaning of the term."[7] If then, as Kojève put it, "it is materially impossible to say something else and more than what Hegel has already said, although it is relatively easy to say less," why should one write anything after Hegel's System of Science? Because, Kojève explained, Hegel's language has to be "clarified," Hegel's discourse has to be "updated" for the present time. In his Chicago course on Hegel's philosophy of history (Fall 1958), Strauss put it this way:

> Carl Schmitt (...) said that on the 31ˢᵗ of January, 1933, Hegel died. Meaning that the Hegelian tradition was still of immense power, and not only at the universities but also as far the German state was concerned, up to this moment. And the crucial point was simply that the rule of a highly educated civil service was split. (...) The only form in which the Hegelian form of government survived today is that by a French scholar of Russian origin, [Kojève], who wrote probably the best book on Hegel in this generation.[8]

The change in the situation which necessitated an update was the replacement of the rule of the civil service in the Hegelian so-called "rational state" with the rule of the mass party in the nihilistic, totalitarian state.[9]

On which basis did Kojève "update" Hegel? Kojève presented later, as "a revelation" for him,[10] what Alexandre Koyré said about Hegelian time in his course on Hegel's religious philosophy in 1932-1933: the Hegelian thesis which underlies Kojève's interpretation was already brought out:

> *We have arrived at the result*: "Geist *ist* Zeit." (Hegel's text!) Here is the key to the understanding of Hegel. Time and History can be included in the dialectical process and become an essential part of philosophy, because spirit *is* time (or *in* time, as Hegel says in the "Phenomenology"). [...]

> What is eternal, is the unity of past, of present and of future. This is thus *time* which is eternal, and not eternity outside time (cf. "the eternal moment" of tradition). One always opposed time and eternity; one conceived of eternity on the model of an immobile *present*.

---

[7] "Préface à la Mise à jour du Système hégélien du Savoir," dated 23 août 1956, in *Commentaire* (Paris), Vol. 3, no. 9 (1980), p. 132.

[8] Seminar in Political Philosophy: Hegel's *The Philosophy of History*, The University of Chicago, Autumn Quarter 1958, unpublished transcript, lecture 6, p. 112.

[9] Ibid.

[10] Kojève, "Préface à la Mise à jour du Système hégélien du Savoir," p. 132.

For H., eternity is not outside time; time is not a mobile image of eternity, but it *is* eternity; there is no other one.[11]

In his last course (1938-1939), Kojève elaborated his "Note sur l'éternité, le temps et le concept." Relying on Hegel's Jena lectures,[12] Kojève equated with the key statement "*Geist* ist Zeit" the following ones: Time exists insofar there is History, i.e., human existence, "*Man is* Time." Time, oriented toward future, is desire (what is absent, is present insofar it is absent), Man is Desire of Desire (anthropogenic desire, i.e., desire as constituting man in his humanity, desire for a non-natural object, to be obtained from an active negation, i.e., work– see *ILH*, pp. 12 ff.), "Man is Desire for Recognition" (by other consciousness, other human beings as self-consciousness) and eventually "historical evolution which finally comes to the universal and homogeneous State and to the absolute Knowledge that reveals the complete Man achieved in and by this State. In short, to say that Man *is* Time, is to say all that Hegel says of Man in the PhG."[13]

At the beginning of his first course, Kojève made already quite clear the orientation of his reading:

> For Hegel, essence is not independent from existence. So man does not exist outside history. Hegel's Phenomenology is therefore 'existential' as Heidegger's. And it must serve as basis for an ontology. [This ontology, in the Logic, is in fact anthropological; it is therefore distorted when it interprets Nature. It is not universal, in spite of what Hegel thought: it is an ontology of Man ('Spirit') and not of Nature.][14]

Kojève's rejection of Hegel's dialectic of Nature, and his affirmation of ontological dualism, can be traced back to Heidegger's influence: according to Kojève, only with Heidegger's *Sein und Zeit* has Hegel's *Phänomenologie des Geistes* been made understandable.[15] Kojève's emphasis on the Hegelian atheistic anthropology was influenced by his reading of Heidegger's *Sein und Zeit* (being-toward-death). In his description of the fundamental philosophical types, Kojève described Hegel and Heidegger as representatives of the true philosophic

---

[11] Fonds Kojève (Bibliothèque nationale de France, Réserve des manuscrits occidentaux), box X, Kojève's notes taken at Koyré's course, 17/III.33, folio 1, verso, and fol. 2, recto (all the documents which are quoted from the Fonds Kojève have been written in French, except the letters of Strauss).

[12] Alexandre Kojève, *Introduction à la lecture de Hegel* (Paris: Gallimard, 2nd ed. 1962), p. 367 (trans. James H. Nichols, *Introduction to the Reading of Hegel* [ed. Allan Bloom, New York: Basic Books, 1969], p. 133).

[13] *ILH*, p. 371 [139]. See the references given by Strauss in *OT*, n. 59 p. 125.

[14] *ILH*, p. 39 (the brackets appear in the original).

[15] See *ILH*, p. 527 n. 1; *Essai...*, p. 165. In a 1931 manuscript, posthumously published in French translation, *L'Athéisme* (trans. from the Russian by Nina Ivanoff, Paris: Gallimard, 1998), the influence of Heidegger appears to be significant on Kojève's atheistic anthropology of the being-toward-death, whereas Hegelian dialectics is absent.

possibility, which is still to be developed.[16] However, against Hegel's "monistic error" (applying dialectical ontology to both Man and Nature), Kojève took sides with Heidegger, who after Kant was the first who raised the problem of dualistic ontology.[17] Heidegger's *Sein und Zeit* was, according to Kojève, the most important attempt since Kant to elaborate a dualistic ontology which would supersede Hegel's impossible monism.[18] In his "Note sur Hegel et Heidegger" (1936),[19] Kojève approved (against Hegel) Heidegger's "resolute acceptance of ontological *dualism*, of the essential and ontologically irreducible difference between human-being (*Dasein*) and natural-being (*Vorhandensein*)." Should we then assume that Kojève simply expounds Heidegger's position in the guise of a commentary, or of an "update," of Hegel? Kojève departs from Heidegger on important points: nature (the human appropriation of nature, which is a removal from authenticity for Heidegger, is the condition for Man's accomplishment according to Kojève). Kojève rejected what he held to be Heidegger's attenuation of human active negation (*ibid.*, pp. 38-40), and Heidegger's "regression" from Hegel to the Presocratics.[20]

Kojève had nevertheless to acknowledge that Hegel's anti-natural trend, which he emphasizes, was not constant in Hegel.[21] Kojève made quite clear he did not plan to confine himself to a commentary of what Hegel said. He openly vindicated his hermeneutical violence: "[…] my work had not the character of a historical study; it mattered relatively little to me to know what Hegel himself meant in his book; I gave a course of philosophical anthropology using Hegelian texts, but saying only what I considered to be the truth and dropping what seemed to me to be, in Hegel, an error."[22]

2. Leo Strauss's twofold objections to Kojève's neo-Hegelianism

In his letter to Kojève dated September 11, 1957, Strauss stated his two main objections in a short formulation: "[…] we are poles apart. The root of the question is I suppose the same as it always was, that you are convinced of the truth of Hegel (Marx) and I am not. You have never given me an answer to my questions: a) was Nietzsche not right in describing the Hegelian-Marxian end as the

---

[16] See *ILH*, pp. 338n [102 n.1] and 527n [259 n.41].

[17] See *ILH*, pp. 485n ff. [213-215 n15]. Cf. the indication of this problem by Strauss in *What is Political Philosophy?* (Chicago: The University of Chicago Press: 1959), pp. 39f.

[18] *ILH*, pp. 485-487n, cf. 527n.

[19] Ed. Bernard Hesbois, in *Rue Descartes*, vol. 7 (juin 1993), pp. 37f.

[20] See *Essai d'une histoire raisonnée*, pp. 165f.

[21] *ILH*, p. 498.

[22] Letter to Tran-Duc-Thao, 7 octobre 1948, Gwendoline Jarczyk and Pierre-Jean Labarrière, eds., in *Genèses*, vol. 2, no. 1 (1990), p. 134.

'last man'? and b) what would you put into the place of Hegel's philosophy of nature?"[23]

Strauss first elaborated these objections in his letter to Kojève dated August 22, 1948. Fulfilling Kojève's wish, Strauss gave him his opinion about the *Introduction à la lecture de Hegel*: "Aside from Heidegger, probably hardly one of our contemporaries has written as comprehensive and at the same time as intelligent a book. In other words, no one has pleaded for modern thought in our time as brilliantly as you."[24] He raised two main objections to Kojève's neo-Hegelian thesis: Kojève would not succeed in getting rid of the philosophy of nature (history would not be a self-sufficient standard for understanding the world and man), and the End-State as described by Kojève could not bring about a complete and true satisfaction to human beings, who are irrational:

> The account as a whole arouses the impression that you regard Hegel's philosophy as absolute knowledge, and reject the philosophy of nature together with its implications as a dogmatic and dispensable residue.[25] One is therefore all the more surprised to find you admit that the probative force of the Hegelian argument (the circularity of the system) is absolutely dependent on the philosophy of nature (291 bottom [98 bottom]; 400, par. 3; 64). (*Ibid.*, p. 237.)

As Strauss already implied in his 1932 review of Carl Schmitt, the problem raised by the possible world-state, and the kind of men who would rule it, has to be referred to the question of the nature of man, which modern thought claimed to decide definitively[26].

3. Kojève's answers to Strauss's objections

1) First objection: what will replace Hegel's philosophy of nature?

a) First answer:

Following Koyré, Kojève could not take seriously Hegel's dialectical philosophy of nature, which rejected Newton and modern physics in general. He suggested an articulation of the "classical" philosophy of nature with the "Hegelian" (Heideggerian) conception of man in an unpublished footnote of "Tyrannie et Sagesse," in which he repeated his rejection of Hegel's dialectical philosophy of nature. Kojève favored the Ancient (i.e., Platonico-Aristotelian) philosophy of nature – seemingly as a concession to Strauss:

---

[23]   *OT*, p. 291.

[24]   Ibid., p. 236, trans. modified.

[25]   See *ILH*, e.g. pp. 378 [146f.], and 489ff. [216ff.].

[26]   "Comments on *Der Begriff des Politischen* by Carl Schmitt" (1932), in appendix to *Spinoza's Critique of Religion*, trans. Elsa M. Sinclair (New York: Schocken Books, 1965), pp. 343ff. (Kojève underlined much of this section in his copy of this book). See also below, n.27.

Personally I think that the thinkers of Antiquity were right (against Hegel) when they admitted that the *natural* Being (the Cosmos) is eternally identical to itself and 'perfect' at once. But I think with Hegel (and against the thinkers of Antiquity) that man creates himself in the course of history and 'perfects' himself only at its end. Now, since man fits into Being and is part of it, the Hegelian reasoning relative to Truth remains valid: man can reach Wisdom only in participating in History. – One can, certainly, not accept this Hegelian way of seeing things. But one can avoid it only if one denies that the *being* of man creates itself as historical action. Now to deny it, is to deny that history has a *meaning*; to deny it, is to deny, as well, and just thereby, this something one calls *liberty* and consequently, to deny it, is to remove all genuine *meaning* to individual existence itself.[27]

However, the classical view of nature is essentially related to the classical view of man. If man's humanity results from the realization of the anthropogenic desire, of man's negation of nature, then the view of being as eternally identical to itself cannot be held anymore, because being is transformed by man: this led Kojève to a sheer contradiction (which he tried to articulate in his *Introduction*) between the perfection of the natural Being and its continuous destruction-transformation by the work of Man. Kojève does not deny that there is an "innate nature" in Man, but he contends it is only an "animal characteristic" that has nothing to do with liberty, which is negation of nature.[28] If Man creates himself in the course of History by his work, i.e., by negating and transforming Nature, then the conception of natural Being as "perfect at once" and "eternally identical to itself" could hardly be held. This "synthesis" cannot therefore succeed. Kojève may have been aware of such a dead end, since he did not go with this attempt later on.

b) Second answer:

In a footnote of his *Introduction*,[29] Kojève sketched another way out of the difficulty raised by Strauss, by articulating the atheistic conception of man (Hegelian anthropology correctly understood thanks to Heidegger's *Sein und Zeit*) with a synthesis from the greatest philosophies of nature:

I see no objection to say that the natural world eludes *conceptual* understanding. Indeed, this would only mean that the existence of Nature is revealed by mathematical algorithm, for example, and not by concepts – that is by *words* having a meaning. Now, modern physics leads in the end to this result: one cannot *speak* of the physical reality without contradictions (…). Hence there would be no *discourse* revealing the physical or natural reality (…). Therefore, it may be necessary to combine Plato's conception (for the mathematical,

---

[27] Manuscript of "Tyrannie et Sagesse," fol. 31 verso (Fonds Kojève, *loc. cit.*). Cf. *ILH*, pp. 378n f. [147 n.36], 485n f. [212 f.n.15], and 434n [158 n.6]. – See also Kojève to Strauss, October 29, 1953 (in *OT*, pp. 261-262), in answer to the sending of *NRH*: "Regarding the issue I can only keep repeating the same thing. If there is something like 'human nature,' then you are surely right in everything." (Ibid., p. 261.)

[28] *ILH*, pp. 492 [219f.] and 494 [222].

[29] *ILH*, pp. 378-379n [147n. 36].

or better, geometrical substructure of the World) with Aristotle's (for its biological structure), and Kant's (for his physical, or better dynamical structure), while reserving Hegelian dialectics for Man and History.

However, in a final sentence which appears in the typescript but not in the printed text, Kojève wrote: "But I confess I do not know how one could combine these conceptions which seem to exclude each other."[30] This then hesitating sketch of another solution became the subject matter of his update of Hegel.

In his *Introduction*, Kojève expounded the advent of the Wise Man as mortal Man-God at the end of history.[31] The Absolute Knowledge of the Wise Man is the result of his recapitulation of the whole process of human thought in its historical dialectics: this Absolute Knowledge exhibits itself in the ultimate Book. The material form of this book was Hegel's 1830 *Encyclopedia of Philosophical Sciences*, the System of Science. Kojève's project was meant to be a paraphrase of this work, as an update of the Hegelian system of knowledge.

The historical-philosophical Introduction (the later Third Introduction) to Energo-logie is mostly devoted to an articulation of this problem: how to update Hegel's energo-logie (philosophy of nature); how to account for ontological dualism (importance of Kant). Kojève's treatment of Kant is of central importance, not only because of its length (about half of the first version of the third, historic-philosophical Introduction has been devoted to Kant), but above because, by emphasizing the separation between nature and liberty, Kant made visible this crucial problem of ontological dualism.

In his "Introduction à la Mise à jour de l'énergo-logie hégélienne" (unpublished part of the first version of the Third, historico-philosophical Introduction, 1952), Kojève elaborated on the contribution of contemporary physics. The main purpose of Kojève's update was to replace Hegel's dialectical philosophy of nature (and all previous "philosophies of nature") with an Energo-logie which would take into account contemporary physics. Heidegger's dualistic ontology was a first attempt in this direction.

In order to achieve the intended articulation, Kojève's Energo-logie should rely on an achieved physics: "I have personally the impression that Physics has reached, around 1950, a degree of perfection which excludes any truly revolutionary upheaval."[32] (Kojève's opinion that physics is achieved amounts to the repetition of a similar assertion at the end of the 19th century.) However, as Strauss pointed out in his "Epilogue," a prominent feature of modern science is the infinite progress it claims to achieve:[33] the very basis of physics might be put into question in some unpredictable future. If Kojève is unable to make

---

[30] Fonds Kojève, box X, F/VII/17.

[31] *ILH*, pp. 388n, 508n.

[32] "Energo-logie, Introduction historico-philosophique," f. 602 (Fonds Kojève, box XV).

[33] *Liberalism Ancient and Modern* (New York: Basic Books, 1968), pp. 211f. It is significant that Kojève never wrote his planned update of Hegel's philosophy of Nature ("Energo-logie").

the articulation between nature and liberty, it means that he does not really go beyond Heidegger's position, and this is likely what Strauss intended to suggest in alluding to Heidegger in the conclusion of his "Restatement:" from Kojève's presuppositions, it would not be possible to come to another *coherent* conclusion than Heidegger's.

2) Answer to the second objection: the problem of the Last Man

Kojève did not address at length Strauss's second objection (the anthropological objection);[34] besides, he did not achieve the planned anthropological part of his update of Hegel. However, in his letter to Strauss dated September 19, 1950,[35] Kojève stated that two classes of rational beings should remain at the end of history (Kojève therefore gives up the "classless" society): "mortal Gods" (Wise men) and "animals" (the common run of men), which endorses Strauss's objection as regards the necessity of enforcement action in the "final" State.

The Additional Note in the second edition of the *Introduction à la lecture de Hegel*,[36] which contains the "supplement on Japan" that Strauss was "anxious to see,"[37] takes implicitly for granted Strauss's objections against Kojève's description of the final State. Besides humanity's return to animality, which Kojève has come to consider as an already present certainty and not as a future possibility to be achieved,[38] his speculated "Japanese," i.e., purely snobbish, post-historical human beings who would still play with the problems in separating "forms" from "contents" without transforming them, eventually come down to Nietzsche's last men: they will not be able anymore to perform any serious action according to "values that have social or political content."[39] With the end of history as Kojève means it, i.e., with the end of the negating activity of man who creates himself, liberty and the sense of individual existence simply disappear.

Kojève's remarks on Japanese snobbism may be considered as an attempt to find some outlet for the aspiration of spirited men: men could play as if great deeds were still to be performed; they could perform an aesthetic imitation of

---

[34] Kojève acknowledged that the question whether there is a "human nature" remains open in his letter to Strauss, October 29, 1953, *op. cit.*, p. 261.

[35] *Op. cit.*, p. 255.

[36] See *ILH*, "Note de la Seconde Édition," pp. 436-437 [159-162]. A manuscript of this additional note, which bears a few corrections, is to be found in the Fonds Kojève, box XI, in a folder titled: "2e édition de l'Introduction à la lecture de Hegel Note additionnelle (Japon) (14.I.62)."

[37] Strauss to Kojève, October 4, 1962, *op. cit.*, p. 310.

[38] From a "militant" position, according to which Hegelian philosophy is not a "discursive revelation," but a "project" to be achieved and proved by action (see Kojève, "Marx, Hegel, and Christianity," trans. Hilail Gildin, *Interpretation: A Journal of Political Philosophy*, vol. 1, no. 1, 1970, p. 41), Kojève shifted to a "triumphant" and "ironic" position in his later works: see *ILH*, "Note de la Seconde Édition" and Michael S. Roth, *Knowing and History* (Ithaca: Cornell University Press, 1988), pp. 139ff.

[39] *ILH*, p. 437 [162].

such deeds. But playing at great deeds cannot be confused with really perform-
ing such deeds. No place would be granted for *thumos* and for aspiration to great
deeds (cf. Kojève's analysis of Desire and of the tyrant; the question of amour-
propre – desire for wealth and power, love of glory). However, Man does not
simply want to be recognized as equal, but to be admired as superior:[40] therefore,
fundamental aspirations of Man could not be entirely fulfilled by the End-State
as described by Kojève. By endorsing Strauss's conclusion, Kojève admitted that
the Absolute Wisdom has not yet been completed, therefore that his contention
regarding the present realization of the End State is false.

Strauss pointed out to the contradiction between the achievement of human
recognition, liberty and equality, on the one hand, and the reduction of man to
animality,[41] on the other:

> In a way, Spengler said that which is only implied in Hegel. I think I am aware of this
> point, but it leads to one terrible thing: That the history of the world which in its totality is
> said to be perfectly satisfactory to reason (the overcoming of contradictions, all tragedies
> redeemed at the end because all the tragedy was needed to this end) would result in final
> tragedy because man has made all these infinite efforts unconsciously, with a view to the
> establishment of the perfectly just society, and then when this society has come into being
> it was the moment of the beginning of decay and absolute degradation of man the history
> of the world would be tragic then and this is absolutely opposed to what Hegel meant. Is
> this not so?…or how do you think Hegel could answer?[42]

Kojève's account of the End of History displays again the inner tensions of
messianism, even secularized: the end is there, but is not completely achieved
yet; the end will necessarily come, but it must be helped to come.[43] Hegel's teach-

---

[40]   Cf. Kojève on unconscious satisfaction in *ILH* pp. 278-279: the "Chinese" ideal (stu-
pefaction due to the security of comfort, as described by Nietzsche, *Fröhliche Wissenschaft*
I, § 24).

[41]   See "Tyrannie et Sagesse," p. 257 n.1 ("Tyranny and Wisdom," in *OT*, p. 162 n.6).

[42]   Course on Hegel's philosophy of history, p. 74. Strauss did not dispute Kojève's interpretation of Hegel's "end of history," as is shown by his criticizing Collingwood's interpretation of Hegel's end of history as "unknowable future," with the example of America (ibid.,
pp. 75 and 89 f.).

[43]   In his letter dated April 17, 1959 (handwritten in English, Fonds Kojève, box XX),
Allan Bloom objected: "Recent political events have weakened some of my conviction concerning the ultimate economic rationalization of our one world. I am sure that this has been
the trend and that in modern thought there is nothing to oppose to the notion that there are no
real political problems, that the rational science of supply and demand has taken the place of
the 'myths' of morality and the state. But because we have no good reason not to accept this
development, does not mean that we will and that the political issues will not stay with us in an
utterly perverted and irrational form. […] I am told the party has more power than ever before
and that there is no thought of a settlement with the West in any fundamental sense, as you
predicted it. This is utterly unreasonable, I know; the regime of virtue and work demanded by
K[hrushchev] can only endure on the constant artificial stimulation of external crisis. But who
says he can't do that indefinitely. I know your thought does not depend on one political event

ing is the final teaching, however it has to be revised. In order to prove his thesis, Kojève should have articulated his anthropology with a new, non-Hegelian theory of phenomena (Energo-logie). However, Kojève only wrote an introduction to such a theory: his note in his *Introduction* about dualistic ontology simply suggested a work plan. Therefore, Kojève did not really go further into the dualism which he pointed out.

In the central part of his *Introduction* ("Note sur l'Eternité, le Temps et le Concept"), Kojève exhibited the four fundamental alternatives: Parmenides-Spinoza, Skepticism, Plato-Aristotle-Kant, Hegel-Heidegger (only Heidegger was named in the typescript). If Kojève was able to prove that there will be no surprise in the future, no essential change in human action and thought, his position would become much stronger. But Strauss contends there is a permanent possibility of "surprise," that is to say a permanent possibility of fundamentally new answers to the fundamental alternatives or problems.[44]

Strauss did not hold Kojève's answers to be successful, as is shown by his final statement about Kojève's position and its crucial difficulty, in his seminar on Plato's *Laws* at the St. John's College, Annapolis (Md.), in 1971-1972:[45] in the context, he replied to the alleged "blindness" of Plato and Aristotle as regards the vanishing of the *polis* as living political form: the victory of the despotic rule of empires over the *polis* did not change their political knowledge; they already knew about these political forms as alternative. Strauss sent then back the blame to the Moderns:

> Many people in modern times believe that we can now figure out the future of mankind – a future which may be either glorious or degrading; in other words, that there will be no surprises. But there are always surprises, as we have seen often enough in our lifetimes. And I think even the younger ones have observed such surprises. Now if one cannot know what will be, can one at least know what one ought to wish to be? In other words, what one ought to do, how one ought to live? Now as Plato frequently refers to the *logos* and to the intellect, *nous – logos* is in Latin *ratio* – so we can say that he is aiming at the society as is the society ruled by reason, the rational society. That I believe we must never for one moment forget.

---

or another coming out the way you expected, but it has some connection as you have so often avowed. But this is wondering." – The meaning of history as expounded by Kojève could be interpreted in a different way: see, e. g., Spengler's historicist account of the "Imperial Age" as the stage of a cyclic development, in every higher culture, in which "there are no more political problems" (*The Decline of the West*, trans. Charles F. Atkinson [London: George Allen & Unwin, 1928], vol. II, p. 432).

[44] Consider, e.g., "Existentialism," in *Interpretation: A Journal of Political Philosophy*, vol. 22, no. 3 (Spring 1995), p. 306.

[45] Unpublished transcript from tape record, lecture 19, p. 1.

Strauss emphasized to his auditors the impossibility of a final system which would articulate the fundamental alternatives. He made also clear that the goal of a rational society should not be disregarded, despite the irrational consequences of modern interpretations of this goal. Having formulated the problem area, Strauss summarized as follows Kojève's notion of the End-State and the anthropological issue implied by it:

> In our time someone I knew quite well, and some others here present knew, Alexandre Kojève, has restated the notion of the rational society quite impressively. And he spoke of the universal and homogeneous society, meaning by that, the rational society, which because it is rational, this was his privilege to believe, is bound to come. The universal and homogeneous state is a kind of combination of Hegel and Marx; the state is obviously not Marxist – and the universal and homogeneous, that comes from Marx. A society that is homogeneous means classless and beyond racialism, as we can say – every human being is a full member. No poor in that state, foreign or civil, nor poverty, but full development of everyone's capacity – and that means, in a language that never Hegel nor Marx nor Kojève used but which is perfectly proper, the coincidence of virtue and happiness – the full development of man's capacity, which is not impeded. This is the perfect satisfaction for man and in this sense happiness. The difficulty which he encountered is this: according to this view, this is of course a timeless stage of human development, hence there will no longer be any great tasks for men, no historical tasks. There will be only some mopping-up operations. But the main point is settled. Now the potentialities are exhausted; and therefore we are in this interesting situation, that the highest peak of humanity is at the same time the beginning of complete emptiness. I believed he never solved this difficulty. Now to come back to the classics. They did not expect in any way a universal and homogeneous state. A universal state – that would mean there is no self-government; and hence the government must be despotic. As for the homogeneity, the absence of classes or difference of races, maybe, this is not possible because of scarcity.

Strauss comes then to a comparison between Hegel-Kojève and Plato as regards the crucial problem, the achievement of the quest for wisdom:

> … in Plato there is no notion of historical tasks. You see, for Hegel, and therefore also for Kojève, there is a history in which the great individuals formed, as it were, the different epochs of history. Great historic tasks. No such task is anymore possible. Or differently stated, especially with a view to Kojève. The end of history means that philosophy has become wisdom – it is no longer a quest for wisdom, but wisdom. So all that men can do is to study Hegel's *Logic* and *Phenomenology*, over and over, and no new thought of any consequence is possible. Whereas in Plato's *Republic* of course there is no end to philosophy, even in the *Republic*, let alone in the *Laws*.[46]

According to Strauss, the possibility of philosophy, of the ascent of human soul from the given opinions toward truth, is enabled by a pre-philosophical "glimpse of the eternal order."[47] However, the progress toward wisdom, toward

---

[46]   *Ibid.*, p. 3.

[47]   "Restatement," *op. cit.*, p. 68. Cf. *Natural Right and History* (Chicago: The University of Chicago Press, 1953), p. 124.

the knowledge of the whole, which the philosopher can experience,[48] should remain an "uncompletable ascent."[49]

---

[48] *OT*, pp. 101-102; "Restatement," p. 66.

[49] Strauss to Voegelin, 10.12.50, in *Faith and Political Philosophy. The Corresponden-ce Between Leo Strauss and Eric Voegelin*, 1934-1964 (University Park: The Pennsylvania University Press, 1993), Barry Cooper and Peter Emberley, eds, p. 75 ("classical philosophy understands itself as the uncompletable ascent from proteron pros hemas to proteron physei"), with Strauss to Kojève, May 28, 1957, in *OT*, p. 279; *NRH*, p. 125; *The City and Man* (Chica-go: Rand McNally, 1964), pp. 20-21.

Piotr Nowak

CARL SCHMITT AND HIS CRITIC

1.

Political Theology, one of the earliest books of Carl Schmitt, begins as follows: "Sovereign is who decides on the exception."[1] And next: "Sovereignty is the highest, legally independent, underived power."[2] As we see from the opening, this small book is dedicated to the problem of sovereignty, hence of power. Each power in its foundation has to be sovereign that is independent and free. It means, the real test for any new power as well as for the traditional one is the borderline, extreme situation when the power makes the final decisions without any external advice or suggestions. The borderline situation according to Schmitt is "(...) a case of extreme peril, danger to the existence of the state,"[3] or simply to existence, to the life of human being. The sovereign not only recognizes the situation as an exception; he also matches up the means that allow him to bring back the normal situation. Here the first ambiguity arises: would not the sovereign tend to create exceptions that would confirm by definition his sovereignty? If so martial law rather than situation of normalcy would constitute the sovereign's natural environment; whereas each period of "normality" would be some kind of degeneration. "For a legal order to make sense, a normal situation must exist, and he is sovereign who definitely decides whether this normal situation actually exists (...) The sovereign produces and guarantees the situation in its totality. He has the monopoly over this last decision."[4] Still we don't know whether "normality" should be understood in terms of peaceful coexistence of free people or, on the contrary, in terms of a state of emergency where the sovereign is always ready to act in order to protect his own substance. I would suggest that (paradoxically) "normality" here means the exception. My suspicion is confirmed by the Schmitt's explicit formulation:

---

[1] Carl Schmitt, *Political Theology. Four Chapters on the Concept of Sovereignty*, trans. G. Schwab (Cambridge: Cambridge University Press, 1988), p. 4.

[2] Ibid., p. 17.

[3] Ibid., p. 6.

[4] Ibid., p. 13.

The exception can be more important to it than the rule, not because of a romantic irony for the paradox, but because the seriousness of an insight goes deeper than the clear generalizations inferred from what ordinarily repeats itself. The exception is more interesting than the rule [the normal situation]. The rule [the normal situation] proves nothing; the exception proves everything: It confirms not only the rule but also its existence, which derives only from the exception. In the exception the power of real life breaks through the crust of mechanism that has become torpid repetition.[5]

Schmitt appears here as siding with life, or else as the thinker who doesn't want to slumber along with a sleepy, liberal civilization submerged in mechanical repetition. The sovereign, at least as Schmitt characterizes him in *Political Theology*, is the very one who wants to stimulate the human ant-hill, who pierces it with the stick and who doesn't want to give the people peacefulness and satisfaction.

2.

In section four of *Political Theology* we already find the arguments that will be developed in the most famous of Schmitt's books, i.e., in *The Concept of the Political*. We read there: "No medium exists (...) between catholicity and atheism. Everyone [each of them – PN] formulated a big either/or, the rigor of which sounded more like dictatorship than everlasting conversation."[6] In this sentence ascribed to Cardinal Newman transpires Schmitt's well known theory called "decisionism." According to it "(...) the decision as such is (...) valuable precisely because as far as the most essential issues are concerned, making a decision is more important than how a decision is made. 'It is definitely in our interest – these are the words of de Maistre – not that a question be decided in one way or another but that it be decided without delay and without appeal.'"[7] This is the language of striving, of conflict. What Schmitt seeks to establish here is a careful distinction between, on the one hand, what is mine and friendly and on the other, what is not mine and (therefore) hostile. The problem Schmitt faces is symptomatic for his theorizing. As he rightly writes modern culture is haunted by idle talk and chatter, that instead of going to war one is looking for a mere conversation in which the whole world transforms itself into the big brother house of the vulgar majority. According to Schmitt "(...) it was characteristic of bourgeois liberalism not to decide (...) [to bring about the battle – PN] but instead to begin a discussion."[8] At this point one can naïvely wonder, and I'm doing this, why is it better to go to a "decisive bloody battle" instead of engaging in sometimes a boring and occasionally fruitful dialogue? Yet to Schmitt any prospect of dialogue

---

[5] Ibid., p. 15.
[6] Ibid., pp. 53-54.
[7] Ibid., pp. 55-56.
[8] Ibid., p. 59.

seems foreign if not disgusting on account of the idle stagnation to which it leads. The only thing needful is a decision, no matter of what kind. First we have to decide; later we will see if the decision made was good or bad one. We are not talking here about the decision necessary to purchase a new car, but about the kind of decisions that deals with the fundamentals of our existence. Using Schmitt's example, because of its ultimate, either/or character the question whether "Christ or Barabbas?" cannot be negotiated or voted for. Hence, according to Schmitt all compromises are acceptable but those that deal with fundamental, metaphysical questions. Carl Schmitt

> (...) considered continuous discussion a method of circumventing responsibility and of ascribing to freedom of speech and of the press an excessive importance that in the final analysis permits the decision to be evaded. Just as liberalism discusses and negotiates every political detail, so it also wants to dissolve metaphysical truth in a discussion. The essence of liberalism is negotiation, a cautious half measure, in the hope that the definitive dispute, the decisive bloody battle, can be transformed into a parliamentary debate and permits the decision to be suspended forever in an everlasting discussion.[9]

Today the danger for political life comes not from consumption, technology or bureaucracy narrowly understood but first and foremost small talk, for which the subject, the way of argumentation and the truth are entirely irrelevant.

3.

Although *Political Theology* contains all the subjects typically considered by Schmitt, including the ontology of decision, the problem of sovereignty and the critique of liberal democracy, it remains in the shadow of Schmitt's best known book, namely *The Concept of the Political. The Concept* represents the most famous (or infamous, depends who is reading) articulation of Schmitt's theory of the need for the enemy, to which I shall now briefly turn.

Let me begin by repeating something that is commonly known. According to the author of *The Concept of the Political* the difference between a friend and an enemy is both final and irreducibly one. Other differences are merely visible manifestations of that fundamental difference, the political difference *par excellence*. In other words one could say that starting from Hobbes's *bellum omnium contra omnes* ("war of all against all") as his point of departure, Schmitt aims at challenging contemporary reluctance to admit that politics is a matter of life and death. Although if we still insist that in the world exist dozens of other distinctions that are more fundamental than the political one, usually we forget that they are derived from the elementary division into enemies and friends that is a strictly political one. "The political enemy need not be morally evil or aesthetically ugly; he need not appear as an economic competitor, and it may even be

---

[9] Ibid., p. 63.

advantageous to engage with him in business transactions. But he is nevertheless the other, the stranger; and it is sufficient for his nature that he is, in a specially intense way, existentially something different and alien (...)."[10] Therefore the enemy is the stranger, somebody who doesn't belong to us, the person with whom we can share a meal or a bus ride, but not our values. In this place the question arises who decides who is the enemy and who is not. How is one to recognize the enemy if there are no criteria – economic or moral – which allow us to do this? It is in the state of emergency, in an exceptional, borderline situation of the Last Judgment that one usually arrives at the knowledge about who is an enemy and who's not, as Schmitt asserts in a manner overloaded with pathos. These are the moments when no one is allowed to sleep or take the side of the fake "normality." Therefore our enemy will be this one whom we have chosen as the enemy. "Each participant is in a position to judge whether the adversary intends to negate his opponent's way of life and therefore must be repulsed or fought in order to preserve one's own form of existence."[11] Strictly speaking, no one but me could decide who my enemy is. I have to do it alone as quickly as possible, otherwise I will be killed. The decision should be taken together with the bloody means that let me overcome the stranger.

4.

One of the main characters in Joseph Conrad's novel *The Secret Agent* is "the incorruptible Professor." He goes for a walk throughout the London's streets with a bomb and dreams about the destruction of Greenwich Observatory. The reason why he is going to blow up the Observatory is very simple: "mankind does not know what it wants" – but Professor does know of course. The book ends with the following fragment:

> And the incorruptible Professor walked, averting his eyes from the odious multitude of mankind. He had no future. He disdained it. He was a force. His thoughts caressed the images of ruin and destruction. He walked frail, insignificant, shabby, miserable – and terrible in the simplicity of his idea calling madness and despair to the regeneration of the world. Nobody looked at him. He passed on unsuspected and deadly, like a pest in the street full of men.[12]

Does this description fit the image of Carl Schmitt? For sure he wasn't "incorruptible Professor" – "frail, insignificant, shabby, miserable." And the truth is he wasn't the naïve dreamer, but a very powerful and tough person, whose thought shaped the mentality of a numbers of activists of NSDAP party. He was born in

---

[10] Carl Schmitt, *The Concept of the Political*, trans. G. Schwab (Chicago: The University of Chicago Press, 1996), p. 27.

[11] Ibid.

[12] Joseph Conrad, *The Secret Agent. A Simple Tale* (London, 1992), p. 283.

1888, in a very orthodox Catholic family. At first he was going to be a priest but finally had chosen the faculty of law and in a short period of time became one of the most significant antiliberal jurists of his time. Schmitt "(…) went further than other [German intellectuals who supported the Nazi in the early days of the Third Reich – PN] becoming a committed, official advocate of the Nazi regime. Under the patronage of Hermann Göring, he was appointed to the Prussian State Council, received professorship in Berlin, and edited an important legal journal."[13] In 1936 he wrote at the conference six pages under the title "German Jurisprudence in the Struggle against the Jewish Spirit." It's enough. There are few facts that support my confession that Schmitt is not the prince of my favorite tale. These facts also indicate that he wasn't an innocent, mentally ill intellectual with the obsession of blowing up the Greenwich Observatory. In the thirties he was dynamite in the literary sense of the word. So, one could ask, why do I deal with dynamite? Do I want to have fun with fireworks as usually boys want to have it? Quite opposite. I assume that nowadays – after Sept. 11 – Schmitt's writings can tell us and in fact they are telling something new about the world, especially about our attitude to this event. I would even risk and say that this way of argumentation has a tremendous power over us as well as over politicians (especially in the States) like Donald Rumsfeld and Paul Wolfowitz or influential publicists (like Samuel Huntington). Now, I will try to explain what I'm talking about.

5.

In his book, Mark Lilla correctly said that, "On the nature of friendship, central theme in classical political thought, there is hardly a word to be found in all Schmitt's writings. We are left with the impression that friendship arises only from shared animosities."[14]

The Concept of the Political teaches that possibility of the ultimate deadly battle does not alone constitute the essence of the political. *The Concept of the Political* also refers to the preceding r e c o g n i t i o n of the basic situation, namely who is or may turn out to be my enemy, whom – at least for the time being – I don't need to fear. In other words, the primary duty of the politician is to identify the enemy, to describe the direction from which one could expect any danger. Then he could act.

So, who is our enemy, the enemy of the West, of the European civilization? No doubt this question is widely discussed now. According to Schmitt and many important politicians, well known by their names, an enemy is e v e r y o n e who doesn't share my values. If we take into consideration the realm of business alone we could make a pact even with the dark forces. But to believe into the same system of values together with a devil – no, it's impossible. Differences of inter-

---

[13] Mark Lilla, *The Reckless Mind. Intellectuals in Politics* (New York, 2001), p. 50.

[14] Ibid., p. 56.

est could be explained and decided – one can merely state the clash of different systems of values, but cannot decide it without eliminating of an enemy. In our new century the first people, I guess, who learned the meaning of Schmitt's message were infamous hijackers who crashed the planes on the skyscrapers of WTC in NY. Second was Oriana Fallaci who in a furious article under the emblematic title *The Rage and the Proud* excluded the possibility of any form of agreement with the "infidels." What then is to be done when there is no chance for a peaceful affirmation of the existing differences? Schmitt claims that only war can save us, only conflict can reawaken the dormant source of values. For this reason one should mobilize both the people as well as philosophical concepts by bringing them back to their basic, militant character. And what then? The picture is less than encouraging. On the one hand culture based on strict values cannot do anything without exclusion of the others, doesn't matter if we define the Other as a Jew or mad cow. The exclusion is the principle of culture. On the other hand, technological development provides the conditions for such exclusion. The exclusion will be total, because totality of the exclusion is technically possible and from the perspective of the endangered values – also desirable. The only thing is to specify who – after the Jews and the mad cows – will be the target of the next Holocaust. It's not difficult to guess…

What is the conclusion that comes out of all this? Nowadays – the ghost of Schmitt calls us from his grave – we must relearn from the beginning the forgotten language of myth, we have to take a stance, to decide "either-or," to give up on the courtesy of "political correctness." And how can we resist to listen and to act when even the ex-president of the United States encouraged us, using the language of the moral crusade? One could argue that this way of thinking is a pure cynicism. Perhaps it is. "When being reproached for immorality and cynicism" – Schmitt insists – "the spectator of political phenomena can always recognize in such reproaches a political weapon used in actual combat."[15] If we translate Schmitt's language of political incorrectness into the average idiom we obtain the following formula: "All the people who tolerate Muslims' violence and barbarism for the sake of their 'human rights' or different kind of sentimental humanism are my and our enemies, the enemies of the whole civilized world."

We should know that Schmitt (as well as his followers) is not prepared to open a discussion; the possibility for which he cuts off from the beginning. According to his method of reasoning, everyone is "black" who "sticks with" "the blacks" (whatever "sticking" may mean); everyone is "an Arab" who asks about the meaning of "the collective responsibility" with reference to bombarding the inhabitants of Afghanistan; everyone is "white" who argues that Robert Mugabe is simply stupid.

Now, at the end of my presentation I would like to confess my helplessness with regard to the books of Carl Schmitt. Their uncomplicated, "military" dis-

---

[15] Schmitt, *The Concept of the Political*, p. 67.

course appears to be very convincing. It appeals to my hidden fears more than to my mind. Nonetheless *nolens volens* it achieves its purpose: I begin the mobilization. I begin to think that nothing must be wrong with my strong determination to handle the dangerous encounter. Why should I merely look at my enemy and do nothing? When some dilemmas arise in my head I hear the voice of Schmitt who calls me: "go and fight!" I cannot pretend that I remain deaf for this voice or that it is irrelevant and doesn't convince me. It does. But if you are convinced by yourself that Schmitt is right, if you are permanently arguing and striving against him, it's not the same situation when somebody else (let's say, the helpers of ex-president Bush) tries to convince you that the author of *The Concept of the Political* is right. This is completely different situation. The problem lies in the difference between on the one hand thinking and philosophy, on the other between order and ideology.

"The nation can only say 'yes' or 'no'" – Schmitt writes in *Legalität und Legitimität* – "but it cannot advise, deliberate or discuss, it cannot govern or administrate (…) First and foremost it cannot ask the questions, it can only answer them 'yes' or 'no' (…) The question is posed only from above, the answer comes only from below."[16] I got the strong impression, now it is stronger than before, that there exists an order of questions set from above; questions which need to be answered immediately and unthinkingly "yes" or "no," "be" or "not to be." I understand that after Sep. 11 we deal with an exception, an unusual and perhaps an extreme situation. Nevertheless I would like to know who is he who set those questions, how does he look like, and neither least nor last, is he prepared to talk about their meaning? And – the more important question – is he my enemy or ally? These are the questions and according to Schmitt, no one is allowed to set them apart from the politicians, the secret agents of the enigmatic being called the national unity.

6.

Carl Schmitt, like Hobbes before, was considered to be an intellectual pariah for many years. After a brilliant academic career in the twilight of the Weimar Republic, and a short but intense period of support from German Nazism from the early 1940s until the defeat of Hitler, Schmitt fell into complete oblivion. After the war, subject to the uncompromising procedures of Denazification, he spent 18 months in the captivity of the Allies, even though no charges were leveled against him (which must have been agonizing for a lawyer, more than the sole fact of being kept in captivity). "When we want to put a dog to sleep," he used to repeat, "we say that it went rabid." After release, he returned to his home town Plattenberg, where he was a relative unknown, and died at a venerable age.

---

[16] Carl Schmitt, *Legalität und Legitimität* (München-Leipzig, 1932), p. 92.

In a conversation with his personal biographer Joseph W. Bendersky, Schmitt described his work on Hobbes as his magnum opus.[17] Those familiar with his other works, for example *Hamlet or Hekuba*, or most famously of all *The Concept of the Political*, may disagree with this verdict. Schmitt's *The Leviathan in the State Theory of Thomas Hobbes. Meaning and Failure of a Political Symbol* maintains charm and attraction for reasons other than its philosophical magnitude, matching that of *Political Theology*. The reason why the book is so exceptional for us is that it is full of personal references: and here we find some of the points of intersection between our two authors becoming more explicit.

Let us consider what both Schmitt and Hobbes have in common, apart from a rather obvious admiration for the ancient virtue of prudence, the similarities in their careers that we touched on above, and rejection by their contemporaries. They certainly share a few concepts, first formulated by Hobbes and then filled with new meaning by Schmitt: *"bellum omnium contra omnes,"* "protection in exchange for obedience," "man is a wolf to another man" – these are only a few. Nonetheless, I believe that what the two authors really share is their "anthropological axiom" – their similar understanding of "human nature."

Both start from the same question: "Is man by nature good or evil?" Or – in other words – what is his essence? For both, the idea that a man is evil ("dangerous") by nature is the main anthropological assumption.[18] The assumption is twofold: this evil means corruption, weakness, lack of knowledge, all deriving directly from human imperfection (*humana impotentia*); but evil is also animal power, will power, and will to fight (*naturae potentia*)[19]. The second evil is not a moral wrong – rather, it is that evil is brutality, a natural roughness, or impulsiveness. For Hobbes, the human beast – guided by the primary impulse – is evil but in an innocent way. Hobbes rejects the idea of sin, assuming that the datum, the so called natural state, is absolute, unrestrained human freedom. Therefore, "human" evil is the evil of an innocent beast, the vitality embodied in one of Robert Musil's characters, Moosbrugger, who is to be trained by setting standards of decency that he must not transgress. "But if man's dangerousness is only supposed or believed in, not genuinely known, the opposite, too, can be regarded as possible, and the attempt to eliminate man's dangerousness (which until now has always really existed) can be put into practice."[20] In a way, Hobbes is an "opti-

---

[17]   Joseph W. Bendersky, "Schmitt and Hobbes, *Telos*, Fall 1996, p. 124. See Carl Schmitt, *The Leviathan in the State Theory of Thomas Hobbes. Meaning and Failure of a Political Symbol*, trans. G. Schwab, E. Hilfstein (Westport, CT: Greenwood Press, 1996). See also Carl Schmitt, "The State as Mechanism in Hobbes and Descartes."

[18]   Schmitt, *The Concept of the Political*, p. 58.

[19]   I reconstruct this aspect of Schmitt's reasoning based on the masterly critique by Leo Strauss, "Notes on Carl Schmitt: The Concept of the Political," in *The Concept of the Political*, trans. J.H. Lomax, pp. 83-107, which can be described as the attempt to defend Hobbes against Schmitt's "Hobbesianism."

[20]   Ibid., p. 96.

mist," a forerunner in the field of human relations. Indeed, following Strauss's line of thinking, one must admit that Hobbes is a true liberal! And this is where I would see the first difference between Hobbes and his 20th century incarnation. Let us assume – just for a test, suggests Schmitt – the innocence of evil that we have seen posited by Hobbes. Then what is good, and is it also innocent? Or maybe good is part of evil? In that instance, the two values no longer refer to each other: they no longer make any moral difference, a distinction which Schmitt considered essential. Meanwhile, good means rationality, perfection, obedience. This is why we should think that evil is not to be identified with the prevailing animal and physical side of humanity (which constitutes the fiction of the "state of nature"), but with moral excess, corrupted will, "the malice of rage" (to use Heideggerian terminology).

Hobbes describes the state of nature as a state of permanent tension, a general hostility of all towards all. This is, to repeat, yet another experiment in reasoning. Thus, while Hobbes absolutizes the fight of individuals and finds in this struggle the basic dimension of human freedom, for Schmitt this struggle is political in nature and is carried on by nations. Nations, not individual people, live in the state of nature. The state – suggests Schmitt – must ensure protection of its citizens, but it is nowhere said that there has to be peace. Strictly speaking, wars are waged by states for no other reason than ensuring internal stability and political unity. The state was created in order to prevent civil war, and this is in fact its basic function. No political action is taken outside the state, because the state is the only subject of freedom. How free a given state is – and this truism cannot be repeated enough – influences the freedom of individuals. In other instances, the state is only a "night watchman" in the service of its more powerful citizens. Hobbes (it is his recurring neurosis) spots enemies everywhere. Literally. Conversely, political activism according to Schmitt must be directed against enemies but also to win friends, or at least allies. The essence of political activism is in recognizing who is the enemy and who is not, then fighting to the bitter end.

The second issue which sets apart both thinkers is that of courage. Schmitt requires the citizens to be ready to devote their life to the leviathan. Hobbes is not so sure. A deserter ("slave") keeps his right to life, because death constitutes *summum malum* – it is the worst of all evils, as it is irreversible and irrevocable. The desertion puts honor at risk (this is true), and it should not lead to the conclusion that it is something wrong or unjustified. Civil obedience is conditional; it can be renounced when one is forced to risk one's life or soul. Thus, courage is not a virtue. The virtue is what constitutes a burgher; it is the virtue of prudence, striving for peace by working hard and growing rich, and exercising freedom without detriment to other people. This is Hobbesian liberalism. Schmitt, on the other hand, in describing the duties of the state's citizens, uses military vocabulary and categories, such as enthusiasm, instincts, unity, irrationality, fight, fear, mobilization. At this point, Schmitt breaks away from Hobbes: he is no longer continuing the other's work; moreover, Schmitt undermines this part of Hobbes and questions the unconditional right to life.

Let us repeat: for Hobbes, the state of nature is a constant struggle against adversity, against physical and social power, the influence and wills of other people. In this sense, the state of nature is impossible. One cannot live in such conditions. According to Schmitt, however, the state of nature does not concern individuals but separate totalities, states which have deadly enemies (deadly – because a political conflict is always a struggle for life and death) as well as potential allies and neutral states. The state of nature defined in this way is not a fiction. However it may become a fiction when the world is completely depoliticized. Let us look into that.

The state, as Schmitt understands it, is normally inactive, and activates only as a response to a threat to its existence. This is a situation of internal disorder (as in the case of a riot or general strike[21]), or external aggression. Unlike in the thesis of permanent oppression in the state of nature, in this thesis emergencies do not happen that often. However, the modern state, as we saw it emerging from the ruins of the project of the League of Nations, has come to penetrate the life of individuals, control it and regulate it (biometric passports, identifications, GPS, constant redefinition of the borderline between life and death, etc.). Today, the state is integrated into the system of international relations and its external borders are normalized, diminishing their political significance. But as we remember, the main political activity of the state is always to distinguish between a friend and an enemy – only that now the enemy is sought for within a state. This relocation requires new enemies to be created, in order to be later found. The universal, world state ("a world state (…) could only be loosely called a state,"[22] Schmitt claims) is organized this way, so that it may reach the souls of citizens, right down to their most private recesses. The total state "immerse[s] itself indiscriminately into every realm, into every sphere of human existence. [It] altogether knows absolutely no domain that is free of state interference because it no longer is able to distinguish anything."[23] This is the inhumane abomination of the modern Behemoth. This creature has neither face nor name; it is intangible, it is "nothing." Hobbes pictured the mechanics and the workings of the power apparatus of the modern state. But it was Schmitt who penetrated the beast from the inside, to find the direct opposite of the Leviathan, age old and demonic.

---

[21]   See Walter Benjamin, "Critique of Violence," in Walter Benjamin, *Reflections: Essays, Aphorisms, Autobiographical Writings*, P. Demetz and E. Jepchott, eds. (New York: Schocken, 1986), pp. 291-292.

[22]   Schmitt, *The Concept of the Political*, p. 57.

[23]   Carl Schmitt, *Starker Staat und gesunde Wirtschaft*, in G. Schwab's *Introduction* to *The Leviathan in the State Theory of Thomas Hobbes. Meaning and Failure of a Political Symbol*, p. x.

Till Kinzel

POSTMODERNISM AND THE ART OF WRITING: THE IMPORTANCE OF LEO STRAUSS FOR THE 21ST CENTURY

One may well wonder what the conjunction of the terms "postmodernism" and "the art of writing" in the title of my paper is meant to convey. Everybody knows, of course, that Leo Strauss advocated a peculiar kind of analyzing and interpreting texts, which means a special art of reading, based on the recognition of the fact that some writers in the non- or preliberal past employed an art of writing. This art of writing, in Strauss's view, is intimately connected to what philosophy is. In fact, the art of writing, also called philosophical esotericism, is, according to Strauss, a logical corollary of the original understanding of philosophy. What is the reason, however, to link the art of writing in Strauss's sense with postmodernism? And why should all this matter in the 21st century, when liberal democracy seems to be safely entrenched in the most important parts of the world? I will leave aside, at least for the time being, the question of the relation of the art of writing to liberal and non-liberal forms of government (or regimes, as Strauss liked to call them). Rather, I first want to concentrate on what is perhaps the primary task for those who want to ensure that Strauss's insights do not become lost or distorted beyond recognition in contemporary academic life. Talking about Strauss and the art of writing within the context of postmodernism or postmodernity shall serve to highlight the extremely strong obstacles and prejudices to Strauss's understanding of philosophy that constitute today's academic common sense (though one can hardly say it is part of a common sense tradition of philosophy). The obstacles would seem to be so strong, because, in spite of all of Strauss's efforts, the currently dominant forms of "cultural studies" are highly disparate but still at one in their extreme historicism or culturalism, denying all transcultural standards as well as the very ability of human beings to overcome, in thought, the limitations of their time. In order to illustrate the limitations of thought allegedly imposed on human beings by their respective social context, the eminent French thinker and postmodern skeptic, now almost turned into a classic, Michel Foucault, developed the metaphor of a fishbowl. We are, he claims, enclosed in the discourses of our time as if in transparent fishbowls and we contemporaries do not know what kind of fishbowls these are. We do not even know that such a fishbowl exists. The discourses which constitute our respective fishbowls are, as Foucault says, our one "historical apriori."[1] In a different way, the French psychoanalyst Jacques Lacan, famous for his claim that the unconscious is structured like a language, could be said to have developed his theory in part in confrontation with Strauss's book *Persecution and the Art of Writing*. Lacan mentions Strauss's book in his essay *The Agency of the Letter in the Unconscious* but shifts the ground of his argument in such a way as to turn Strauss's argument on its head.[2] He does so by going Freud one better and highlighting exactly what Strauss was trying to draw into the question, namely the way that writers are not the masters of their words but rather the servants of some mysterious unconscious that speaks through them (I simplify for the sake of clarity). The influence of Lacan's thought on the discursive field of cultural studies, of what, in Foucault's terminology, constitutes our contemporary fishbowl, can hardly be overestimated.

Even though some might claim that postmodernism as a quasi-philosophical fashion is already old hat, I still would argue that the basic underlying theoretical claims, which are more or less updated and theoretically sophisticated versions of historicism, constitute the very heart of the matter in "cultural studies" as they are practiced today. And as the cultural studies approach is now the reigning paradigm in academia, one would do well to take it seriously not only as a potential for certain kinds of interesting research – studying the interior decoration on the walls of the cave[3] – but also as a way of thought that effectively keeps people from understanding philosophy as it was originally understood. This, in my view, is the crucial issue one needs to confront in today's academic "world of discourse," a world that fails to see that philosophy as originally understood is not just one theory among many – which would make it possible to integrate it into cultural studies as just one more approach to consider – but a whole way of life. This way of life is in the decisive respect incommensurable, for it is distinguished from all other ways of life by its intransigent nature in searching out the limitations of one's self-knowledge, an intransigence, I would suggest, that leads philosophy well beyond the by now facile recognition that everything is socially and/or discursively constructed, as the case may be.

---

[1]   Paul Veyne, *Foucault. Der Philosoph als Samurai* (Stuttgart: Reclam, 2009), pp. 20, 35.

[2]   Cf. on this issue Annabell Patterson's two instructive books, *Censorship and Interpretation. The Conditions of Writing and Reading in Early Modern England* (Madison: University of Wisconsin Press, 1990); *Reading Between the Lines* (London: Routledge, 1993).

[3]   See Leo Strauss, "Religiöse Lage der Gegenwart," in Leo Strauss, Heinrich Meier ed., *Philosophie und Gesetz – Frühe Schriften* (Stuttgart: Metzler, 1997), pp. 389, 462. See also the letter by Strauss to Karl Löwith from 20 August 1946 in Leo Strauss, *Hobbes politische Wissenschaft und zugehörige Schriften – Briefe – Gesammelte Schriften*, vol. 3 (Stuttgart: Metzler, 2001), p. 666.

The challenges to the way of reading that implies a certain way of life promoted by Strauss are also related to another concept which has become a cornerstone of postmodern theories of interpretation even before postmodernism appeared on the scene. This concept is the notion of the so-called "intentional fallacy," first put forth by literary scholars William K. Wimsatt and Monroe C. Beardsley in 1946.[4] Wimsatt and Beardsley's attack on the so-called intentional fallacy and thereby on interpretive intentionalism tout court was tremendously successful, liberating readers and scholarly interpreters from the limitations of having to ascertain the author's communicative intentions. It was thus in fact regarded as a kind of heresy to presuppose, if only in a heuristic way, a coherence of the text that reflects the coherence of its author's thoughts.

Wimsatt and Beardsley, however, restricted their remarks to "work(s) of literary art" as opposed to, e.g., philosophical texts. This initial and very sober limitation of their critique of intentionalism was soon abandoned with the advent of poststructuralism and the way it was interpreted to subvert the usual distinction between literary and philosophical texts. Jacques Derrida and Richard Rorty, it would seem, gave credence to the view that the boundaries between these different sorts of texts were unclear and therefore philosophical texts could be read in much the same way as literary texts – and perhaps vice versa.

The importance of Leo Strauss in this context can hardly be overestimated. His work presents a serious and powerful challenge to the reigning orthodoxies about how to read texts. Leo Strauss's art of writing and reading presents to the readers of the 21st century a deconstruction – before deconstruction was made into a hot topic by Derrida – of the historicist versions of hermeneutics that disregard or deny the possibility of understanding an author as he understood himself. The reconstruction of a non-historicist understanding of philosophy might well be helped along by a closer study of Leo Strauss's art of reading and writing. For Strauss's form of hermeneutics, as Klaus Oehler, a student of Gerhard Krüger, emphasizes, "is the most radical attack on the phenomenalistic, subjectivist, historicist, and deconstructivist hermeneutics that can be conceived."[5] One should not, however, underestimate the current tendency or very powerful prejudice for all sorts of non-philosophical contextualizations. The currently fashionable injunction in what were once the humanities to "always historicize" and "always contextualize" expresses the very efficient current dogma that tends to deny the

---

[4] William K. Wimsatt Jr. and Monroe Beardsley, "The Intentional Fallacy," in Vincent B. Leitch ed., *Norton Anthology of Theory and Criticism* (New York: Norton, 2001), pp. 1374-1387. On Wimsatt and Beardsley and the fashionable denial of the role of authorial intention see Robert Grant, "Fiction, Meaning and Utterance," in Robert Grant, *Imagining the Real. Essays on Politics, Ideology and Literature* (Basingstoke: Palgrave Macmillan, 2003), pp. 130-133.

[5] Klaus Oehler, *Blicke aus dem Philosophenturm. Eine Rückschau* (Hildesheim: Olms, 2007), p. 187.

possibility of philosophy in the original sense.[6] In fact, the "method" of historicization today is the most effective way to neutralize philosophy's insistence that truth be the ultimate concern for those who wish to gain knowledge.[7] It is thus in the nature of the case that the *philosophical* contextualization that Leo Strauss wanted to foreground is hardly ever taken into consideration these days. Philosophy, however, should also be considered as perhaps the most important context within which certain authors have to be placed.

Leo Strauss's rediscovery of *philosophical* esotericism (as opposed to all other kinds of esotericism) is identical with the refutation of historicism, of the view that all people, including the philosophers, are sons of their times. Leo Strauss was passionately concerned about the possibility of what he calls "attachment to detachment" – and I would suggest that it is the art of writing that makes this attachment to detachment possible for those who are addressed by the philosopher's, by philosophical eros. The art of writing is the means to make the attachment to detachment of the philosopher into something more than a private hobby.

Strauss was impelled by his philosophical eros to move towards the most radical form of philosophizing by critically analysing early modern philosophers such as Hobbes and Spinoza. The understanding of political philosophy that Strauss presents hinges on the necessity to find an answer to the question "Why philosophy?" which, however, first of all needs to be made thematic itself. "The philosophers," Strauss says, "as well as other men who have become aware of the possibility of philosophy, are sooner or later driven to wonder 'Why philosophy?'"[8] It is surely no accident that Strauss not only brings up this question in his classical statement on "Classical Political Philosophy" but also and especially in what I regard as the much more important article, in "Farabi's *Plato*," which, together with various other highly revealing articles, has never been reprinted in book form in one of Strauss's collections (at least in English). As Strauss could easily

---

[6]   Contextualizing methods of interpretation have been developed by Quentin Skinner who explicitly opposes Leo Strauss's way of reading philosophical texts. See Quentin Skinner, "Meaning and Understanding in the History of Ideas," *History and Theory* 8, no. 1 (1969), pp. 3-53. Skinner's rejection of Strauss's view is connected to his philosophical conviction, derived from R. G. Collingwood, that "there simply are no perennial problems in philosophy: there are only individual answers to individual questions, with as many different answers as there are questions, and as many different questions as there are questioners." (p. 50). Cf. also the useful article by Rafael Major, "The Cambridge School and Leo Strauss: texts and contexts of American political science," *Political Research Quarterly* 58, no. 3 (September 2005), pp. 477-485; and see also Emile Perreau-Saussine, "Quentin Skinner in Context," *Review of Politics* 69, no.1 (2007), pp. 106-122.

[7]   See, on the crucial issue of the "historical point of view" vs. the truth, Josef Pieper, "Was heißt Interpretation?," in Josef Pieper, Berthold Wald ed., *Schriften zum Philosophiebegriff* (Hamburg: Meiner, 1995), pp. 226-227.

[8]   Leo Strauss, "On Classical Political Philosophy," *Social Research* 12 no. 1/4 (1945), p. 115.

have included these essays – among them "The Spirit of Sparta," "The Intention of Rousseau," "Collingwood's Philosophy of History," and "On a New Interpretation of Plato's Political Philosophy" – one wonders why he did not do so. All the more reason to study these articles and essays with utmost care, for they contain important clues as to Strauss's own art of writing, which, it goes without saying, he first had to practice in order to perfect it. A further indication for the importance of "Farabi's *Plato*" in Strauss's oeuvre is provided by the fact this article includes a motto in German that is taken from Lessing who obviously played a crucial role in Strauss's rediscovery of the exotericism of *at least* all ancient philosophers.[9] Lesssing, in this quotation, says that the same thought can be of wholly different value in another context.[10] Strauss's reference to Lessing who, as he would later claim, had then always been at his elbows,[11] links his early concern for the theologico-political problem since his dissertation and up to his editorial work for the Mendelssohn-Jubiläumsausgabe, to his mature concern for the nature of political philosophy.[12]

"Farabi's *Plato*" also includes a reference to the crucial question "Why philosophy?" that puts the most radical self-questioning of philosophy on the agenda. Because asking the question "Why philosophy?" implies for the philosopher the probing of what is most emphatically his own, it cannot be severed, as Strauss explains in "Farabi's *Plato*," from self-knowledge.[13] Philosophy cannot be philosophy without this form of questioning that takes up the questioning precisely if and when the philosopher has begun to take certain things for granted. It is not the least this particularly austere and at times harsh self-questioning of which one can safely say that it distinguishes as such the intelligent minority, as Strauss calls it, from the intelligentsia. If and in so far as the philosopher is defined by being

---

[9] Leo Strauss, "Persecution and the Art of Writing," *Social Research* 8, no. 1/4 (1941), p. 494; Leo Strauss, "Exoteric Teaching," in Leo Strauss, Thomas L. Pangle ed., *The Rebirth of Classical Political Rationalism. An Introduction to the Thought of Leo Strauss* (Chicago: University of Chicago Press, 1989), pp. 63-71.

[10] Gotthold Ephraim Lessing, "Leibniz von den ewigen Strafen," in Gotthold Ephraim Lessing, *Gesammelte Werke* VII (Berlin: Aufbau, 1956), p. 464. See on this Georges Tamer, *Islamische Philosophie und die Krise der Moderne. Das Verhältnis von Leo Strauss zu Alfarabi, Avicenna und Averroes* (Leiden: Brill, 2001), p. 114.

[11] "A Giving of Accounts. Jacob Klein and Leo Strauss," in Leo Strauss, Kenneth Hart Green ed., *Jewish Philosophy and the Crisis of Modernity. Essays and Lectures in Modern Jewish Thought* (Albany: SUNY Press, 1997), p. 462.

[12] See on this Leo Strauss, "Einleitung zu 'Morgenstunden' und 'An die Freunde Lessings'," in Leo Strauss, Heinrich Meier ed., *Philosophie und Gesetz – Frühe Schriften – Gesammelte Schriften*, vol. 2 (Stuttgart: Metzler, 1997), pp. 528-605; cf. also Strauss's explicit recognition of the "geistigen Freiheit Lessings" for which he could not find any Jewish equivalent at his time, i.e. in the 1930s. See Leo Strauss, "Eine Erinnerung an Lessing," in Strauss, *Philosophie und Gesetz*, p. 608.

[13] Leo Strauss, "Farabi's *Plato*," in *Louis Ginzberg Jubilee Volume* (New York 1945), p. 366.

that person who is able to resist the constant urge to take something for granted, to rely on self-evident truths, Strauss's understanding of the philosopher does not lead to easily digestible self-evident truths. On the contrary, as Strauss notes, what is self-evident (*selbstverständlich*) is always essentially not understood: "Was aber 'selbstverständlich' ist, das ist im Grunde immer *unverstanden*."[14] Precisely because understanding is the calling of the philosopher, he has to search out precisely what is not understood. The task of the philosopher is to understand freely what has been transmitted to us as self-evident. The fact that the philosopher cannot take anything for granted and that he therefore is wary of claims of self-evidence, does not necessarily mean that there are no self-evident things. But as even those things that have been taken to be self-evident by certain people have been questioned by others – thereby implying that they are in fact not self-evident – it is notoriously difficult to start out from indubitably self-evident claims.

It is, first and foremost, the concern of Strauss to educate those who are capable of doubting their own principles in a principled way. The defense of the philosophical way of life that I take to be of the utmost concern for Strauss has to be understood with an important proviso: the defense of a certain thing or cause or way of life is secondary to internal justification of it as it appears to the philosophers. The philosopher needs to confront the question "Why philosophy?," but he needs to do so in a way that does not exclude maintaining a self-critical stance. A most revealing passage in this respect can be found in "On a New Interpretation of Plato's Political Philosophy," a highly puzzling text, as witnessed by Löwith's uncomprehending reaction to it in the correspondence.[15] Strauss here explains:

> Defensibility is not truth. The world abounds with defensible positions that are irreconcilable with one another. To limit oneself to the defense of a position means to claim the advantages of prescription; but one cannot enjoy those advantages without exposing oneself to the reasonable suspicion that one is defending a vested interest of some kind or another which does not bear being looked into by an impartial third. To claim the advantages of prescription is particularly unbecoming for the adherents of the modern principles – principles that are inseparable from the demand for the liberation of one's mind from all prejudices. The very resolution to defend a position may be said to entail the loss of a most important freedom, a freedom the exercise of which was responsible for the success of the modern venture: defenders cannot afford radically to doubt. Adherents of the modern principles who lack the ability to take a critical distance from the modern principles, to look at those principles not from their habitual point of view but from the point of view of their opponents, have already admitted defeat: they show by their action that theirs is a dogmatic adherence to an established position.[16]

---

[14]   Strauss, "Religiöse Lage der Gegenwart," p. 390; cf. p. 389 on what follows.

[15]   See letter from Karl Löwith to Leo Strauss from August 14, 1946, in Strauss, *Hobbes politische Wissenschaft*, p. 659.

[16]   Leo Strauss, "On a New Interpretation of Plato's Political Philosophy," *Social Research* 12, no. 1/4 (1945), p. 327.

Strauss here sums up in a nutshell many of his radical Socratic tenets, especially the view that every position that can be construed as primarily a defense (of the West, of revelation, of Leo Strauss, of X) is as such a non-philosophical position. For the defense of something always entails an interest that may prevent the act of questioning to be as radical as necessary, including even the questioning of the presuppositions of one's own cherished predilections.[17] To defend Leo Strauss in this sense can therefore not be the philosophically appropriate approach (though it may well be in order politically) – and for this reason one should keep in mind the well-known Socratic warning: "I would ask you to be thinking of the truth and not of Socrates" (*Phaedo* 91c). But as almost everybody will also be aware of, to care for the truth about philosophy necessitates reflection on the problem of Socrates that is encapsulated in the fate of Socrates.[18]

This attitude of being willing to doubt in a more radical way than the methodical Descartes managed to doubt, can be irritating and may appear to be fruitless and pointless. Especially from the point of view of those critical of philosophy, equating philosophy's radical questioning and open-ended orientation towards the truth, this kind of doubt may very well appear identical with or similar to, i.e., in any case very close to, nihilism. The "most important freedom" to doubt can turn into the *belief* that this freedom to doubt can now be taken for granted. This, however, is precisely what Strauss suggests we should not accept. In fact, taking anything in philosophy for granted may well lead to an ossification of even the most radical principles of modern philosophy, such as Descartes' *cogito*.[19] Strauss pursues a most radical understanding of philosophy in so far as he urges us not so much to defend as to understand the true nature of philosophy, for, as he says, "defenders cannot afford radically to doubt." Strauss's conception of philosophy is meant to provide for exactly this possibility: To preserve an awareness of the ever to be renewed necessity not to stop thinking which, to all intents and purposes, is identical with asking questions. These questions always already include, or imply, the crucial question, "Why philosophy?," which cannot be answered without giving an answer to the question, "What is philosophy?," *ti estin he philosophia*? The answer to this question hints at the core of Strauss's philosophical concerns, for it is this question which animates even much of the young and younger Strauss, even before he explicitly developed his later famous notion of political philosophy after he had moved, as some would have it, from being the pre-Straussian Strauss to being *the* Leo Strauss. A most fascinating reflection on

---

[17] Cf. Thomas L. Pangle, *Leo Strauss. An Introduction to His Thought and Intellectual Legacy* (Baltimore: Johns Hopkins University Press, 2006), pp. 44-45, 125.

[18] Cf. Allan Bloom, *The Closing of the American Mind* (New York: Touchstone, 1988), pp. 310, 382.

[19] Cf. Gerhard Krüger, "Die Herkunft des philosophischen Selbstbewußtseins," in Gerhard Krüger, *Freiheit und Weltverwaltung. Aufsätze zur Philosophie der Geschichte* (Freiburg/München: Alber, 1958), pp. 11-69.

the importance of Socratic questioning – showing Leo Strauss's full awareness of the radical conclusions to which Socratic philosophizing was bound to lead – can be found in "Cohen und Maimuni" (1931), which, unfortunately, has not yet been translated into English and therefore remains outside the purview of many readers of Strauss in the English-speaking world.[20] "Socratic philosophizing means: questioning." However, in order to truly ask a question, one must seriously be interested in finding or receiving an answer – absent this the practice of asking questions would be nothing but an empty game any half-intelligent and obnoxious youth can come up with. For Strauss, at this point in time, Socrates' claim to know nothing cannot be taken at face value, for it is evident that Socrates knew many things. The big question is: how can Socrates maintain that he knows nothing even though he knows certain things? How can he still maintain his questioning (*in der Frage bleiben*) (p. 411)? Strauss argues that Socrates wants to maintain his questioning attitude, because it is essential for a humanly lived life to ask questions. However, one may very well ask all kinds of questions, most of them clearly trivial and meaningless, as Strauss asserts when he laconically remarks: "Fraglich ist vielerlei." (p. 411) – that is to say that many things can be regarded as questionable, regardless of their intrinsic importance. The philosophical point of view, however, is that this questioning cannot be a questioning just about anything, as was also, at the same time, intimated by Strauss's contemporary Gerhard Krüger.[21] It has to be a questioning concerning the most important and weighty matters. This cannot be the question concerning what is below the earth or above the skies, but only the question concerning how one should live, what the right way of life is. Strauss has thus reached a point in his argument where he needs to intimate some answer to the question of what the right way of life is.

In conclusion it seems proper to return to one of Leo Strauss's shortest but at the same time also most revealing and relevant texts, especially his review of Julius Ebbinghaus, but also a highly important footnote in *Philosophie und Gesetz*.[22] Taking up Plato's allegory in the *Republic*, Strauss there famously talks about the so-called second cave in which we have fallen not so much because of the tradition, he says, but because of the tradition of polemics against the tradition. This second cave of which Strauss speaks in the 1930s thus constitutes our modern

---

[20] Leo Strauss, "Cohen und Maimuni," in Strauss, *Philosophie und Gesetz*, pp. 393-436.

[21] See Gerhard Krüger, *Philosophie und Moral in der Kantischen Kritik* (Tübingen: J. C. B. Mohr, 1931). Krüger ends his book on the following note, thus in some way pointing out the path Strauss would take in the direction of unconditional philosophical questioning: "Wirklich unbedingt aber wird die Frage nur sein, wenn sie, *im Wissen um die geschichtliche Leidenschaft, das Gute erfragt. Die Antwort* auf diese Frage – und so auch die christliche Antwort Augustins – sei dahingestellt. Daß die entscheidende Frage *wahr* bleibt, auch wenn sie *keine* Antwort findet, kann den, der so fragt, das Beispiel des *Sokrates* lehren" (p. 236).

[22] Leo Strauss, "Besprechung von Julius Ebbinghaus, Über die Fortschritte der Metaphysik," in Strauss, *Philosophie und Gesetz*, pp. 437-439; *Philosophie und Gesetz*, in ibid., pp. 13-14 n. 2.

predicament. It illustrates our situation which is not so much a natural situation as an unnatural situation.[23] This situation is paradoxical, for it necessitates the use of unnatural means in order to retrieve something of the natural horizon that constitutes the starting point for philosophy as originally understood. This cave is thus, in Strauss's view, a pit beneath the pit, from which we can only ascend by means of "lesendes Lernen," learning by reading. Strauss explicitly states that philosophy as such must not necessarily change, though "the way in which the introduction to philosophy must proceed" has to change "with the change of the artificial or accidental obstacles to philosophy." In our time, Strauss then suggests, these obstacles have to be removed by a special kind of hermeneutics:

> The artificial obstacles may be so strong at a given time that a most elaborate "artificial" introduction has to be completed before the "natural" introduction can begin. It is conceivable that a particular pseudo-philosophy may emerge whose power cannot be broken but by the most intensive reading of old books. As long as that pseudo-philosophy rules, elaborate historical studies may be needed which would have been superfluous and therefore harmful in more fortunate times.[24]

This all-important essence of Strauss's conceit – learning by reading – shows clearly that Strauss could not have regarded himself as just a scholar. For the mere scholar would not only not want to get out of the second, not to mention the first, cave. He would also not be able to see the second cave *as* a cave.

Whichever way we look at the problem of Leo Strauss and the issues that are entailed by it – we need to read him in order to understand him – and in order to read him we need to make up our minds about the issues of reading that are tied up with political philosophy. Strauss's art of reading rejects in the most principled manner possible the suggestion that it is impossible to understand an author as he understood himself. This is why his approach differs decisively from those offered by the likes of Kant, Dilthey or Heidegger who raise the possibility of understanding the authors better than they understood themselves.[25] If one does not

---

[23] Strauss's understanding of our situation in the image of the second cave has profound implications for our understanding of the state of "cultural studies." Cf. Till Kinzel, *Platonische Kulturkritik in Amerika. Studien zu Allan Blooms "The Closing of the American Mind"* (Berlin: Duncker & Humblot, 2002), pp. 195-210.

[24] Leo Strauss, *Persecution and the Art of Writing* (Chicago: The University of Chicago Press, 1952), p. 155. The difficulties to overcome the 'artificial' obstacles that Strauss mentions should not be underestimated. There are however ways in which, e.g. in fields like literary studies, Strauss's hermeneutics could serve as a stepping stone to philosophy as originally understood. Cf. Lawrance Thompson, "Review of *Persecution and the Art of Writing*," *Modern Philology* 51, no. 3 (February 1954), pp. 208-210.

[25] See, e.g., Kant, *Kritik der reinen Vernunft*, B 370; Wilhelm Dilthey, *Der Aufbau der geschichtlichen Welt in den Geisteswissenschaften* (Frankfurt/M.: Suhrkamp, 1997), p. 268 (referring to Schleiermacher's "daring sentence," e.g., to be found in Friedrich Schleiermacher, "Die Allgemeine Hermeneutik," E 12, in *Ermeneutica*, Milan: Bompiani, 2000, p. 198, where he says that the aim of hermeneutics consists of understanding in the highest sense which in-

accept the principle that one can understand a thinker as he understood himself, there is no way to escape the "lazy interpretative subjectivism" of which Klaus Oehler speaks in this context.[26] We need to think about the art of writing and reading that is the corollary of Strauss's analysis of the two related questions "Why philosophy?" and "What is political philosophy?"[27] It is impossible to understand what Strauss's recovery of the art of writing and reading implies[28] if one does not confront the question "why political philosophy?." This question is the more abstract but nevertheless always concrete form in which the problem of Socrates reappears after philosophy had been invented.

Seth Benardete well understood how much the seemingly merely hermeneutical question of the right kind of reading has to do with what philosophy is. He attributes to Strauss the view that "what philosophy is seems to be inseparable from the question of how to read Plato."[29] Both questions – what philosophy is and how to read Plato – are tied to each other by what makes philosophy possible and what makes people want to read Plato in the first place – philosophical eros.[30] Benardete also has another sentence that perfectly links Strauss's to Plato's Socratism in their shared conviction that one needs to start and re-start again so as "to begin at the beginning in the interpretation of Platonic dialogues." To begin at

---

cludes understanding the writer better than he understood himself); see also *Martin Heidegger, Die Grundprobleme der Phänomenologie* (Frankfurt/M.: Klostermann, 1989), p. 157.

[26] Oehler, *Blicke aus dem Philosophenturm*, p. 187. Oehler also points to the similarities between Strauss's hermeneutics and those of Rudolf Bultmann with which Strauss became acquainted in the 1920s, according to Oehler.

[27] Pace Eugene Sheppard, *Leo Strauss and the Politics of Exile* (Waltham: Brandeis University Press, 2006), p. 5. Sheppard attempts to provide a historical explanation for the art of writing instead of a philosophical rationale and thus regards Strauss's notions of esotericism as "perhaps the major pillar" of his thought which, of course, it is not. Cf. Leo Strauss, "On a Forgotten Kind of Writing," in Leo Strauss, *What Is Political Philosophy? and Other Studies* (Chicago: University of Chicago Press, 1988), p. 227.

[28] Cf. Arthur Melzer, "On the Pedagogical Motive for Esoteric Writing," *The Journal of Politics* 69, no. 4 (November 2007), pp. 1015-1031; cf. Leo Strauss, "The Spirit of Sparta or The Taste of Xenophon," *Social Research* 6 no. 1/4 (1939), p. 535. Strauss here points to the fact, later taken up in a remarkable way in his article criticizing John Wild's new interpretation of Plato, that "the classical authors became the most efficient teachers of independent thinking."

[29] Seth Benardete, "Leo Strauss on Plato," in Seth Benardete, *The Argument of the Action. Essays on Greek Poetry and Philosophy* (Chicago: University of Chicago Press, 2000), p. 407.

[30] See Strauss, *What Is Political Philosophy?*, p. 40, where Strauss refers to the fact that philosophy, despite its seeming ugliness or Sisyphean character, "is necessarily accompanied, sustained and elevated by *eros*." Cf. his remark elsewhere that "philosophizing is surrender to the truth without concern for one's dignity and without concern for even the noble, since the truth is not simply noble or beautiful but in a certain sense ugly." See Leo Strauss, Seth Benardete ed., *On Plato's "Symposium"* (Chicago: University of Chicago Press, 2001), p. 93.

the beginning is just another way of saying that one should not take anything for granted when it comes to philosophy. Benardete continues:

> Only if one comes to them [i.e. the Platonic dialogues] with the innocence of a naïve zoologist does one come sufficiently prepared. This innocence is the interpretative equivalent of Socratic ignorance.[31]

This sentence contains within itself a Strauss-like paradox. It may not be wholly superfluous to remind ourselves of the fact that Socratic ignorance was not only connected to self-knowledge but also to irony. This form of Socratic ignorance may also be the proper way to begin at the beginning when studying Strauss. Not assuming that one already knows what is what, this kind of learning by reading may well turn into what Strauss surely thought it was – a philosophical activity that points to the fact that philosophy is not philosophy if it is not understood as a way of life. In his article on *Persecution and the Art of Writing*, Strauss quotes from William Blackstone's *Commentaries on the Laws of England*. Blackstone here puts forth the notion, in the context of high treason to be sure, that writing is a form of action (*scribere est agere*).[32] Before writing, however, comes reading, and in the present circumstances it is first and foremost the art of reading which Leo Strauss practiced that has to be our concern. To be concerned about reading in this sense is a necessary corollary of one's passion for philosophy. Studying the art of writing is an exercise in attachment to detachment from the here and now in order to philosophize in the here and now, maybe even to become a philosopher. The task of philosophical education for the 21st century may thus well be to teach especially students the art of reading. Reading is a form of action in behalf of philosophy: *Legere est agere*.[33]

---

[31]   Seth Benardete, "Leo Strauss' *The City and Man*," in *The Political Science Reviewer* 8 (1978), p. 6.

[32]   William Blackstone, *Commentaries on the Laws of England: A Facsimile of the First Edition of 1765-1769*. (Chicago: University of Chicago Press, 1979). Quoted in *The Founders' Constitution*, Philip B. Kurland and Ralph Lerner eds., Volume 4, Article 3, Section 3, Clauses 1 and 2, Document 8, http://press-pubs.uchicago.edu/founders/documents/a3_3_1-2s8.html, The University of Chicago Press (last accessed 30 September 2009).

[33]   Cf. Leo Strauss, "Persecution and the Art of Writing," p. 488, with Leo Strauss, *Persecution and the Art of Writing*, p. 144: "It is a general observation that people write as they read. As a rule, careful writers are careful readers and *vice versa*. A careful writer wants to be read carefully." In light of the reference to William Blackstone in Strauss's article from 1941, Strauss's decision to put pen to paper concerning writing and reading between the lines would seem to indicate that he was fully aware of the fact that he was *doing* something, that he was acting on behalf of philosophy.

Laurence Lampert

LEO STRAUSS'S GYNAIKOLOGIA

Readers drawn to Leo Strauss have good reason to pay close attention to two books that by themselves might seem to have little to recommend them, as distant as they seem from the customary issues of intellectual life today (they are commentaries on Xenophon), and as superficial as they at first seem (they appear more like mere paraphrase than anything else Strauss wrote). But Strauss said in a letter to Gershom Scholem a year before he died that "my two books on Xenophon's Socrates… are not the last thing I have written, but I believe they are the best" (Strauss 2001, 764-765). Within his best two books, in his Preface to the second, *Xenophon's Socrates*, Strauss singled out the first, *Xenophon's Socratic Discourse*, as the more important: he wrote and published his interpretation of the *Oeconomicus* first, he said, "because that work is, it seems to me, the most revealing and at the same time the most misunderstood of Xenophon's Socratic writings."

Xenophon narrates his *Oeconomicus* after uttering a single sentence of his own, its first: "I once heard him discourse on the management of the household as well, in about these words." After that he relates only the words of Socrates or Kritoboulos except for "Socrates said," "Kritoboulos said," and the like. Xenophon's sole sentence implies his presence in the audience for the conversation he narrates. As for his own audience, initially it is anyone who can read, but it narrows to those who can stay interested in a book so many have judged tedious and trite; ultimately it narrows to the fewest who come to see that it has hidden marvels addressed just to them. Strauss too mastered this art of audience selection in his best books; they are masterpieces of the art of appearing less great than they are.

Within the conversation Xenophon narrates between Socrates and Kritoboulos on gentlemanship, Socrates narrates a conversation he held at an earlier time with Ischomachos after asking Kritoboulos if he wanted to hear "from the beginning how I once came together with a man who seemed to me really to be one of those men to whom the name of gentleman is justly applied?" (6.12). Socrates' narration occupies the second two-thirds of the *Oeconomicus* (chapters 7-21).

Strauss supplied his own title, *Gynaikologia*, to each of the first four chapters of Socrates' narration, adding to each a number, a different subtitle, and the number of the corresponding chapter in the *Oeconomicus*:

Gynaikologia – I: Marriage according to the gods and according to the law (Chapter VII);

Gynaikologia – II: Order, I (Chapter VIII);

Gynaikologia – III: Order, II (Chapter IX);

Gynaikologia – IV: Cosmetics (Chapter X).

Strauss's book, like Xenophon's, has twenty-one chapters. Its chapter headings prominently display the number of Xenophon's chapter but leave his own unnumbered. Strauss gave a reason for saying that the *Oeconomicus* was Xenophon's most revealing work: "in its central chapter Socrates is directly contrasted with a perfect gentleman." In his own book Strauss moved Xenophon's central chapter, the eleventh, slightly off center, making Xenophon's central chapter follow his own central chapter, his eleventh, the final chapter of his *Gynaikologia*. Can this little shift be significant? Emerging from a study of Strauss's *Gynaikologia* is a recognition that he lavished special care on centers – of individual chapters, of the *Gynaikologia*, and of his whole book. These centers show that Strauss mastered a technique he had long appreciated in classical authors, the literary art of centering, a silent way of highlighting what matters most. It is a laconic art of so controlling the flow and pace of an argument that it attains its greatest insights at peak, central moments, pausing at the peak to gather and share what the flowing commentary has made almost available. There is grandeur in this art of centering that is anything but mechanical; it depends as much on the willingness of the reader to grant his author the role of instructor as it depends on the grace of the author to give his reader access to what he has learned. The density and precision of these moments at the center are, it seems to me, the best measure and most pleasing reward of Strauss's philanthropy, his chosen way of giving what he has been granted.

Gynaikologia – I: Marriage According to the Gods and Law

Strauss prepares to discuss Socrates' narration of his conversation with Ischomachos by saying that it brings "to light and life a unique event of his past," his once and for all "discovery of what perfect gentlemanship is" (129). (The phrase *perfect gentleman*, Strauss explained, is "the ordinary English translation of a Greek expression which more literally translated means 'a man who is noble [beautiful, fair, fine] and good'" [128].) Strauss's *Gynaikologia* treats the first four chapters of Socrates' narration of that unique event which occurred at a much earlier time than his conversation with Kritoboulos.

The first subject of the first chapter of the *Gynaikologia* is Ischomachos's "management" of his wife, his education of her. The first stages of his educating her strongly excited Socrates' curiosity: "on no other occasion does Socrates in the *Oeconomicus* express his eagerness to learn in such strong terms" (132). A "comparison" dominates Strauss's account of the first chapter, Ischomachos's comparison of his wife's position in the household to that of the queen bee in a beehive. Strauss measures how that comparison is apt and inapt.

Ischomachos made his comparison of the queen bee at the very start of what Strauss calls his "lecture" to his wife (137), his very first lesson following his very first questioning of his young wife on why she thinks he chose her. Responding to her question of what she might do "to help in increasing the household," Ischomachos says, "By Zeus ... just try to do in the best manner possible what the gods have brought you forth to be capable of and what the law praises." "And what are these things," she asks (7.16-17). They are works comparable to the works that "the leading bee of the hive has charge of," he answers first, launching into a long, uninterrupted lesson for her on what marriage is according to the gods and according to the law. He ends recalling his opening comparison: "And it seems to me ... that the leader of the bees also toils in this way to accomplish the works that the god has ordered her to do" (7.32). Only then does his wife speak again: "'In what way ... are the works of the leader of the bees similar to the works I must do?" Their following dialogue shows why Strauss gave a warning when Ischomachos first introduced his comparison: it "is obviously liable to misunderstanding and even to misuse" (135). Strauss focuses on that liability in the final paragraph of his chapter.

Strauss reports Ischomachos's reply that "the wife can be compared to the queen bee since both control even the outdoor work of the members of the community while they themselves always stay indoors" (138). He notes that Ischomachos emphasized that "the queen bee does not suffer the bees to be idle" but was silent on the drones. Having noted that inaptness, Strauss says that "Ischomachos' comparison of the two kinds of females is apt in many points, although not all of them are immediately convincing to his bride" – could they *become* convincing in ways she can't anticipate? Strauss intimates his affirmative answer by concluding his chapter with three ascendingly significant ways in which its aptness may have seemed questionable to her.

"For instance," the queen bee's control of the upbringing of the progeny: "when the young ones are fit to work, she sends them out under a leader to found a colony." The wife may be led to wonder whether she is to send out her children "to found a colony under a leader other than herself (or her husband)."

"Furthermore," the comparison leaves it unclear whether Ischomachos believes that the queen bee takes care of the sick bees as the good wife takes care of the sick servants. But when his wife speaks of taking care of the sick as most rewarding because "it makes the servants grateful and enhances their good will," he returns "to the image of the queen bee" to say that the bees become so attached to the queen bee who takes care of them that "when she leaves the hive, none thinks of staying behind, but all follow her." Strauss wonders "whether in the case of divorce all servants will leave together with the wife" (139).

"Above all," the comparison of the wife with the queen bee "suffers from the fact that it does not provide a proper place for the husband and master." Strauss notes that "Ischomachos saves the comparison as well as he can by surreptitiously admitting that his wife is indeed the ruler of the maidservants rather than of the menservants" but what Strauss notes last is most telling, for Ischomachos states "powerfully and movingly that if she proves manifestly superior to him, she will be the mistress of him who is the direct ruler of the menservants, even and especially after she has ceased to be young and of youthful bloom." The first lesson Ischomachos's wife ever learns from her husband begins and ends with a most memorable comparison. Introduced to "counteract his wife's extreme modesty and diffidence," "to reassure her," Ischomachos's queen bee comparison may, on that unforgettable occasion, have planted a seed of possible supremacy in a potential queen.

Study of all four chapters of the *Gynaikologia* allows these possible inaptnesses of the queen bee comparison to display their full aptness because such study explains something Strauss is bent on emphasizing about Socrates in the *Gynaikologia*: so far from being a perfect gentleman or wanting to be, Socrates is womanly. In application to Socrates, comparisons that at first seem open and homely come to sight as harboring a hidden and exalted sense.

Gynaikologia – II: Order I

"Order I," the first of two chapters on order, concerns "the usefulness and beauty of order for human beings" (140-1); the second, "Order II," "concerns…the order itself" (146). The two chapters are also linked by the way they begin: "Both chapters open with a question of Socrates concerning the effect of Ischomachos' teaching on his wife" (146). Socrates' question is his sole speech in the first of the chapters: "Did you notice, Ischomachos … that she was stirred to diligence by these things?" "Yes, by Zeus," says Ischomachos, moving at once to another subject of his instruction, a "lecture" occupying the rest of the chapter, a lecture he was careful to give under the most favorable circumstances, for she had just failed him: being unable to find something in her sphere that he wanted, "she blushed deeply, she was annoyed with herself" (140). Ashamed and condemning herself, she will not let it happen again after hearing her husband's lectures on order.

His lecture conveys the usefulness and beauty of order through "examples," three at first, chorus, army, and trireme. Strauss shows each to be both apt and inapt. Part of their inaptness stems from their being in motion whereas order as understood by Ischomachos "belongs to rest rather than motion;" in addition, they contribute to disorder. Despite the partial inaptness of his examples Ischomachos "turns to admonishing his wife to join him in putting all their belongings into their proper place so that they will be always available for use" (141).

"Ischomachos is not quite satisfied with the three examples" and gives a fourth and last example that Strauss calls "most apt" (142) and "most revealing" (144). It is most apt because "Ischomachos is concerned with instructing his wife in how to establish and keep order among their implements and utensils" and this example is the order of utensils on a great Phoenician merchantman. Ischomachos addressed this example, by name, to Socrates; it "is to instruct, to educate even Socrates" (142). On the Phoenician merchantman, "the very survival of everyone on board depended on ... the most beautiful and most accurate order." This demanded "the utmost care, especially on the part of the man in charge." That man, the boatswain, a petty officer on a merchant ship, "already possessed perfect knowledge of where everything was placed and how much there was of it." Despite having that knowledge, he was observed by Ischomachos "inspecting everything as to its being handy in every situation that might arise." "Wondering at this examination" (8.15), Ischomachos tells Socrates, he "asked him what he was doing." Strauss summarizes what Ischomachos reported as the direct speech of the knowing and inspecting man in charge responsible for the survival of everyone on board: he "told him that there is no time to search for the needed things when the god raises a storm at sea, for the god threatens and punishes the slack; one must be satisfied when the god does not destroy those who do no wrong; when he saves those who do service very well, one must be grateful to the gods." The boatswain's view of how gods act distinguishes three kinds of humans, the slack, those who do no wrong, and those who do service well. His view of the gods' actions prompts him to intense watchfulness over the order established on board ship. Ischomachos "finds no fault" with the boatswain's view and Socrates "is silent throughout the chapter." Strauss himself speaks up to contrast the boatswain's view with Ischomachos's: "the boatswain is more certain than Ischomachos about the gods punishing (and therefore noticing) the slack." Strauss can compare the two views because he had, in the previous chapter, reported Ischomachos's view of the gods' noticing and punishing: "if a man acts against the divine or natural order ... his disorderly conduct is perhaps noticed by the gods and he is punished for it" (137). On that occasion Strauss spoke up for a silent Socrates to say "Ischomachos is less certain of the gods' omniscience than is Socrates." Strauss can know Socrates' certainty because Xenophon said in the *Memorabilia* that "Socrates believed that the gods know everything, what is said, what is done, and what is silently deliberated" (1.1.19). Strauss leaves it to his reader to figure out just how Socrates' certainty in the *Memorabilia* is related to his silence in the *Oeconomicus*.

Strauss adds to his statement that the boatswain is more certain than Ischomachos about the gods punishing the slack: "he is as doubtful as Ischomachos about evil befalling only the bad, i.e., about whether one can speak in strict parlance of divine punishment" (143). He then turns to the implications of the most apt example for the issue of order. "In the boatswain's statement, and hence in the whole chapter, order is not presented as in any way rooted in something divine; it is presented rather as being altogether of human origin; the gods are mentioned only as disturbers of order." In this first of two chapters on order, Strauss ends his paragraph on the boatswain's view of the gods and order: "One could say that order is presented here as devised against the unpredictable actions of the gods."

These reflections on the gods noticing and punishing and on the gods and the origins of order – reflections on the theology and ontology implicit in Ischoma-chos's most apt example of order – fall in the central paragraph of the second chapter of the *Gynaikologia*. Strauss's reflections on Ischomachos's implicit view of the gods and origins fell in the central paragraph of the first chapter of his *Gynaikologia*. There, he noted that Ischomachos urged his wife "to do as well as she can what the gods enabled her to do by bringing her forth, and what in ad-dition the law praises" (135). And he noted that "Ischomachos does not ascribe divine origin to the law." Then, based on Ischomachos's statement about the gods bringing forth his wife (*ephusan*, from *phusis*, nature), he generalized: "What the gods have generated, what owes its being to the gods, is 'nature' as distinguished in particular from law." In the present central paragraph, stating the boatswain's view of the gods and order, Strauss generalized the boatswain's view of the mer-chantman, the sea, and the god raising the storm, saying that order is presented as wholly of human origin, as not in any way rooted in something divine, and as devised against the unpredictable actions of the gods. Order in Ischomachos's view as refined by the most apt example, is of wholly human origin and nature, in constant motion, is subject to disorder potentially destructive to all human devising. Setting out these views in these two central paragraphs Strauss waits till the central paragraph of the third chapter of his *Gynaikologia* to contrast them with Socrates' "teaching" (147-149). He thus spreads across the three centers of his *Gynaikologia* chapters the exalted themes of gods, nature, order, and human action. Only in the third will he complete his treatment and intimate the ends Socrates' teaching serves.

But as to centers, paragraph four of the second chapter on the *Gynaikologia* occupies a special place: following the central paragraph of the chapter which invoked the central paragraph of the previous chapter and prepared the central paragraph of the next chapter, it is itself a central paragraph, the eleventh of the twenty-one paragraphs of the *Gynaikologia*. What could *it* center after a center that had such profound implications for the questions of gods, nature, order and human action?

Paragraph four interrupts Strauss's commentary on Ischomachos's lecture be-cause Ischomachos's most apt example reminds him of something Socrates said about Cyrus while making his case for farming with Kritoboulos. "Ischomachos' story of the Phoenician merchantman and its boatswain reminds us of Socrates' story of Cyrus and his pleasure garden." The central paragraph of the *Gynaikologia* contrasts two competing stories of order, the perfect gentleman's and the philosopher's: it does what Strauss said Xenophon's central chapter in the *Oeconomicus* did: "in its central chapter Socrates is directly contrasted with a perfect gentleman," a contrast that is "the most revealing" matter in the most revealing of Xenophon's Socratic writings (Strauss 1972, "Preface"). What does Strauss's contrast reveal? It consists of five different contrasts. After stating them Strauss separates Socrates from Ischomachos's teacher while linking Socrates to both Ischomachos and Cyrus: "Socrates has, so to speak, nothing in common with the Phoenician boatswain, whereas he has very much to do with Ischomachos, the model gentleman, and with Cyrus, the model ruler." The absoluteness of "nothing in common" calls attention to the vagueness of "has very much to do with" – what does the latter mean? The next sentence, one of two to close the paragraph on imperatives, suggests the answer: "We must therefore wonder whether in his view Ischomachos or Cyrus occupies the higher rank." To be told to wonder how Socrates ranked the two is to be told to wonder just how Socrates has very much to do with each as model: is either *his* model? Strauss said that Socrates has no intention of becoming a perfect gentleman: he does not take a gentleman as his model. Does he take a ruler as his model? Strauss ends his paragraph on a second imperative: "We must leave it open whether the contrasts just pointed out are of any use for settling this issue." If we don't want to leave it open, if we wonder how Strauss's five contrasts may be of use in settling this issue of Socrates' model, we can learn that they settle entirely just how Socrates has very much to do with Cyrus as model ruler.

First contrast, the ordered thing: a pleasure garden; a merchantman.

Second contrast, the orderer: "a man who is almost a king;" "a nameless boatswain," a "man in charge" (142) taken as a model orderer by the perfect gentleman.

Third contrast, order and adornment: This central contrast seems at first to consist of a single sentence: "In the Persian story the order belongs together with Cyrus' resplendent adornments of all kinds; in the Phoenician story the splendor is altogether replaced by utility." This contrast mixes order, adornment, and utility. *Order* is a pleasure garden and a merchantman. *Adornments* are "resplendent ... of all kinds" and splendor altogether replaced. *Utility* altogether replaces splendor on the merchantman – and in the pleasure garden? That the order of adornments in the pleasure garden also has a utility seems to be implied by saying that splendor is "*altogether* replaced" by utility on the merchantman. Just how adornment and utility belong together in the order of the pleasure garden seems to be the issue Strauss addresses in his supplement to the central contrast, for he adorned this contrast with the central footnote of his chapter – and a central footnote to a central contrast of the central paragraph of the *Gynaikologia* promises to be both revelatory and dense. It consists of two sentences telling the reader three things to do: "Cf. Socrates' identification of the beautiful or noble with the good in *Mem*. III.8.5-7; cf. *Mem*. IV.6.8-9. Cf. Plato, *Republic* 458e4." We are to compare the mix of order, adornment, and utility with two passages that add an element to the mix: the *good*. And we are to consult Plato.

What does Socrates' identification of the beautiful or noble (two translations of *kalos*) with the good in the first *Memorabilia* passage mean? When Strauss commented on this passage in his later Xenophon book, he called the identification a "paradoxical thesis" and gave the reason Socrates stated it: it "stems from the attempt to reject the excess of the noble over the good as irrational" (Strauss 1972, 76, see 73-76). Socrates stated a paradoxical thesis about the good because his interlocutor attempted to reject as irrational any aspect of the noble that exceeded the good as he understood it. His interlocutor was a philosopher, Aristippos, and Strauss suggests that Socrates' conversation with him can be read as substituting for a conversation with Plato (Strauss 1972, 73-74). Socrates conversed earlier with Aristippos in the *Memorabilia* (II.1), attempting unsuccessfully to persuade him to take political life seriously. Aristippos, a philosopher holding the good to be pleasure, stuck to his view that that meant living as easily and pleasantly as possible. To reject the excess of the noble over the good as irrational is one piece of Aristippos' failure to take political life seriously, for political life depends upon an excess of the noble over the good construed as pleasure. Socrates would not have failed to persuade Plato to take political life seriously and to embrace the paradoxical identification of the noble and the good (Strauss 1972, 32-39; see Strauss 1963, 92-102). Socrates, teacher of young aspirants to perfect gentlemanship while not himself a gentleman, and counselor of philosophers on the seriousness of political life, argues for a view of the good that has a utility for political life as ordered by the gentlemen. Arguing for that view has a utility for Socrates too, he whose "story" can tell of a ruler in a pleasure garden with resplendent adornments of all kinds: Socrates takes political life so seriously as to go to the trouble of adorning himself with a paradoxical thesis about the good that ranks the life of the gentleman highest by granting it its irrational excess of the noble over the good; it is a good for him, a rational man, to grant that irrational excess.

When Strauss discussed the second passage of the *Memorabilia* referred to in his footnote (IV.6.8-9; Strauss 1972, 119-120), he referred back to the first passage in order to show how Socrates' shifting usage regarding beautiful and good indicates the limited purpose of each exchange: each serves Socrates' purpose of educating his interlocutor while both together can educate companions who heard both or who read both in Xenophon.

And the Plato passage Strauss's footnote told one to consult? In commenting on the footnote's first *Memorabilia* passage Strauss did what he told the reader of his footnote to do, compare Plato, *Republic* 458e4. It shows the relation between utility and the sacred: "in a properly constituted city only the most useful marriages are the holy ones" (Strauss 1972, 76). Plato indicates that the sacred can be useful to a philosopher as a resplendent adornment useful to the city.

The central footnote therefore suggests the following interpretation of the central contrast of the central paragraph. Utility for Socrates the philosopher dictated that his good – enjoyment of the pleasure garden of indulging the unquenchable passion of inquiry into the order of the beings – be protected by resplendent adornments that include taking political life so seriously as to trouble himself to identify the noble with the good and to bring in the sacred to secure the way of life of the gentleman by persuasive arguments. The central contrast will prove itself central in a literal way too: it must be supplemented by the second half of the *Gynaikologia*: the center of the next chapter will present the kind of resplendent adornment that completes the previous chapter-centers by supplying a new teaching on the gods, nature, order, and human action, and the final chapter completes the argument by showing what such adornment is: "cosmetics." The central contrast does not leave it open: in Socrates' view the model ruler occupies the higher rank and Socrates will, in an exalted sense, model his own behavior on that of the model ruler.

Fourth contrast, closeness to the original. Ischomachos actually saw the order in his story and heard the orderer whereas Socrates neither saw nor heard but got his story through intermediaries. Therefore, "one could say that ... Socrates is closer to the original" of the Phoenician story which he got directly from Ischomachos than to the original of his own. To question Socrates' closeness to the original of his own story is to invite the question, who is *its* original? The answer: *Xenophon*. Xenophon saw Cyrus's pleasure garden, he heard Cyrus speak, and he wrote what he saw and heard in an adventure story bound to make him famous, his *Anabasis of Cyrus*. And he wrote the book showing how Cyrus the Great could be considered a model ruler, his *Cyropaedeia*. And he wrote the book containing "Socrates' story" and every other story of the *Oeconomicus*. Why would Strauss draw a contrast that points, yet merely points, to Xenophon as the actual original for "Socrates' story"?

In his commentary on "Socrates' story" Strauss had indicated Xenophon's role by highlighting the compulsions on a story-teller to make his story persuasive (116-118). Aiming to persuade Kritoboulos of the nobility of farming by giving him a model to imitate, Socrates began with what "people say" of the great Persian king: that he believed farming and the art of war belong to the most noble and necessary pursuits and that he devoted himself to both. Socrates had "to prove the truth of the rumor" and did so first by an argument whose adequacy Strauss wondered about. Other items about "Cyrus, the most famous king," took Socrates to a story that "would convince Kritoboulos fully that Cyrus – the most glorious of all the Persian kings" was as proud of his farming as of his being a warrior "if he could be sure that the story is true." But the hero of that story is not the most famous king: "Socrates is...compelled to speak...of the younger

Cyrus." There's another problem: "Even of the younger Cyrus, Socrates did not have first-hand knowledge." And here Strauss states, "but Xenophon had, and Xenophon, we remember, was present at the conversation between Socrates and Kritoboulos on household management." Not saying directly that Xenophon is the original, Strauss moves to yet another problem. Bringing in the younger Cyrus cannot by itself solve the problem of persuasion because the younger Cyrus had less authority than the Great Cyrus: "Socrates is therefore compelled to improve somewhat on the younger Cyrus' record." Even improving on the record is not enough: "above all, [Socrates was compelled] to conceal as much as possible the fact that the younger Cyrus is not the same individual as the first Cyrus." Strauss then compares the smoothness of the transition from the first Cyrus to the second with Xenophon's transitions from the *Memorabilia* to the *Oeconomicus* and from Thucydides' *History* to the *Hellenica*, transitions whose lack of evident smoothness raise questions. Having thus brought in Xenophon as the one with first-hand knowledge and as an author whose way of writing invites questions, Strauss says, "Besides, many Greeks might have found it difficult that a barbarian should be held up as a model for the Greeks." How was this final difficulty handled? "*Xenophon* was therefore compelled to make his Socrates make the greatest contemporary Greek authority – the Spartan Lysander, the victor in the Peloponnesian War – establish the authority of the younger Cyrus." By allowing Socrates' problem of persuasion to be seen as Xenophon's problem, Strauss allows his reader to see just who was under compulsion in all this story-telling, this improving and concealing and making authoritative for the sake of persuasion: Xenophon, who had first-hand knowledge, was compelled by his purposes in his *Oeconomicus* to make his character, Socrates, say what it was necessary to say to persuade his character, Kritoboulos. Having named the original of Socrates' story, Strauss returns to his customary level of narrative: "Socrates does this by retelling a story...." Xenophon disappears but now as always invisibly present, an author compelled to make his Socrates make the necessary adjustments to persuade his Kritoboulos of the nobility of farming through stories about the model ruler Cyrus. "Socrates" is from now on Xenophon's Socrates outfitted by Xenophon with the appropriate stories, for some of which he is the only possible author.

A notable feature of this particular story makes Xenophon the emphatic original of "Socrates' story." (Strauss does not mention this feature but it is available to any reader of Xenophon and Xenophon has had few readers like Strauss. Even if Strauss did not notice, it fits and reinforces the argument he is making in the fourth contrast.) By having Socrates tell Kritoboulos about an already dead younger Cyrus, Xenophon fixes the dramatic date of their exchange: it must be after September, 401 when Cyrus was killed at Cunaxa. But that fact turns Xenophon's first sentence, his only sentence in his own name, into a puzzle: he could not have been present when Socrates conversed with Kritoboulos between September, 401 and July, 399 when Socrates was executed because he was in Asia Minor where he had gone in March, 401 with the express purpose of observing Cyrus – as he says in his *Anabasis*, the very book in which he relates the details about the death of Cyrus that he assigns to Socrates in his *Oeconomicus*. Present at the death of Cyrus, he uses details to which he was an eye and ear witness to point to his absence from a discourse he opened by seeming to claim he was present. Xenophon must want his reader to suspect that he opened his *Oeconomicus* with a correctable fiction. But why? Perhaps to suggest that he had been present on a different occasion when Socrates discoursed on the management of the household in "*about these words*," slightly different words each time for Socrates' retelling of the unique event through which he discovered what perfect gentlemanship is. Xenophon thereby implies that he was present in such an attentive way that he could know what Socrates would say on similar occasions at which he could not have been present. His first sentence indicates the character of all his sentences: based on Xenophon's authority as eye and ear witness they say what Socrates would say on such an occasion – and what he would say always opens access to something different that he also means, access through informed inference correcting a first impression. Xenophon's "presence," phantom though it be, is inexpungeable from the paradigm Socratic discourse: that discourse must picture a Xenophon present because the discourse that educates the many Kritobouloses to gentlemanship also invites the rare Xenophon into the pleasure garden of philosophy while training him in training gentlemen. Xenophon stakes his claim to Socratic authority on the ease with which he invents Socratic speeches for occasions on which he can only seem to have been present. Xenophon, master of persuasive story-telling, is the original of "Socrates' story" in the emphatic sense that Socrates could not possibly have heard it or told it. But Xenophon's story is no less authoritative, no less Socrates' story, for that.

Xenophon may also play with his impossible presence at the other conversation recorded in the *Oeconomicus*, Socrates' much earlier conversation with Ischomachos. Choosing to set that conversation in the colonnade of Zeus the Deliverer, Xenophon set it in a colonnade that came to feature, Pausanias reports, a painting of the Athenian cavalry in support of the Spartans at the battle of Mantineia in 362; the most notable figure among the Athenians in that painting is Grylos, son of Xenophon (Pausanias, 1.3.3-4). That battle is the final event Xenophon described in his *Hellenica* (7.5.15-27); he made it a valedictory for the great Theban leader who fell there, Epaminondas, while making no mention of his son.

What does Xenophon's being the actual original of "Socrates' story" have to do with the issue Strauss's contrasts settle, Socrates' view of the relative rank of model gentleman and model ruler? As told by Xenophon, Socrates' story helps his Socrates persuade a young Greek to pursue the way of life of the gentleman by ennobling that life through a fiction of a model farmer who is actually a model ruler. Socrates' story shows that Socrates ranked ruling higher than gentlemanship by showing a story-teller win a kind of rule over a young gentleman. Socrates has no intention of becoming a gentleman but he is by deed a ruler whose instrument of rule is authoritative story-telling. Xenophon assigns his Socrates a story of which he is the original; he imitates in writing Socrates' purpose in speaking; doing what Socrates did, he facilitates rule by the philosopher Socrates. (Strauss later assigns "Socrates' story" its proper place when, after Socrates has told a story of which he is the original and the subject, Strauss can say that Socrates' story of the horse of Nikias the foreigner "is as characteristic of Socrates as the stor[y] of Cyrus [is] of Lysander" [160].)

Fifth contrast, adornment and the divine: "The Persian story is silent on the gods, although it is adorned with an oath; the opposite is true of the Phoenician story" – it is silent on oaths, although it is adorned with actions of the gods. The *adorned* of the fifth contrast is a reminder of the central contrast. In the pleasure garden that is the order of the model ruler, order belongs together with adornments that include the kind that is an oath, the one spoken by a Persian ruler being an oath to Mithras (118). On the merchantman that is the model of order of the model gentleman, such splendor is altogether replaced by utility; the man in charge speaks of the gods as disturbers of order and utters no oath because his gods are unreachable by oath.

Strauss's five contrasts show that Socrates judges the model ruler higher in rank than the model gentleman and suggest that Socrates aspired to rule out of the pleasure garden of philosophy. How can a *philosopher* rule? As Cyrus who was almost a king ruled, the contrasts answer, through resplendent adornments that belong together with his pleasure garden. The resplendent adornments a philosopher can outfit himself with in order to rule are authoritative stories underwriting useful oaths to gods. Socrates' story about the gods is the theme of the central paragraph of the next chapter; that a philosopher learns to rule through adorning stories is the theme of the final chapter of the *Gynaikologia*, "Cosmetics." The central paragraph of the *Gynaikologia* really is central: it gathers what preceded it, anticipates what follows, settles the central issue of rank, and shows that and how the philosopher rules.

The contrasts, as compact and subtle as they are, give every appearance of doing what Strauss's final sentence orders, leave it open whether model ruler or model gentleman holds the higher rank for Socrates. But they settle it after all, settle it with the reserve Strauss mastered. "We must leave it open" must therefore state an imperative that Strauss both took as a compulsion and addressed to his reader: Leave it open.

Gynaikologia – III: Order II

Strauss begins the third chapter of his *Gynaikologia* calling attention to the close connection between the two chapters on order as "appears immediately from their contents." That connection is "in addition…indicated by…the beginnings of the two chapters," each opening "with a question of Socrates concerning the effect of Ischomachos' teaching on his wife." In the first, his teaching stirred her "to greater care: the care as such antedated the lecture" (146). In the second, she promised to take care and asked her husband "to bring their things in order in the manner stated by him: her concern with order did not antedate the lecture." Antecedent care and lack of antecedent concern with order mark Ischomachos's "nice or sweet bride" (133). Do they also mark the apparent innocent asking a perfect gentleman what perfect gentlemanship is? Socrates asks Ischomachos "how he brought their things in order for her" (146). Antecedent care drove nice and innocent Socrates to ask and a concern for order is kindled in him by hearing Ischomachos's way of "separating his indoor things into tribes in order to establish order within his house" (147).

After calling attention to the close resemblance between the beginnings of the two chapters on order, Strauss begins his central paragraph of his second chapter on order with a sentence bearing a close resemblance to the one beginning the central paragraph of his *Gynaikologia*. Both interrupt his commentary because something of Ischomachos's reminds him of something of Socrates': there, "Ischomachos' story…reminds us of Socrates' story," here, "Ischomachos' separating his indoor things according to tribes in order to establish order within his house reminds us of Socrates' separating the beings according to races or kinds in order to discover the order of the whole" (147). As the resemblance indicates, this central paragraph takes up and completes that central paragraph which intimated that Socrates took Cyrus in his pleasure garden as his model. Moreover, the central paragraph of the first chapter of the *Gynaikologia* set out Ischomachos's idea of order and the central paragraph of its second chapter set out the boatswain's idea of order – *this* central paragraph sets out the order of the whole according to "Socrates' most comprehensive teaching." This central paragraph takes up and completes the theme of order present in the two previous central paragraphs and in the central paragraph of the *Gynaikologia*: this is the peak of peaks.

Strauss quotes Xenophon's *Memorabilia* for Socrates' separating the beings according to kinds: Socrates "never ceased considering with his companions what each of the beings is" (147). Commenting on this passage two years later, Strauss noted a subtlety preserved in an alternative manuscript: "Perhaps Socrates never ceased considering what each of the beings is silently 'in the midst of his companions' (the reading of B), even if he did not consider it 'together with his companions'" (Strauss 1972, 116-157). On this reading, Socrates left it to his companions to participate in his silent consideration of the beings: a Xenophon could participate, a Kritoboulos not. Silent participation leads to "the center of

Socrates' life – a center of which [Xenophon] does not speak owing to the limitation he has imposed on himself especially in the *Memorabilia*" (Strauss 1972, 117). Strauss too silently leads his reader to the center of Socrates' life in this central paragraph, for being reminded of Socrates' separating by Ischomachos's puts him under a compulsion: "We are forced to wonder whether Ischomachos' separating his indoor things according to tribes is not the model for the peculiarly Socratic philosophizing" – *the peculiarly Socratic philosophizing* is the center of Socrates' life. In this last of his central paragraphs in the *Gynaikologia* Strauss crafts his sentences to raise questions that their progress answers, leading one into the center of Socrates' life. The paragraph is an instructional exercise on the model of Socrates' silent instruction, artful dialogue with his reader allowing one to consider just what the philosophizing peculiar to Socrates is and how he attained it.

Was Ischomachos Socrates' model for his attempt to discover the order of the whole in its races or kinds through his method of dialectics? Strauss recalls two matters that may suggest he was: Socrates approached *him* in order to learn what perfect gentlemanship is, and *his* example par excellence of order was meant to educate even Socrates. To learn what a perfect gentleman is is to learn a lot: "the question regarding the perfect gentleman may be said to comprise all the questions regarding human things which Socrates was always raising." Strauss names two, those concerning the pious and the noble, adding that "these questions call for separating, for instance, what is pious from what is noble." This suffices for him to say, "It seems then that Ischomachos was in a manner the source, not only of Socrates' substantive knowledge of the human things, but also of his way of acquiring that knowledge, of his 'method.'" This unbelievable conclusion needs a defense and Strauss adds that it is not as surprising as it first sounds for this reason: "Socrates' most comprehensive teaching, his teaching which transcends the human things, deals with the whole order of the cosmos, the order that serves the benefit of men and is due to the god's *oikonomein*." The god, Socrates teaches, manages a household, the cosmos, in an orderly fashion that serves human benefit. Is Ischomachos the source of this teaching, Ischomachos who, though he manages a household, holds a different view of the gods? (137)

Strauss's sentence on Socrates' most comprehensive teaching, so stunning in its suddenness and scope, generates a caution: "It is true that the teleotheology is exposed to difficulties." Socrates' teaching is a *teleotheology*, a label Strauss invents that captures in a single word its two basic claims: Socrates teaches a theology and a cosmology that maintain that gods manage a cosmos end-directed for human benefit. Instead of relating that teaching to its ostensible source, Strauss's point till now, he exposes its difficulties for the rest of the paragraph before finally, at its end, suggesting how to resolve them. He begins with two difficulties from the *Memorabilia*. First, Socrates contradicts his own teleotheology by claiming that "the divine has no needs." The contradiction means less than an unclarity:

"Above all, it is not clear how Socrates' theology is connected with the 'What is…' question which he never ceased raising." *Above all,* how is Socrates' separating the beings according to kinds in order to discover the order of the whole *connected with* his teaching on the whole? An initial answer may be indicated by Strauss's temporary shift from "never ceased considering" (148, 150) to "never ceased raising" (149, 148): could Socrates raise in the midst of his companions a "What is…" question he had considered to its end?

Turning then to the *Oeconomicus* for two difficulties it presents for the teleotheology, Strauss says, "Ischomachos indicates some doubts regarding the teleotheology." Well, not exactly. Ischomachos never heard the teleotheology in his sole conversation with Socrates. But he did indicate a view of the gods different from Socrates' teleotheology, a fact that raises a question about how that teleotheology could have its source with him. Strauss goes on: "In particular, in the section devoted to 'order' there is almost complete silence about the god or the gods." The complete silence is Socrates' and Ischomachos's; the Phoenician boatswain spoke of the god. Ischomachos found no fault with what he said though it expressed greater certainty than he had about gods punishing and therefore noticing the slack: did he welcome such a view of order? But that view gives "even less support for the teleotheology than before" for while the boatswain "is as doubtful as Ischomachos about evil befalling only the bad," he does not present order "as in any way rooted in something divine…the gods are mentioned only as disturbers of order" (143). Where does silent Socrates stand? "As for Socrates, he speaks in the *Oeconomicus* of the gods as at least as much disturbers of the philanthropic order as its supporters; he is silent during Ischomachos' lectures on order; later on he says that the gods do not rule the year in an ordered manner."

The two difficulties in the *Oeconomicus* invite the solution obvious from the structure of the *Oeconomicus*: an old Socrates is reporting on an event earlier in his life. If Socrates sought out Ischomachos as a younger man than the one who taught the teleotheology in the *Memorabilia*, then hearing Ischomachos' lectures on order could well be how he learned what needed to be taught. Strauss's final sentence of the paragraph confirms this solution and begins the process that brings this peak into full view. Strauss was "therefore tempted to wonder whether the Xenophontic Socrates was not, like the Platonic Socrates, dissatisfied with the simple teleology – anthropocentric or not – which at first glance seems to supply the most rational solution to all difficulties and turned for this reason to the 'What is…' questions or to 'the separating of beings according to kinds.'" Xenophon's Socrates must then be construed developmentally, as Plato's Socrates presented himself in Plato's *Phaedo*. The "simple teleology" that young Socrates abandoned must then be literally separable from the teleotheology he would later come to teach – it lacked the *theoi*. Using Plato's account of Socrates' development to interpret the *Oeconomicus* suggests that Socrates' conversation with Ischomachos is Xenophon's representation of the Socratic turn showing a young Socrates turning to his own method of inquiry, to the "What is…" questions. Seeking out Ischomachos is a *consequence* of Socrates' turn, his pursuit of that particular "What is…" question – What is a perfect gentleman? – which comprises "all the questions regarding human things" (148). Hearing Ischomachos answer this "What is…" question, he learns the proper teaching for gentlemen, a teleotheology that was an anthropocentric improvement on the teleology Plato's *Phaedo* shows him abandoning early, a teleotheology to teach gentlemen that gods order the cosmos as they order their households.

Strauss attached a footnote to this final sentence of his central paragraph. It supplies first two references to the *Phaedo*. They send the reader to the Platonic Socrates' report on his hopes for a teleology which holds that mind, the cause of all things, orders all things for the best whether earth, sun, moon or the rest of the heavenly bodies (*Phaedo* 97c3-98b6), and then to his report that his inability to credit such a cause led him to his "second sailing in search of the cause," his decision to turn away from "looking into beings" and to "take refuge in the *logoi* and look in them for the truth of beings" (99c6-e6). The Platonic template of Socrates' turn fits the Xenophontic Socrates if seeking out Ischomachos is that part of his turn to the logoi that looks for the truth of beings in Ischomachos's lectures educating his wife and finds in them the perfect gentleman's understanding of gods, nature, and order that Strauss put at the centers of his previous *Gynaikologia* chapters. Xenophon and Plato chose formally similar ways to present what each must have regarded as the most important event in the history of philosophy: an old Socrates relates to young companions the turn that led to his mature teaching, silently showing them the way to the center of his life. Strauss combines the two accounts to help show the peculiarly Socratic philosophizing by showing how Socrates' teaching, his teleotheology, arose from his "What is…" questioning.

For after its references to the Socratic turn in the *Phaedo*, the footnote vouchsafes, guardedly, a most illuminating revelation about Plato's Socrates. It invites one to compare "the parallel development on a higher level – the level of the 'kinds' or 'ideas' – and in this sense at a later stage, as reported in the *Parmenides* 130b7-e4." Plato's *Parmenides* reports a development in a still young Socrates slightly older than the one reported on in *Phaedo* for he has already made the turn to the ideas. Plato set his *Parmenides* during Parmenides' famous visit to Athens with his follower Zeno in August, 450 (Nails, 308-9): this higher and later stage of Socrates' philosophical development occurred when he is about nineteen. At the start of this stage, having understood the kinds to be ideas, he is, as Plato presents him, a brash, even rude young thinker who believes he has solved the problem of kinds with his doctrine of transcendent ideas, for he wields it like a weapon to strike down the solution to the problem of the one and the many that Parmenides and Zeno had famously advocated for years. In the sole passage to which Strauss directs his reader, Parmenides expresses admiration for Socrates' "zeal for speeches" but he has just crushed Socrates' doctrine with the first of his

fatal refutations of transcendent ideas. He goes on in Strauss's passage to challenge a humbled Socrates, saying that "philosophy has not yet gripped you as
it will, in my opinion. And when it has you will dishonor none of these things;
but as for now, you still look to the opinions of men, because of your age." To
be a "parallel development" to the one in the *Phaedo*, "on a higher level... at
a later stage," this stage too must move from one way of seeking a solution to the
problem of cause to a different one. In this later development the young Socrates
is compelled by Parmenides' argument to move beyond his youthful doctrine of
ideas to a more satisfactory if unstated view peculiar to Socratic philosophizing,
the future Parmenides said was possible for him. But this leads to a puzzle in
Plato: *Phaedo* shows Socrates making his refuted doctrine of ideas part of his
teaching on the last day of his life as he presses his "safe" doctrine of ideas on
a young Cebes worried about reason's ability to ground what he believes in, the
immortality of his soul. Adding this Plato comparison to the final sentence of
his paragraph allows Strauss to leave to his reader actual entry to the peculiarly
Socratic philosophizing: the Plato comparison suggests that Xenophon's mature
Socrates offered his teleotheology as Plato's mature Socrates offered his doctrine
of ideas, as a teaching a variant of which he had earlier held but which he had
learned was exposed to difficulties, to logical refutation, but which he came see
as both salutary for young gentlemen and useful for prospective philosophers.
The complexities of Strauss's last central paragraph can be unknotted as Strauss's
conscious act: he bunched into simultaneity events he knew to be chronologically
separate. He did what Xenophon and Plato did, built in temporal complexities
to tax the reader and educate through their solution. The solution is to pull the
complexities apart into their proper chronological sequence; so separated they
allow Socrates to be viewed developmentally. The *Gynaicologia* shows Socrates learning what would make him the teacher of a teleotheology. The pivotal
event following his turn to the "What is..." questions was his conversation with
Ischomachos; learning what perfect gentlemanship is, he learns what would be
salutary for gentlemen to be taught.

With Plato's help a Socrates in process emerges from Strauss's culminating
central paragraph, a Socrates becoming the Socrates of the peculiarly Socratic
philosophizing. With Plato's help Strauss answers his question on the connection between Socrates' theology and his "What is..." questions: his "What is..."
questions are connected to his theology as its source. Asking "What is a perfect
gentleman?" led him to the proper theology for gentlemen, a teleotheology in
which the gods so order the cosmos as to serve the benefit of gentlemen, primarily
by allowing them to speak in strict parlance of divine justice. The teleotheology
did in a manner have an Ischomachean origin: his view of gods, nature and order
invited a Socratic corrective. Socrates as theologian tamed the gods into human
service; he ruled the unruly gods by making their hitherto unpredictable actions
predictable or moral. Teaching the teleotheology without mentioning its difficul-

ties allowed Socrates in the midst of his companions to silently raise questions about the kinds of being and about the highest beings and how that kind of being might be related to the whole of beings.

But if Socrates' mature teleotheology is that part of the peculiarly Socratic philosophizing that is a politic teaching for gentlemen – Socrates' political philosophy – what was Socrates' actual mature view of things, the "substantive knowledge of human things" to which his "method," his "What is…" questions, led him, knowledge that Strauss suggests also had its source in Ischomachos? This too Strauss treats with great brevity in a last sentence added to the footnote added to the last central paragraph: "The 'What is…' questions are meant to dispose of the questions regarding the 'material and efficient causes' of the natural species." Strauss completes the triumvirate of Socratics who established the Great Tradition: for all their differences in presentation, Xenophon, Plato, and Aristotle remained true to the peculiarly Socratic philosophizing. More importantly, the sentence indicates how the "parallel development" reported in Plato's *Parmenides* helped solve the problem of cause, for it explains the purpose of the "What is…" questions by exploiting a precise ambiguity in "dispose of." In the now most common sense of *dispose of*, the "What is…" questions are meant to *set aside entirely* unsettling questions regarding material and efficient causes of the natural species and, though this is unspoken, locate their causes wholly in formal and final causes; they are meant to set aside the dangerous inquiries of the Greek science of nature by dealing with the causes of natural species teleotheologically. But *dispose of* in its initial primary sense means *to set things in their proper or fitting order* – separating the beings according to their natural kinds in order to discover the order of the whole. The peculiarly Socratic philosophizing does not set aside the genuine science of nature with its investigation of material and efficient causes but shelters such an investigation within causes that can seem alternative to it but are supplementary to it. In formal and final causes Socratic philosophy investigates the natural and inescapable cognitive activity of humans that orders material events and things into kinds or ideas. Part of the inescapable structure of that activity is teleotheological: it invents imaginary kinds and imaginary causes to read the cosmos as fulfilling the imaginary purposes of imaginary beings. The footnote to Strauss's final central paragraph shows that while the peculiarly Socratic philosophizing was taken up in various ways by Xenophon, Plato, and Aristotle it remained a never ceasing consideration of nature and human nature sheltered behind a salutary teaching on nature and human nature that it knew to have difficulties.

The final sentence of Strauss's footnote introduces the next paragraph as that part of Strauss's report on the peculiarly Socratic philosophizing that reports Socrates' investigation of nature. It describes, if incompletely, a Socrates who completed the parallel development on the higher level anticipated in the *Parmenides* passage. Strauss begins this paragraph by accounting for his central paragraph:

it was "a deliberate exaggeration" (149) to suggest that Ischomachos could be the source of both Socrates' substantive knowledge of the human things and his "method" but it was needed as a corrective for those "concerned with 'the Socratic problem.'" To correct their supposition that Socrates learned nothing from Ischomachos, Strauss acted as if Socrates learned everything from Ischomachos. Those concerned with the Socratic problem missed Socrates' attempt "to discover the order of the whole by distinguishing the kinds of beings that make up the whole." Consequently they missed the matter of greatest importance: Socrates' "finding out what each of those kinds is." That quiet *finding out* anticipates Strauss's statement of what Socrates' investigation of nature actually came to conclude about nature and human nature. Yes, Socrates blamed those who engaged in the inquiry into the nature of all things, but for what reason? (150) Not because they inquired but because their publicly stated answers made the whole enterprise look laughable or criminal. Strauss infers from Socrates' blame the "sane and sober" view of beings as a whole the blame implies: there are a finite number of kinds; the kinds themselves neither change nor come into being or pass out of being. A Xenophontic inquirer, Strauss only implies the most arresting result: every particular being comes into being and passes out of being, including the beings with the highest kind of being.

Strauss's final sentence on the peculiarly Socratic philosophizing accounts for the false appearance that Socrates limited his inquiry to the human things: "this appearance is ultimately of importance only because it points to the humble ("Ischomachean") origin of the philosophizing peculiar to him." The philosophizing peculiar to Socrates originates in his turn to the human without exhausting itself in the human; it discovers the human place in nature by discovering nature through the human. Thus Socrates became himself, a teacher whose public teleotheology educated the gentlemen while igniting the genuine education of those like himself passionate to understand. The philosophizing peculiar to Socratic is a teaching on the whole and a continuing investigation of the whole under the notion of kinds or ideas. It is political philosophy and philosophy, a teaching and an investigation carried on simultaneously in the highest refinement of speech, Socratic dialectic through which Socrates taught a teleotheology and never ceased considering what each of the beings is in the midst of his companions. Strauss's peak of peaks is a lovely structure, a central paragraph on the apparent peak, a linking footnote, and a second paragraph on the real peak, an inescapably, naturally clouded, never to be conquered peak. Strauss beautifully engages in the philosophizing peculiar to Socrates.

Ischomachos's lectures to his wife are the deepest retrievals of the *Oeconomicus*. In its timeless narrative present, the *Oeconomicus* is Xenophon's report: he narrates it all. His first retrieval reports an earlier dialogue between Socrates and Kritoboulos. Within that dialogue is a second retrieval, Socrates' report to Kritoboulos and the others of his earlier dialogue with Ischomachos. Within that report is a third and deepest retrieval, Ischomachos's report to Socrates of his earliest educating of his wife. The pauses Strauss built in at the centers of his commentary on Ischomachos's report show that the structurally deepest retrieval retrieves Socrates' deepest subject. Socrates' steering plus Ischomachos's eagerness to report his success combine to make Socrates an auditor of the perfect gentleman's implicit and inchoate understanding of nature, his conviction that he brings order to what the gods bring forth. He stands within nature as a maker, full of care, diligent, inventive, over against a nature unpredictable and wild but yielding like an unformed female to forceful interventions by the male. Strauss's careful centering assigns Socrates' corrective teaching on nature, his teleotheology, its proper role: as civically salutary it is fixed at the center, as rationally precarious it is a start. Strauss simply states what the "What is…" questioning attained and intimated in the interstices of the teleotheology, Socrates' finding out of natural kinds and imaginary kinds, an implied ontology according to which the process that nature *is* generates always transitory beings distributed across a hierarchy of natural kinds. The study of nature finds out those kinds plus humanly-generated kinds (tribes?) which the turn to the logoi also reveal, kinds that can be said to be "natural" as unwittingly generated by the care-full being. Subject to witting modification by a knower who knows their origins, they can be shaped into useful implements for ordering the care-full being. The centers of the *Gynaikologia* make the teleotheology a fit teaching for one who takes Cyrus in his pleasure garden with his resplendent adornments as model regal ruler for ruling gentlemen. Homely Xenophon exalts; most exalted is knowing; exalted too is the ruling knowing necessitates.

Gynaikologia – IV: Cosmetics

It can be no accident that Strauss pushed back Xenophon's central eleventh chapter to make his own eleventh chapter central. Instead of simply following Xenophon's twenty-one chapters, he added a chapter at the start and then, in order to end with twenty-one, he folded Xenophon's seventeenth and eighteenth chapters into his own eighteenth chapter. Strauss's central eleventh chapter has no center; it is a block of four paragraphs, three of commentary, one of judgment on Ischomachos's education of his wife. The chapter as a whole shows why Strauss contrived to place cosmetics at the center of his best book.

Ischomachos is eager to report and Socrates eager to hear other examples of his wife's obedience (153, 132). One example proves enough. After hearing it Socrates puts a stop to Ischomachos, leaving the *gynaikologia*, Strauss says, incomplete. Why is one example enough? Strauss emphasizes that Ischomachos's *report* on his wife's virtue interests Socrates at least as much as that virtue itself. If this one example is enough to exhaust Socrates' interest in the perfect gentleman's attempt to educate his wife, it must teach him the last lesson needed on both the gentleman and the virtue he reports.

Strauss's first paragraph elaborates Socrates' contrast of two kinds of reproduction of originals, Ischomachos's report on his wife's virtue and Zeuxis's portrait of a beautiful woman. Socrates' contrast "can easily induce one to think that the beauty of a living human being can be surpassed by a painter's imitation, while the virtue of a living human being cannot be surpassed or even rivaled by a poet's or a writer's imitation." Strauss ends his paragraph on a third reproduction of an original, another report on the virtue of a human being: "We surely do not go wrong if we assert that Xenophon regarded his reproduction of Socrates' virtue for more than one reason as inferior to that virtue itself, one reason being that in publicly presenting Socrates' virtue he could not assume that he was speaking only to friends." If Xenophon's report on his subject's virtue is inferior to that virtue itself, is Ischomachos's report on his wife's virtue inferior to hers? He lacked Xenophon's stated reason for making his report inferior to his wife's virtue. Was his report perhaps superior to his wife's virtue? What is his report and what is her virtue?

Strauss notes that the cosmetics Ischomachos's wife used reappear in Xenophon's writings (154-155). In Socrates' rendering of Prodicus' story, Vice beautified herself to seduce Herakles (*Memorabilia* 2.1.22): she acted to make her complexion appear whiter and rosier than it was and her bearing seem straighter than its nature. And Cyrus the Great "acted, according to Xenophon, in order to beguile his subjects" (155) with those cosmetics; Xenophon applauds Cyrus for using them and counseling his commanders to use them, platform shoes to "seem to be taller than they are...color beneath their eyes so that they might appear more beautiful eyes than they are, and rubbed-on colors so that they might be seen as having better complexions than they had by nature" (*Cyropaedia* 8.1.41). Vice used the cosmetics as a means of seduction, Cyrus as a means of rule. Ischomachos's wife used them for seduction but, obedient to her husband's lecture, she never used them again because his lecture taught her that they repelled him. "The perfect gentleman Ischomachos has no use for such practices," Strauss says, practices which attempt to "improve on her being, the truth, her nature" (154). Ischomachos takes a "firm stand ... for nature, or truth, against deception" (156). Socrates learns from Ischomachos's report that the perfect gentleman wants being, truth, and nature as they are – and that he believes he knows what they are.

What does Socrates learn about the virtue of the wife from her husband's report? Strauss began his chapter with Socrates admiring her "masculine mind" while swearing like a woman (153). Her masculine mind, Strauss explains, "revealed that virile concern with one's own that makes human beings good defenders of their own." Strauss speaks a second time of her masculine mind though Xenophon did not: when Ischomachos threatened to deceive her by pretending to be richer than he is, she "broke in 'straightway,' 'at once,'" "she becomes lively," "since she must repel the thought that her husband might deceive her about his property by boasting or by concealment; she thus shows again how masculine her mind is in regard to her own" (155). Virile in defending her own, is her mind simply masculine? In a dialogue with her educating husband that Strauss paraphrases in detail she shows that her means to the goals of her masculine mind cannot be and are not masculine but are as they must be feminine, indirect and subtle, guileful and beguiling. She "broke in" to her husband's speech to deploy the one means she had of securing an advantage over him: she says (Strauss reports) that "she could not love him from her heart, from her soul, if he were a man who would do such things." She speaks of love from the heart, he speaks of sharing each other's bodies. He "clinches the issue" with a comparison, the last of the *Gynaikologia*, about what the gods have done: just as the gods made horses most pleasant to horses and cattle to cattle and sheep to sheep, "so human beings regard the genuine body of a human being most pleasant." Strauss notes the "lack of parallelism" in the comparison but says it "is justified by the fact that nature enables human beings, as distinguished from the brutes, to invent and use cosmetics." Strauss uses the word *cosmetics* for the first time in his "Cosmetics" chapter when he makes *nature* replace *gods* and cosmetics *natural* for humans. He ends his paragraph on how Ischomachos spoke of nature and cosmetics. After showing "in the section on order that men can and to some extent even must improve on nature, Ischomachos now calls his wife back from an unnecessary and undesirable deviation from nature, from a deviation which originates in the wish to deceive." Strauss summarizes the last three chapters of his *Gynaikologia*: "after having devoted the section on order to genuine beauty, he speaks in the subsequent chapter of spurious beauty." Cosmetics, Ischomachos judges, are spurious beauty that deviates from nature and originates in the wish to deceive.

Socrates, a student of nature, neither approves nor questions "[t]he firm stand taken by Ischomachos for nature, or truth, against deception" but eagerly asks, "By the gods...what did she reply to this?" Her replies can "end...the *gynaikologia*" (156) because they teach Socrates a certain cosmetics. Strauss makes his point by strict consistency in employing the language of appearance, not of being, truth, or nature. Ischomachos's wife never again used these cosmetics but "*tried to present herself undisguised* and in a becoming manner" – her becoming manner is her success in her conscious effort to present herself undisguised. For she asked her husband "how she could *come to sight* as beautiful in truth and not merely in appearance" – she asked him what appearances would meet his standard of truthful beauty. His simple advice led to this: "by *acting* thus, the wife will *look more attractive* to her husband than her maid." Looking more attractive by acting, "she will *be* superior anyway...by the voluntary character of her submission." She *is* superior but is her submission voluntary, she who must submit as the maid must submit? Ischomachos assures Socrates "that his wife *still behaves now* as he had taught her then." Compelled to submit in a household ruled by her husband, a man with the law on his side, she learns the necessity of appearing voluntarily submissive to his standard of being, truth, and nature, making it the standard of her appearance. Knowing her situation and learning her husband's demands, she makes herself a master cosmetologist and her ostensible master her cosmetics' beguiled victim.

Through Ischomachos's report on how she learned to act, the perfect gentleman's wife teaches Socrates the indispensable lesson in cosmetics for one who is superior to the perfect gentleman but under his rule: abjuring cosmetics that cannot withstand proximity she outfits herself in the invisible cosmetic of obedience to his standard of being, truth, and nature. Hiding a willful opacity in apparent transparency, she guarantees his willing transparency. Self-commanding in seeming obedience to a commanding she is powerless to counter directly, she counters indirectly, in a wily way, acting and entirely winning over her unmusical perfect gentleman husband, that man of rectitude proud of his model wife, eager to recite examples of her obedience. His deluded report on his wife's pleasing appearance of obedience offers Socrates insight into the way of life of the gentleman: sedate and secure in its self-confident mastery, its trust that it can lecture order into malleable nature, it proves easy prey to a deception that knows the uses of counterfeit obedience. Its morality-fuelled conviction of its own rightness stamps it with obtuseness, with insensitivity to artfulness, to a cosmetic willingly and knowingly deceptive. Ischomachos's report on his wife's virtue displays the vulnerability of his own vaunted virtuousness. His report on his wife's virtue, like Xenophon's report on Socrates' virtue, is inferior to that virtue itself. (His report may also surpass his wife's virtue. If Strauss is right in identifying her in his final paragraph of the *Gynaikologia*, she is wanton in the inward license she allows herself and the outward actions they lead to. She is "a quite remarkable wife" and Strauss paraphrases words Andocides used at his trial to describe the actions of "that most impudent hag" (158).

Socrates "behaves like a woman in contrast to the masculine character of Ischomachos' wife" (153). But Ischomachos's masculine wife behaved like a woman in virtuous obedience – and her example taught a Socrates who resembles her in the essential respect: being ruled by the more powerful in the household that is the city of the perfect gentlemen. Socrates behaves like a woman; he learns from her example the virtue of seeming obedience and seeming transparency to what rules him. But it was "the masculine character of Ischomachos' wife" that led her to abjure the very cosmetics adopted and recommended by the model ruler. Did she abjure Cyrus's means to gain Cyrus's end? The aptness of the first comparison of the *gynaikologia*, the queen bee, shows that she did: the "mistress of the house" (156) proves to be "mistress of him who is the direct ruler" of the outside things (139); "she proves to be manifestly superior to" her "husband and master" (139). When Strauss recalls Cyrus again to cite his use of cosmetics (155), he recalls the model ruler who ranks higher than the perfect gentleman. Manly Socrates learned from Ischomachos's wife how to achieve Cyrus's end: his masculine mind is inwardly manly in outwardly using feminine means to secure his end of rule. The "masculine mind" of Ischomachos's wife reveals "that virile concern with one's own which makes human beings good defenders of their own." As a philosopher Socrates is not attached to his own city or household but is willing to measure and abandon them in favor of the foreign if it is rational to do so. As a philosopher Socrates defends what is genuinely his own; he is manly in his masculine mind, his interior resolve to defend philosophy itself, passionate pursuit of the "What is…" questions. He learns from Ischomachos' wife: her husband's report on her virtue teaches him both that a certain womanly obedience is necessary for the inner freedom indispensable to philosophy, and that the limit on her outward freedom does not preclude a kind of rule over her apparent ruler. To defend what falls to him by natural right of superior wisdom, he must gain rule over the ruler of the outside things through cosmetics.

The centers of the first three chapters of Strauss's *Gynaikologia* show that Socrates' defense of his own through rule over the gentlemen can be effected in one way only: he can rule the human whole through a persuasive teaching on the whole that will be welcomed by the gentlemen. Human action springs from human belief about the human place in nature. Ischomachos believed that the gods generated nature, whereas law that orders relations among humans is not of divine but of human origin (134-135). His belief was refined by the boatswain's belief that order is altogether of human origin and sails like a great merchantman on a sea on which a god can raise a storm that punishes all equally the slack (142-143). Having learned the power of these beliefs about nature and the gods and the human effort to establish lasting order; having asked, answered, yet not pronounced one question in particular about the kinds of being, What is a god?; and, not least, having learned a concern with order from his own precarious place in the household; Socrates crafted a novel teaching on gods, nature and the human. According to his teleotheology, the whole is a moral order that serves the benefit of men and is due to the god's *oikonomein* (148-149).

Strauss crafted his book to have its central chapter show what that teaching is: cosmetics. Offered to the upright pillars of society, it is an instrument of rule over society's rulers that gives the philosopher who offers it a respectable place in society; Socrates rules the "outdoor," rules actions, by coming to rule the "indoor," thoughts about god and nature. Socrates the philanthropist gives the gentlemen the gift of a teleotheology, an implement of order altogether of human origin. His philanthropy is a double act of philosophy: it preserves the pleasure garden of philosophy in the midst of the city of the gentlemen while opening it to those naturally suited to enter. From here, from the rule flowing out of the philosopher ruler's pleasure garden, the full aptness of the first comparison of the *Gynaikologia* can be recovered on just those points where Ischomachos's wife thought it might be inapt – only to the queen bee comparison did Ischomachos's diffident young wife break her silence and perhaps her awe to raise a question about his

first ever lecture to her (137). The queen bee controls the upbringing of the progeny, sending them out when mature under a leader to found a colony (138). The
bees become so attached to their queen through being healed by her that when
a divorce occurs all will leave with the ruling queen. It is the master's place to
be ruled by the one who proves manifestly superior to him, the mistress, the female master who rules the direct ruler of the menservants. The queen bee image
proves most apt for the exalted, a philosophical ruler. For this reason, perhaps,
Strauss moved Xenophon's center off-center and put cosmetics at his center: his
is not the manly deed that founds the precarious teaching to shelter philosophy
in its productive hive; his deed recovers that founding in its cosmetic character.
Strauss's recovery of cosmetics belongs at the center of his book as the way in
to the genuine center, what Xenophon centered, the *Andrologia* that shows what
a real real man is.

Judged by the categories Strauss assigned Ischomachos, the teleotheology is,
as a cosmetic, *spurious beauty*, the beauty of a deviation from nature that originates in the wish to deceive. Could the spurious beauty of the cosmetic harbor
a genuine beauty of nature accessible to Socrates but judged repulsive by adher-
ents of spurious beauty? Strauss suggests in a most economical way that it does,
that nature as it is shines with genuine beauty. His last sentence of his central
chapter and his last sentence on Xenophon's central chapter contrast Ischomachos's attempt to educate his wife with Socrates' refraining from any effort what-
soever to educate his. Was Socrates able to change his reaction to nature's unchangeable conduct because he found in it and loved in it genuine beauty?

References

Nails, Debra. 2002. *The People of Plato: A Prosopography of Plato and Other Socratics.*
Indianapolis: Hackett Publishing.

Pausanias. 1971. *Guide to Greece.* Vol. 1. Trans. Peter Levi. Harmondsworth: Penguin Books.

Strauss, Leo. 1963. *On Tyranny: An Interpretation of Xenophon's Hiero.* Ithaca: Cornell U.
Press.

_____. 1970. *Socrates' Socratic Discourse: An Interpretation of the Oeconomicus.* Ithaca:
Cornell U. Press.

_____. 1972. *Xenophon's Socrates.* Ithaca: Cornell U. Press.

_____. 2001. *Leo Strauss: Gesammelte Schriften. Band 3.* Herausgegeben von Heinrich und
Wiebke Meier. Stuttgart: Verlag J.B. Metzler.

CONTRIBUTORS

Paweł Armada is Assistant Professor (adiunkt) of political science at Jesuit University of Philosophy and Education in Krakow, Poland. He is the author of a large monograph entitled *Szkoła myślenia politycznego Leo Straussa* (*The Straussian School of Political Thinking*) and a co-translator of Leo Strauss's *On Tyranny* into Polish. He was one of the organizers of the conference *Modernity and What Has Been Lost*.

Jürgen Gebhardt is Professor of Political Science at the Universität Erlangen-Nürnberg. He has also taught at Universität München, Harvard University, Ruhr-Univeristät Bochum, University of Virginia, Martin-Luther Universität Halle-Wittenberg, Beijing University. His research focuses on political theory, political philosophy and the history of ideas. His publications include the volumes *Die Krise des Amerikanismus* (1976) and *Americanism* (1992) as well as numerous articles on the history of political ideas, systematic political theory and comparative politics. He is a co-editor of *The Collected Works of Eric Voegelin*.

Arkadiusz Górnisiewicz is a PhD student at the Jagiellonian University (Department of International and Political Studies) in Krakow. He is a Polish co-translator of Leo Strauss's *On Tyranny*. He was one of the organizers of the conference *Modernity and What Has Been Lost*. He is currently working on the philosophical and theological presuppositions of modernity, the problem of European nihilism, and the writings of Karl Löwith.

David Janssens is Assistant Professor in Philosophy of Law in the Department of Philosophy at the Tilburg University. His main expertise is in classical political and legal philosophy. He is the author of *Between Athens and Jerusalem: Philosophy, Prophecy, and Politics in Leo Strauss's Early Thought* (2008).

Till Kinzel teaches at the TU Berlin and TU Braunschweig. He is a Privatdozent für Englische und Amerikanische Literaturwissenschaft. His PhD dissertation was devoted to the Platonic cultural critique in America. He is the author of many publications including the following: *Platonische Kulturkritik in Amerika. Studien zu Allan Blooms* The Closing of the American Mind (2002); *Nicolás Gómez Dávila. Parteigänger verlorener Sachen* (2003).

Laurence Lampert is professor of philosophy at Indiana University, Indianapolis. He is the author of numerous articles and the following books: *Nietzsche's Teaching: An Interpretation of* Thus Spoke Zarathustra (1986); *Nietzsche and Modern Times: A Study of Bacon,*

Descartes, and Nietzsche (1993); *Leo Strauss and Nietzsche* (1996); *Nietzsche's Task: An Interpretation of* Beyond Good and Evil (2001); *How Philosophy Became Socratic? A Study of Plato's* Protagoras, Charmides, and Republic (2010). He has also edited an edition of Francis Bacon's *Advertisement Touching a Holy War* (2000).

Heinrich Meier is Professor of Philosophy at the Ludwig-Maximilians Universität München and Distinguished Visiting Professor in the Committee on Social Thought at the University of Chicago. He is the Director of the Carl Friedrich von Siemens Foundation in Munich. His scholarly interests include political philosophy, history of philosophy and anthropology. He is the editor of Leo Strauss's *Gesammelte Schriften*, as well as the author of the books: *Carl Schmitt and Leo Strauss. The Hidden Dialogue* (1996); *The Lesson of Carl Schmitt. Four Chapters on the Distinction between Political Theology and Political Philosophy* (1998); *Leo Strauss and the Theologico-Political Problem* (2006).

Piotr Nowak is deputy editor-in-chief of the philosophical quarterly "Kronos" and senior lecturer at Bialystok University. He is the author of several books, including one on Alexandre Kojève (*Ontologia sukcesu*). He has co-edited the book *Man and His Enemies. Essays on Carl Schmitt* (2008). He has translated works of Hannah Arendt, Leo Strauss, and the British-American poet W. H. Auden.

Emmanuel Patard is a PhD student at the Université Paris I (Panthéon-Sorbonne). He published a critical edition of Leo Strauss' "Restatement" (1950), together with various unpublished material related to the Strauss-Kojève Correspondence, in a special issue of *Interpretation: A Journal of Political Philosophy*, Vol. 36, No. 1 (Fall 2008). He is currently working on a critical edition of Leo Strauss's essays, lectures, and courses of the New School Period (1938-1948).

Daniel Tanguay is Adjunct Professor of Political Science and Associate Professor of Philosophy at the University of Ottawa. His fields of interest involve political philosophy, social philosophy and contemporary continental philosophy. In recent years he focused on the French return to political philosophy – Claude Lefort, Pierre Manent, Marcel Gauchet, and others. He is the author of *Leo Strauss. An Intellectual Biography* (2007).

Nathan Tarcov is Professor in the Committee on Social Thought, the Department of Political Science, and the College at the University of Chicago. He is Director of the Leo Strauss Center at the University of Chicago. His scholarly interests include history of political theory, education and family in political theory, and principles of U.S. foreign policy. He is the author of *Locke's Education for Liberty* (1984) and numerous articles on Machiavelli, Locke, Strauss, and American political thought and foreign policy; translator (with Harvey C. Mansfield) of Machiavelli's *Discourses on Livy*; and editor (with Clifford Orwin) of *The Legacy of Rousseau* (1996).

NAME INDEX

Achilles 55, 61, 62
Adler E. 70
Aeschylus 57, 65
Agamemnon 57, 60, 62
Alfarabi 30, 80, 139
Aquinas Thomas 50, 80,
Arendt Hannah 14, 15, 83–91, 174
Aristippos 154
Aristophanes 55–57, 64
Aristotle 18, 28–30, 39, 45, 50–51, 58, 80, 90–
    –91, 99, 117, 121, 164
Armada Paweł 13, 14, 18, 73, 173
Aron Raymond 33
Atkinson Charles F. 121
Augustine of Hippo 96, 99

Bacon Francis 99, 101, 173, 174
Bartlett R. 104
Batnitzky Leora 81
Beardsley Monroe C. 137
Benardete Seth 54, 65, 68, 144–145
Bendersky Joseph W. 132,
Benjamin Walter 134
Blackstone Sir William 59, 145
Bloom, Allan 80, 114, 120, 141, 143, 150, 173
Bluhm Harald 70
Blumenberg Hans 101
Bolotin David 50
Bourdieu Pierre 34
Bossuet Jacques-Bénigne 96
Brague Rémi 61, 97
Brainard Marcus 78, 94
Bush George W. 131

Carey George W. 88
Chase Michael 43
Cicero 50, 64–65, 91
Circe 60
Cohen Hermann 142
Collingwood Robin George 120, 138–139

Comte Auguste 96
Conrad Joseph 128
Cooper Barry 123
Cronos 49
Cyrus 76, 152–169

Davidson Arnold I. 43
Davis Michael 54, 70
Demetz P. 134
Democritus 57, 64
Derrida Jacques 137
Descartes René 99, 115, 132, 141, 174
Dewey John 39
Dilthey Wilhelm 143
Doyle Arthur Conan 69

Ebbinghaus Julius 142
Emberley Peter 123
Empedocles 60, 64–65
Epaminondas 157
Epicurus 64
Euripides 57, 64

Fallaci Oriana 130
Fingerhut Bruce 18
Foucault Michel 16, 43, 135–136

Gebhardt Jürgen 14, 83, 88, 173
Gildin Hilail 87, 101, 119
Ginzberg Louis 30, 139
Goldie Mark 51
Gourevitch Victor 37, 93, 111–112
Górnisiewicz Arkadiusz 15, 18, 93, 173
Grant Robert 137
Graham George J. 88
Green D.E. 99
Green Kenneth Hart 46, 77, 139
Gunnell John G. 85–88

Hadot Pierre 43

Habermas Jürgen 36, 105
Havelock Eric 56, 57, 63, 66
Hegel G.W.F. 15–16, 94, 96, 99, 102, 111, 113–
   –122
Heidegger Martin 16, 19, 22, 57, 78, 80, 97, 99,
   100, 104–106, 112, 114–122, 143–144
Henningsen Manfred 90
Heraclitus 60, 65
Herbert Zbigniew 10
Herakles 167
Hermes 60–61
Herodotus 13, 54–55, 60, 65, 97
Hesbois Bernard 115
Hesiod 13, 55–67
Hilfstein E. 132
Hill Melvyn A. 91
Hitler Adolf 94, 131
Hobbes Thomas 101–103, 127, 131–140
Hobsbawm Eric 88
Hogan Maurice P. 89
Homer 55–69
Horace 57–58, 65
Huntington Samuel 129

Ischomachos 147–171

Janssens David 13, 51, 53, 103, 108, 173
Jarczyk Gwendoline 115
Jepchott E. 134
Joachim of Fiore 96

Kant Immanuel 99, 115, 118, 121, 143
Kierkegaard Søren 15, 99, 106
King Elizabeth 94
Kinzel Till 16, 17, 135, 143, 173
Klein Jacob 54–56, 60, 62–63, 139
Kojève Alexandre 9, 15, 16, 29, 49, 67, 77–78,
   93, 100, 103, 108, 111–123, 174
Kritoboulos 147–148, 152, 155–159, 165
Krüger Gerhard 137, 141–142
Kurland Philip B. 145

Labarrière Pierre–Jean 115
Lampert Laurence 14, 17, 77, 147, 173
Large D. 104
Launay M.B. de 106
Leitch Vincent B. 137
Lerner Ralph 145
Lessing Gotthold E. 71, 139
Lilla Mark 88, 129

Loyola St. Ignatius of 39–41
Locke John 35, 51, 174
Lomax J.H. 102, 107, 132
Löwith, Karl 15, 80, 93–109, 136, 140, 173
Lucretius 20, 56, 64–65
Lysander 156, 158

Machiavelli Niccolò 14, 30, 43, 51, 67, 76–79,
   88, 100–102, 111, 174
Maimonides 30, 54, 70, 104
Major Rafael 138
Mansfield, Harvey C. 51, 174
Marx Karl 51, 96, 115, 119, 122
McAllister Ted V. 88
McCurdy Henry B. 88
Meier Heinrich 11–12, 18, 19, 25, 46, 54, 70,
   74, 78, 80, 94–95, 102, 105–106, 136, 139,
   171, 174
Meier Wiebke 54, 80, 106, 171
Melzer Arthur 71, 144
Milton John 59
Morgan George Allen 95
Musil Robert 132

Nails Debra 162, 171
Newman John Henry 126
Nichols James H. 114
Nikias 158
Nietzsche Friedrich 10, 14–15, 20, 27, 29, 30,
   36, 39–41, 77–78, 80, 82, 94, 95, 98–99,
   101–109, 115, 119, 120, 173–174
Nowak Piotr 16, 125, 174

Oakeshott Michael 14, 83–86, 88, 91
Odysseus 55, 58, 60–62, 68
Oehler Klaus 137, 144
Ovid 65

Pangle Thomas L. 89, 104, 139, 141
Parekh Bhikhu 85
Parmenides 56–57, 60, 62, 65, 121, 162–164
Patard Emmanuel 15–16, 111, 174
Patterson Annabell 136
Pausanias 157, 171
Pearson K.A. 104
Perreau–Saussine Emile 138
Petropulos William 87
Pieper Josef 138
Pippin Robert 103

Plato 13–14, 17–18, 20, 27–30, 35, 39, 43, 45, 49–51, 53–56, 58–60, 62–71, 79–81, 84, 86, 90–91, 97, 101, 103–105, 116–117, 121–122, 138–140, 142–145, 154–155, 161–164, 171, 173–174
Platt Michael 53
Polin Raymond 33
Polybius 97
Polyphemus 61
Pope Alexander 57–58

Rawls John 14, 36, 39–40, 85
Ries Wiebrecht 94
Riesterer Berthold 95
Riezler Kurt 57
Renaut Alain 35
Roth Michael S. 37, 93, 111, 119
Rorty Richard 38–40, 137
Rosen Stanley 65
Rosenzweig Franz 57, 65, 105–106
Rousseau Jean-Jacques 20, 29–30, 35, 101––102, 139, 174
Rumsfeld Donald 129

Szlachta Bogdan 18
Schleiermacher Friedrich 143
Schmitt Carl 16, 19, 100, 102, 113, 116, 125––134, 174
Schwab George D. 125, 128, 132, 134
Sheppard Eugene 144
Sinclair Elsa M. 116
Skinner Quentin 138
Socrates 11, 17, 28, 47–48, 53, 55–56, 58, 62––63, 67–69, 76, 78–80, 111, 141–142, 144, 147–171
Sophocles 55, 57, 65
Spengler Oswald 98, 120–121
Spinoza Baruch (Benedict) de 26, 94–95, 104––105, 116, 121, 138

Steiner Gary 105
Stichweh Klaus 100, 106

Tamer Georges 139
Tanguay Daniel 12, 33, 108, 174
Tarcov Nathan 12–13, 43, 100, 174
Taylor Charles 36, 88
Thao Tran Duc 115
Thersites 62
Thompson Lawrance 143
Thucydides 13, 55–56, 62, 65–66, 74–75, 97, 156
Tocqueville Alexis de 98
Toynbee Arnold 98
Tucker Robert C. 51

Vettori Francesco 51
Vergil 58, 65
Veyne Paul 136
Vico Gianbattista 96
Voegelin Eric 14–15, 78, 83–91, 123, 173
Voltaire 96

Wald Berthold 98, 138
Wallace Robert 101
Walsh David 90
Weil Eric 33
Weiss Gilbert 87
Wimsatt William K. 137
Wolfowitz Paul 129
Wolin Richard 100, 105

Xenophon 13, 15, 17–18, 54–56, 58, 62, 66, 74, 76, 78–79, 111, 144, 147–148, 151, 153–154–171

Zeno of Elea 162

SUBJECT INDEX

Ancients and Moderns 13, 15, 53, 71, 97, 105, 112

andreia 55, 62–63

anthropology 39, 114–115, 117, 121, 174

art of writing 13, 16, 20, 31, 45, 50, 51, 53–59, 62–63, 66–71, 77–78, 80, 95, 135–139, 141, 143–145

atheism / atheistic 104, 114, 117, 126

Athens and Jerusalem / Jerusalem and Athens 9–10, 13, 15, 51, 53, 103, 106, 173

atopia 62

authority / authoritative 10, 13, 15, 20–21, 22– –25, 44, 47, 54–55, 63, 74, 76, 81, 85, 88– 89, 91, 156–158

best regime 9, 12, 34–39, 41–42, 48–49, 101– –103

bios politikos 54

bios philosophikos 54

cave 12–14, 17, 30, 43–44, 50–51, 64, 71, 74– –75, 78, 82, 103, 105, 136, 142–143

Christian / Christianity 10, 15, 41, 49, 77, 88, 96–101, 103–107, 119

city 8, 13–14, 37, 42, 49, 50–51, 55–56, 60, 62, 64, 67, 69, 74–75, 77, 79–80, 82, 84–85, 90–91, 94, 100–101, 103–104, 123, 145, 154, 155, 169–170

City of God 49

civil society 48

civilization / civilizing 15, 79, 83, 86–87, 88, 91, 94, 98, 102, 106, 108, 111, 126, 129, 130

comedy 55, 60, 80

communism 10, 33

communitarians 33

community 14, 23, 28, 42, 44, 46–47, 52, 74, 77, 79–82, 90, 95, 109, 149

convention / conventional 43, 47, 48, 50, 61

cosmos / cosmology / cosmological 15, 17, 49, 67, 96–99, 106–107, 117, 160, 162–164

culture / cultural 8–9, 16, 23, 26, 27, 35, 75, 85–87, 95, 121, 126, 130, 135–136, 143, 173

defense of philosophy / philosophical life 10, 12–14, 23, 42, 73–74, 140

diairesis 59

dialectics / dialectical 34, 113–116, 118, 160, 165

dialogue / dialogic 15, 20, 22, 29, 37, 54–55, 60, 62–65, 67, 76, 102, 111–112, 126, 144–145, 149, 160, 165, 168, 174

doctrinairism 35

dualism / dualistic 60, 114–115, 118, 121

eironeia 55, 62

Enlightenment 10, 15, 39, 40, 103, 111

eros 25, 50, 78, 138, 144

esoterism / esoteric 8, 11, 17, 20–21, 54, 57, 66, 68–69, 71, 95, 103, 135, 138, 144,

eternity / eternal 9, 14, 26, 44–45, 77, 82, 96, 99–100, 105–107, 112–114, 117, 121–122,

existentialism / existentialist 15, 19, 25, 78, 80, 97, 99–100, 104–105, 112, 114, 121, 128

facts and values 45

final / End / universal and homogenous state 9, 15–16, 78, 108–109, 111, 116, 120, 122,

gentleman / gentlemanship 79, 147–148, 150, 153–155, 157–160, 162–163, 166–167, 169

God / gods 12, 17–18, 23–25, 49, 59–61, 63– –64, 68, 73–74, 81, 97, 100, 102, 104, 105– –108, 118–119, 148–149, 151–152, 155, 158, 160–163, 166, 168, 170

good / best life 9, 12, 23, 28, 34, 39, 48–49, 101–102

hermeneutics 89, 137, 143–144
historicism / historicist 12, 15–16, 21, 30, 39, 44, 86, 95, 99, 105, 121, 135–138
historicity 90, 99
human soul 10, 13, 23, 37, 39, 41, 62, 64–65, 70, 78, 122, 133–134, 163, 168
human condition 66, 70

ideas [doctrine of] 17, 163
immanence / immanent 9, 100

kalos 154

Last Man / last men 16, 116, 119
Leviathan 16, 102, 132–134
liberal democracy 9, 28, 36–37, 39–40, 53, 73, 127, 135
logoi 55, 162, 166

messianism 120
modernity 7–10, 14–15, 29–30, 38, 43, 46, 70, 75, 77, 83, 86–90, 93–95, 98, 99–108, 139, 173
morality 38, 47–48, 50, 52, 63, 104, 120, 169
mythology 55

natural law / right 12, 34–35, 38, 43–50, 61, 63, 73, 74, 81, 95, 101, 102, 105, 122, 170
nature 12–13, 15–16, 18, 22–23, 26, 28, 31, 34, 37, 39–41, 44–49, 51–52, 56, 58, 60–62, 64, 65, 68, 74, 78, 80, 83, 87, 95, 97–104, 107, 114–119, 128–129, 132–134, 136, 138–139, 141, 152, 155, 162–171
neoconservative 7
nihilism / nihilistic 15, 73, 93, 97, 99, 105–108, 113, 141, 173
nomos / nomoi 55, 61, 63

ontology 105, 114–115, 118, 121, 127, 152, 166

paideia 13, 55
patriotism 28, 50
patriciate 48
pedagogical 71, 144
philosophic(al) life 10–11, 13–14, 19–20, 23––25, 28, 29, 31, 42, 47, 49–51, 54, 63, 65, 73–74, 77, 82, 91, 95
philosophy of history 15, 90, 95–98, 113, 120, 139

phusis 13, 60–62, 68, 152
Platonism 29, 54
poet / poetry 7, 10–11, 13, 25, 53, 55–71, 99, 144, 167, 174
polis 55, 86, 90, 103, 109, 121
[the] political 23, 26, 44, 100, 102, 126–132, 134
political life 14, 24, 26, 28, 42, 49, 54, 73–75, 81–82, 91, 127, 154–155
political order 18, 23, 44–45, 80, 101
political philosophy 8, 12, 15, 18, 23, 27, 33––39, 41–45, 47, 50, 56–57, 62, 67, 69–70, 73–74, 77–79, 84–88, 90–91, 93, 100–101, 108, 112–113, 115, 119, 121, 123, 138–141, 143–144, 164–165, 173–174,
political science 7, 14, 36–37, 41, 74–76, 85, 88–90, 100, 104, 111, 138, 145, 173, 174
political theology 125–127, 132, 174
political theory 14, 35, 36, 77, 84–86, 103, 173
postmodernism / postmodern 11, 16, 40, 135––137
potential philosopher 51, 78
[the] prephilosophic(al) 47, 64, 75
prophet / prophecy 7, 14, 77, 79, 82, 96, 104
protreptic 13, 27, 55

reason / reasoning 13, 24–25, 38, 39, 46, 50, 53, 59, 70, 85–86, 91, 96, 101–102, 117, 120––121, 130, 132–133, 163
relativism / relativist 38, 41, 95, 107, 112,
Revelation 7, 12–13, 24–26, 46, 53–54, 81, 89, 105, 113, 119, 141, 162
[the] salutary 10, 17–18, 28, 66, 68, 163–164, 166

secularization / secular 15, 26, 93, 95–96, 98, 100–101, 105, 120
Seinsfrage 16, 112
sociology / social science 8, 33, 46, 112
Socratic ignorance 145
Socratic question 9, 13, 51, 142
sovereign / sovereignty 24–26, 35, 125–127
state of nature 16, 102, 133–134
Straussian school 8, 173
subjectivism 144

theoi 161
teleotheology 17, 160–171
theologico–political problem 12, 24–27, 46, 70, 78, 94–95, 105, 139, 174

theology 10, 17, 26–27, 46, 63, 96, 98–100, 105, 125–127, 132, 152, 160–161, 163, 174

thumos 69–70, 120

totalitarianism 33, 83, 85, 87–88

tragedy 54–55, 60, 80, 120

transcendent(al) 75, 100, 162–163

tyranny 15, 29, 37, 49, 51, 58, 70, 76–78, 93, 100, 103, 108–109, 111, 116, 120, 171, 173

utility 153–155, 158

virtue 18, 34, 39, 48–50, 55, 62, 75–76, 101––103, 120, 122, 132–133, 166–167, 169

wisdom 9, 13, 35, 37, 45–47, 49–51, 55–56, 58–59, 61–63, 79–80, 86, 97, 103, 117, 120, 122, 170

zetetic 67, 79